*Charles H. Kramer, M.D.*

The Family Institute of Chicago

417 North Kenilworth Avenue, Oak Park, Illinois 60302

# Society without the Father

Alexander Mitscherlich

# Society without the Father

*A Contribution to Social Psychology*

Translated from the German
by Eric Mosbacher

*A Helen and Kurt Wolff Book*
*Harcourt, Brace & World, Inc.*

NEW YORK

First American edition

Library of Congress Catalog Card Number:
65-19066

Printed in the United States of America

Originally published in German under the title
*Auf dem Weg zur vaterlosen Gesellschaft* by R.
Piper & Co. Verlag, Munich

# Contents

CONTENTS

viii

# Personal Acknowledgements

The most pleasing experience that an author is entitled to expect is the first reading of his manuscript by persons who follow his ideas with interest but without giving up their critical independence, that is, with Brecht's 'alienation effect'. I am indebted to two of them in particular: to Dr Peter Brückner, for his numerous suggestions both in relation to the main argument of the book and to matters of detail, and to my assistant Käte Hügel, who never tired of making the various drafts both legible and readable.

I am indebted to the generosity of the Foundations Fund for Research in Psychiatry which made it possible for me to absent myself from daily clinical duties for a substantial period. During this period I received invaluable help and suggestions from Dr Paula Heimann and Dr Michael Balint, and suggestions made by my friends and colleagues Dr John Klauber and Dr Pierre Turquet are also reflected in the foregoing pages.

I count as one of the strokes of good fortune in my life the continual help given me by my friends Dr Willi Hoffer, Professor Piet Kuiper, and Professor Fritz Redlich. I am particularly grateful to Professor Redlich for the patience with which he encouraged me to continue in my many moments of discouragement in face of the enormous complexities of the task.

Innumerable discussions at the clinic enabled me to benefit from the experience of my colleagues and to learn from them, and I express my thanks to them too.

The book would not have been written without long collaboration with my wife, Dr Margarete Mitscherlich-Nielsen, to whom I therefore wish to dedicate it.

# I

# Introductory: The Dynamics
# of Adaptation

*The long years of childhood*

Man comes into the world unadapted and untrained, and he remains in
the nest for a very long time; and the end of the process of human
maturation, in contrast to that of animals who spend a long time in the
nest (or take off quickly), is not a perfect representative of the species,
but an individual moulded by a learning process and familiarized to a
greater or lesser extent with social forms. In many situations he is faced
with decisions of which no one will relieve him. All the same, he is
relieved of a great deal, because for the most part he makes decisions
in accordance with patterns imbibed from his family environment,
social status, or culture. His equipment of innate patterns of behaviour
is only rudimentary. To mention only a few striking examples, he has
no hereditary, ritualized, courtship or mating behaviour, and his
knowledge of how to recognize enemies or nurture the young is not
innate.

*Development of aptitudes and social environment*

How much human behaviour is innate is unknown; all we can be sure
of is that it is far from adequate for the regulation of life among our
fellows. The real regulator, our code of behaviour, is learnt slowly.
Constitutional factors and acquired aptitudes interact. The geneticist
knows, for instance, that uniovular twins greatly resemble each other in
appearance, and also in aptitudes and social character. But in such
extreme instances – in this case the effect of sharing the same genes –

one is apt to overlook how much more complicated is the interplay between individuals, each of whom brings variable hereditary factors into the world, and their environment. The extent to which aptitudes which we so readily take to be hereditary and unalterable can be encouraged or inhibited by environment is shown by a study by Freeman and his colleagues of 125 pairs of siblings who were separated at an average age of five and a half, one of each pair being brought up in a foster-home. At the time of the study the separation had lasted for five or ten years or more. Normal siblings have a 'similarity' ratio of 0·5, but the figure for these children was only 0·25. This 'showed the extent to which children's capacities can be influenced by environmental differences'.[1]

In this connection a significant observation is reported by Margaret Mead. 'Among the Mundugumor people of New Guinea, children born with the umbilical cord wound around their necks are singled out as of nature and indisputable right artists.'[2] In this case a culture has 'arbitrarily associated, in an artificial way, two completely unrelated points: manner of birth and an ability to paint intricate designs upon pieces of bark'. Mrs Mead continues: 'When we learn further that so firmly is this association insisted upon that only those who are so born can paint good pictures, while the man born without a strangulating cord labors humble and unarrogant, and never attains any virtuosity, we see the strength that lies in such irrelevant associations once they are firmly embedded in the culture.' Thus it is not only the intimate family environment, such as that which an adopted child may chance to enter, that has variable effects on the development of capacities; there is also the factor of collective social behaviour. The expectations of a social group can powerfully promote potential aptitudes in one individual and inhibit them in another.

Such social assumptions are of course not completely unknown in our own culture. In families of long-established social status, craftsmen or peasants, for instance, to say nothing of the aristocracy, it is more or less taken for granted that the eldest son will step into his father's shoes; and indeed he very often does so, adapting himself with varying degrees of success and with varying degrees of reluctance, but yielding to the pressure of an environment that has brought him up and trained him to do so. Examples such as these show the importance of the part played by social environment in the development of human character and aptitudes, in the whole formation of the individual. The more flexible a society is, the greater its division of labour and freedom from property ties, and the more mobile it is in consequence, the greater is the individual's chance of being able to follow his own proclivities in the development of his capacities. Indeed, it is only in such a society that the problem of individual proclivities arises. Our own culture offers some scope in this respect, though not nearly so much as is often suggested, but we should not deceive ourselves about our own history or about the situation in many other cultures, in which the social situation of the individual is strictly laid down in advance and his behaviour is prescribed in every detail.

The immediate social environment in which the individual is embedded affects not only his vital decisions, scale of values, and behaviour but also the forms taken by failure to meet social demands. Many illnesses, for instance, are not precipitated by constitution and the effects of nature alone; the social environment also plays its part. This is particularly true of neurotic and psychosomatic illness, which we have learnt to recognize as an attempt, though an unsuccessful one, to solve an individual conflict.[3] The very thorough work of Theodore Lidz[4] has shown the influence of the family environment on schizophrenia, hitherto regarded predominantly from the hereditary aspect. As Luxenburger put it, heredity is not fate, but the threat of fate. It is the social environment that, to an extent we cannot yet measure, determines whether the threat becomes reality. It can help the individual to integrate constitutional socially disruptive trends into his total personality and hold them in check, or it can help the opposite process, encourage antisocial or asocial behaviour or lead to 'illness'.

*Adaptation, closed and open*

Here we can only touch on the question of the influence of heredity on all the problems we have mentioned, but there is one fact which we shall bear in mind. One of the peculiarities of man is obviously that he does not possess a single and definite hereditary way of adapting himself to his environment. On the contrary, he has an extraordinary ability to adapt himself to very different and changing, sometimes swiftly changing, social environments.

As in the course of this book we shall be considering the process of

3

adaptation chiefly from these social points of view, concentrating, that is to say, on only one aspect of this ability, it will be as well to inquire straight away what is meant by adaptation in the broader biological context. Let us take as an example the well-known engineering feats of the beaver, which dams flowing water in such a way as to keep the level above that of the entrances to its burrow, thus protecting the occupants from their natural enemies. These dams are constructed with great artifice and skill, and systems are known which have been maintained for more than seventy years by thirty generations of beavers.[5] Biology offers us theories which more or less satisfy individual workers in the field and state the physical or organic assumptions necessary to explain such performances.[6] They may depend, for instance, on the extent of development of the cerebral cortex. Further, the relatively young science of hereditary genetics has shown that certain capacities – in fact, the ways of behaviour characteristic of a species – are anchored in the genes and their arrangement in the chromosomes. We know that the living organism is essentially a system directed to the maintenance of its own equilibrium (a homoeostatic system), with innumerable feedback mechanisms and reciprocal influencing of the organic functions. Since Norbert Wiener we have talked of 'cybernetic systems', but even in Pavlov's theories the interaction of the neural stimulation and inhibition processes plays a central role.

All this enables a living organism to adapt itself to a specific environment and at the same time – at any rate to some extent – to adapt its environment to itself. Instead of the ingenious beaver, we might have cited the no less astonishing examples of the web-spinning spider or the insects that live in highly socialized communities. In all these cases life seeks to remain constant within the environment peculiar to the species (J. von Uexküll). During this process of adaptation the living creature acquires aptitudes which it uses to try actively to improve its environmental conditions. All these processes of biological adaptation – which certainly represent only one vital process, but a highly important one, as we have believed since Darwin – have one thing in common. They take place extraordinarily slowly and, as has been shown by the Belgian palaeontogist Luis Dollo, are irreversible. Once a process of adaptation, whether physical or of hereditary ways of behaviour, has been completed, there can be no despecialization. In the event of an unfavourable change in the environment to which an organism has adapted itself over the ages (presumably by mutations), it cannot back-pedal and start again, but in extreme cases it will die out and become extinct.

## Adaptation is not progress

All these theories are very persuasive; no better explanations of many processes of adaptation are available. But we should free ourselves of one idea that the nineteenth century seized on with premature optimism and prized highly, namely, that Darwin's evolution implies progress. That is typical anthropomorphism transferring to life processes in general ideas that we have formed for use in our own particular social environment. Upward! Progress! Evolution! Even today the 'common man', in so far as he accepts evolution, probably does so because the theory rides on the coat-tails of that most popular of all gods, Progress. But is evolution progress? asks Garrett Hardin in an excellent chapter of his *Nature and Man's Fate*. He continues: 'Bertrand Russell has wryly remarked: "A process which led from amoeba to man appeared to the philosophers to be obviously progress – though whether the amoeba would agree with this opinion is not known."'[7] Flies which have 'adapted' themselves to DDT are genetically different from the type that prevailed before the introduction of the poison. Are the resistant strains better? They have merely acquired different characteristics in response to an environmental change.

## Cultural adaptation: a process of selective accommodation

Let us now leave the problem of the adaptation of the living creature to its environment and the hereditary ways of behaviour peculiar to its species and look at the human problem of cultural adaptation. Here again the question may be asked: Which is the better adapted, the 'primitive' or the advanced, 'highly civilized' man? And what do we mean by primitive and advanced? We can only counter with the opposite questions: Adapted to what? And what does primitiveness consist of? In the defective adaptation to his environment of a Central European white-collar worker with a two-room flat and typical consumer habits? In what way is he less primitive than an Arapesh from the mountains of New Guinea, that is, a man who belongs to a culture we regard as characteristically 'primitive' and full of hazards? Is either of them better adapted? In fact we are asking the wrong questions. Both, like all mankind, live in *selective* adjustment to their environment. Naturally, as von Uexküll points out, an Indian on the Orinoco lives in a world the contents of which are quite different from those of our highly technical and specialized industrial civilization. Both primitives and ourselves are similarly adapted to the environment – and have characteristic deficiencies in adaptation to it.

Every adaptation to any given natural or cultural circumstances involves both development and inhibition of aptitudes. Our culture has made tremendous advances in mastering the forces of nature. But can it claim similar advances in knowledge of the natural forces inside ourselves? What we regard as primitive is not seldom merely the unknown, or rather the not understood, those things in other people we are unable to project ourselves into and understand the spirit of. It is not only savages who strike us as being primitive in this way, but also many members of our own culture; and we ourselves are in return regarded in the same way by others.[8]

*Four basic components of adaptation to the human environment*

For the purpose of constructing a model enabling us to visualize what is involved, we can distinguish four basic components in adaptation to the human environment:

1. Passive adaptation to existing conditions. This process is obviously associated with the learning of rules, prohibitions, symbols, and in particular speech.

2. As a reflection of this passive adaptation to social life we carry out a similar adaptation within; that is, we adapt our impulses and satisfactions to the requirements of the outside world. 'Passive' in this sense means that we do not just release the impulses that arise in us egoistically and autistically, but shape them in accordance with a pre-existent pattern of behaviour, in which renunciation, postponement, and disguise of aims are often called for.

3. We achieve active adaptation if we succeed in bringing our environment into such harmony with ourselves that our purposes actively contribute to shaping the resultant situations.

4. Active adaptation also has its inner counterpart. We do not blindly

and passively take over prescribed forms of behaviour, but modify them. Certain impulses towards certain individuals in our environment may not fit in with the ideal standards of our society, but we nevertheless permit ourselves to feel and recognize and even express them. Thus we assume the initiative and with it a twofold responsibility – both to ourselves and to our social environment. For society can tolerate only a moderate amount of initiative in our total behaviour if its cohesion is not to be destroyed.

## The limits of social tolerance

Thus life in society is dominated by these two antagonistic trends. Instead of active and passive they can equally well be called assimilative and integrative. We assimilate our social environment. If we carry too far the trend to fuse our initiatives completely with the standards of social behaviour, we develop into social automatons. If we engage in activity that to a greater or lesser extent conflicts with those standards but is nevertheless accepted by our fellows, we are behaving integratively. Activity that meets with no such echo, that ruthlessly ignores standards and offends the susceptibilities of others, is isolated and antisocial.

The transitions between instinctual behaviour, behaviour in conformity with social norms, and behaviour guided by the ego are fluid. The sequence makes increasing demands on the integrative capacity. Individuals with basic urges and perhaps also ego qualities of different strength develop different capacities for integration and different degrees of inflexibility, adherence to taboos, or readiness for change. A decisive influence is exercised in this respect by the prevailing degree of intolerance, insistence on rigid adherence to norms or 'anomy' (Durkheim), lack of leadership or genuine tolerance for individual expressions of life; and the sector in which the basic drives of the individual find one answer or the other is also a factor.

## The dynamics of human adaptation

In view of the enormous number of past cultures and the number that still exist today, it is obvious that the mode and dynamics of adaptation developed by man differ from those of other social animals. Human specialization has avoided developing specialized tools for a special environment such as flippers or fins; instead man has specialized in non-specialization (K. Lorenz). In other words, his speciality is a 'tool-making brain', an inventiveness that compensates for his failure to develop hereditary bodily tools and ways of behaviour. Also these capacities are associated with achievements of the conscious mind, though these are not the work of the conscious mind only, as is shown by every spontaneous idea.

It is also evident that, in comparison with the specializations of other species, which are permanently anchored in the genes, the processes of adaptation in human history take place with very great rapidity; and they can crumble and give way to new forms with the same rapidity. In other words, the processes of human adaptation of affective human behaviour both in social forms and in social styles of mastering the natural environment are incomparably more superficial and transitory than those of the animals.[9] The only characteristic man never shakes off is his biologically determined lack of adaptation, and that seems to be his specialization. But whether this should be regarded as progress in the evolutionary sense, that is, tending to maintain his *status quo*, is at least an open question, particularly when the possibilities of destruction that have arisen from our 'tool-making brain' and lack of adaptation are taken into account.

We can of course never detach ourselves so completely from our subjective human situation as to be able to look impartially at our life, whether biological or intellectual. We cannot avoid judgements of value about ourselves and others, or prejudices about relatively known or relatively or completely unknown features of our own culture, or others that are remote in space or time. But in discussing, as we are trying to do here, the specifically human insecurities arising from man's basic lack of adaptation, we should do well to exercise the utmost tolerance. Tolerance as a method of approach is not merely taking relativity into account and is not apologetic. We can be happy and guilty only in our own culture. But perhaps we can gain knowledge of the particular weaknesses and insecurities to which we are subject, and find ways and means of coping with them to some extent, when we have learnt more from the facts, in particular the fact that there is no such thing as a 'best' human culture, one in which man can finally flourish, and that that culture is certainly not the individual's own. In the sense of Dollo's law, the die is cast. We are fated to be specialists in imperfection. Man does not come into the world with an inherited way of behaviour that in all important matters co-ordinates him with a specific environment, but, as we said at the outset, is born unadapted and untrained. Every one of his cultures he enters as a novice. That is a fact of natural history. Perhaps realization of the necessity of putting up with (cultural) difference was made possible only by the cultural cosmopolitanism of our time, which as a result of the technical development of communications and the imposition by machinery of a uniformity of production and consumption has brought into functional relationship with each other human groupings with totally different histories. Mankind's original social form was that of the 'closed or exclusive group, the horde or clan. . . . The closed group has – or once had – an "ideal standard" different from those of every other group. Only members of the group are initiated into these ideal human standards, they alone have the task of fulfilling the mission of humanity. The Eskimos' name for themselves, for instance, is *Inuit*, which means "we, the most human of all". While the members of the exclusive group are representatives of the ideal standard, all others suffer the opprobrium of non-worth; they are ignorant of, or do not fulfil, the true mission of life. The epithets "barbarian", "heretic", "pagan" – to say nothing of modern, generally politically coloured, examples – express the antithesis to the ideal standard, the "non-worth standard".[10] Since in our fantasy ideas we all persist in our ethnocentric or group-centred ways of thought, one of the 'humiliations' with which we have to cope is that Negroes, Chinese, Jews, and Communists all have the same sense of being in possession of the ideal standard and are inclined to despise us accordingly. Racial characteristics seem more and more to be losing importance as indications of membership of an exclusive group – the internationalization of athletic competition has been one factor in this. The question of what marks of exclusivity will maintain their taboo character in the future, and how the function of the former spatially closed group or clan will be carried over into cosmopolitan industrial civilization, remains entirely open. For it is not to be expected that in these historically entirely novel conditions agreement on a single common standard will come about by general consent. For one thing, the excess of affect that provides the motive force of the perpetual reconstruction of the social world always needs an 'enemy'. Hitherto in human history the perpetual search for an outlet for the impulses condemned to suppression by civilized social life has discharged itself in the most appalling mutual persecutions. It is not easy to see why a single civilization – that is to say, a uniform, world-wide technology and the adaptations imposed by it – should bring about any change in man's primary nature.

## A new function, the extension of consciousness

Man has developed a new function – that of acquiring an understanding of himself enabling him to control, guide, and shape his actions. That puts the conscious into a dialectical relationship with older biological functions, the hereditary nature of which explains unconscious behaviour which imposes itself as a matter of course. How far the conscious extends is obviously not fixed; it varies from individual to individual, from culture to culture, but it can hardly be doubted that in the course of observable history it has encroached on the realm of unconscious mental processes, and has made its greatest advances where, as Alfred Weber says, civilization has gone furthest in covering up the natural with a technical environment, thus creating a 'second natural environment'.

# II

# Adaptation and Insight

*Social renunciation and instinctual surplus*

The culture of the present day is inseparable from its technology. A second factor is the population increase and the formation of new and relatively uniform cultural areas which leap over geographical, national, and language boundaries and adapt themselves to the state of technological progress and the ideas of social value and organization associated with it.

But rivalry, reciprocal hostile valuation, the tendency to look inwards and cut themselves off from disturbing outside influences, reappear in these great societies just as they did in the days of hostility between religious or national cultural groups in the past. The historical novelty is that the means of destruction have reached a degree of effectiveness capable of imperilling human survival. In the past the losses of war were slowly made good by the growth of new generations. But if war can now result in damage to the germ plasm itself, we have reached a point at which biological processes can no longer be relied on to make good the losses. Irreparable destruction of germ plasm could threaten the survival of civilization.

Thus one of man's reactions – his surplus aggressive drive – has survived unchanged all technological developments and social revolutions. The benefits he derives from his so variously organized social groupings obviously do not sufficiently compensate him for the renunciations that they involve. Instead, the instinctual life is subject to vicissitudes imposed by society – among other things, collective pressures that may cause it to regress to the situation that existed at the outset of the cultural process; that is, the originally ruthless basic urges which, stated in psychological terms, aim at total domination of their 'object', namely fellow human beings, partially reappear in crises and conflicts. Those who have more social power are able more easily to satisfy their needs within their society, and those who have less can hope to be able to fulfil their unsatisfied and unsocialized urges at the expense of collectively branded individuals and groups outside their own society.

## Surplus aggressivity

Every group imposes renunciations on its members, and enforced renunciation creates hostility. Hostility disturbs the inner cohesion of the group. To avoid having to impose fresh renunciations, it opens up the only path by which hostility can be acted out. We shall discuss this more fully later. For the time being let us bear in mind that the unending succession of wars of which history tells us indicate a fluid, easily roused, surplus aggressivity the 'rational' justification for which it is the task of religious or social or other ideologies to provide. The belief in progress in this connection that used to be associated with the development of science and technology has turned out to be unfounded. On the contrary, perhaps the present situation shows with special clarity one of the tendencies immanent in human social organization – to relapse from rational into deluded behaviour. The extent of paranoid distortion of reality that afflicts the politics of the present day can hardly be overrated. Here lies the dynamite that might lead to the obliteration of human achievements and the destruction of life itself.

Little is to be gained by self-reproaches or self-assessments masquerading as revelations, such as that man is 'evil' by nature or that one's own race is the 'highest'. Instead, we must try to increase our verifiable knowledge of man, enabling us better to understand the reasons for his 'evilness', his belief in his own omnipotence, resulting from the interaction between social situation and his basic drives; and in this context 'better' can only mean more dispassionately. Man is a scientific and no longer a mere philosophical problem. If science alone cannot answer the question of meaning, at all events it can provide philosophical speculation with more accurate knowledge about the nature of its object.

*Growth and education*

As human beings are known to us only as socially formed, that is educated, individuals, we must first make some distinctions and differentiations in regard to the formative process. No one could have become what he is except as the result of an educative process, and in man this begins at a remarkably early stage; the corresponding stage in related animals takes the form of intra-uterine growth.

Common to both growth and education is that they are dynamic processes. Growth has a definite aim – the achievement of the mature form of the species – and so has education. The latter implies adaptation to a particular model. But this model is determined by the ways of a group or society and is not a firmly rooted peculiarity of the species. The constant factor is not the model but the adaptation. Man can be educated according to all the exceedingly varied patterns that the contemporary social world offers us today; also he has the capacity not just to submit passively to education, but also to educate himself, and this makes it possible for him to transcend and overstep the training facilities offered him in the direction of the truth. As truth is a symbol for something that can be only approached but never reached, from this point of view education is a dynamic process, incomplete and uncompletable. What this means in practice is that by education one can try to avoid delusions about the world, about people, and, above all, about oneself.

*A co-ordinated search*

Because of the enormous risk of deception – particularly self-deception – education can never be complete. Schooling comes to an end, but there is no end to self-education. An educated man can be described as one who has retained his youthful receptiveness to the new and the unknown. He is a seeker of knowledge and of ways to test experience. What he learns about the world and mankind and its history should help him to draw nearer to the truth about himself. One does not know the truth about oneself, one seeks it, and to the end of one's life the search remains unsatisfied.

The dynamic definition of education tells us that it is a search, and increasingly a co-ordinated search. When it declines into a demand for unattainable self-evident certainty, it ceases. Dogmatic certainty is the end of education (not excluding religious education). The educated philistine is as uneducated as the ignoramus.

If education is measured by thirst and curiosity for knowledge and not by its mere possession – agreeable and convenient though that may be – it must be admitted that it is a rarity, or at any rate a very precious thing, and that societies do a good deal – or sometimes make strenuous efforts – to prevent it from arising among mankind.

The factors that lead to education's running on the rocks (to 'education for its own sake', for instance) are numerous. They all end in prejudices that block the path to further discovery. Curiosity about knowledge conflicts with the ban on seeking it (in sanctified taboos, for instance). Where the community-imposed ban on seeking and questioning is the stronger, questioning becomes associated with anxiety. At this point education ends and 'social obedience' becomes the guiding line of behaviour. The breadth or narrowness of an individual's education, the persistence of his quest for knowledge or its extinction, depend both on his own strength of character and on the attitude of the group and its readiness to consider critically its own collective assumptions. In this respect no society is very tolerant, a phenomenon connected with the need to keep individuals in the group; it does so by enforcing its standards.

When one considers the intimidation to which the individual is subjected when he attempts to cast a critical eye on things, in particular the sacrosanct assumptions taken for granted in his own family or social group, in politics, etc., it is impossible to avoid the impression that those who are diverted from their true inclinations by the early assumption of prejudices, or meet with no response to their quest or are shouted down, greatly outnumber those who are ungifted or inflexible by nature.

## Three levels of education

Having thus attempted to emphasize the dynamic element in education, let us make further distinctions and differentiations. In the life of the individual early, pre-critical education, relatively poor in conscious content, can be distinguished from later education that makes increasing use of the critical consciousness. At the beginning of the path lie imitation and unquestioning experience of things. This is followed by identification with models, whom we seek to copy in knowledge, in character, and in relations with other people. Having completed the stage at which we incorporate models into our nature, we are able to move a stage further in the direction of self-realization.

What are the abilities with which the demand for education can be linked, and what aspects of the personality should be developed? In common parlance education implies knowledge, and the reader's first association with the word is the intellectual capacity for acquiring knowledge. Another essential element in the education through which we all pass is education in the expression of affect, that is, in behaviour, first identifying ourselves with others and finally in unhampered self-development. Closely connected with the education of affect, but not identical with it, is social education. By that is meant our capacity to observe critically and accept the multiformity of our fellow-men and our ability to live with them.

This formula, though it describes the co-operative aspects of 'social education', is of course misleading, for it does not take into account the actual power relations, the preponderance exercised by customs and existing standards and the collective pressure to accept them. Passive adaptation to conformity is generally enforced with little sympathy or understanding for the individuality of the person concerned, his individual variations and groping attempts to develop in his own way. Infinitely more often education takes the form of terrorism rather than guidance towards independence. The inconceivable complications and anomalies of the great societies of the present day are skilfully covered up and euphemized by a public opinion that purports to be liberal-minded but in reality exercises a different function – that of papering over the cracks and at the same time rousing sufficient anxiety to prevent the individual from breaking away from the group.

### Dialectical function of education

The means of destruction on the use of which public opinion might once again insist have become so terrible, so destructive to the biological substance, that ways and means must be found of changing the methods of education. Education must fulfil a dialectical role; it must exercise an influence on society and simultaneously provide immunization against it when it tries to impose stereotyped thought and action instead of critical understanding. One of society's most important tasks is to create a public opinion able to weigh pros and cons before decisions are made. 'If public opinion is legitimately to exercise the checking and controlling function that has been ascribed to it by the theory of the democratic state since Locke, its correctness must itself be subject to checks and controls.'[1] That is the purpose that must be served by social education in our cultural field. By means of it the repetition-compulsion of history must be superseded and a new social order established in the absence of which our freedom will turn out to be void of content. Massive resistance to this from existing institutions can be counted on.

The primary educational aim of the traditional religions is the inculcation of faith, and powerful authoritarian ideologies and their institutions surpass themselves in the same fanatical spirit of faith. They have undoubtedly made daily life easier for millions and millions of men. Those who a few decades ago were the mere illiterate objects of history have no reason to worry their heads about the truth of doctrines which have helped them to a life more worthy of human dignity. But the asynchronism of history has put us in a different position. We are faced with the question whether the obedient acceptance of beliefs that we practised so long in history is an adequate response to the degree of differentiation that the historical process has established in our cultural area. There are enough traditionalist forces in our society that see no reason for any revision of the tasks of education. Their methods – the initiation of the individual into untouchable taboos and the imposition of inhibitions of the critical reason – necessarily coincide with those of their sworn enemies, who draw the same certitude from different arguments and use the statistical majority of a manipulated public opinion to demonstrate their rightness. A revolution such as the Russian, for instance, can lead to material improvements, though the methods used differ little in their essentials from those of the régime that it displaced.

One of the principal aims of this book is to show that the maintenance of freedom at the present historical moment depends, not on repetition of the educational maxims of the past, but on a revision of educational practice. Only if we succeed in bringing further into consciousness and overcoming the terrorism – unrecognized as such and at the same time taken as a matter of course – that is exercised in our society by education can we hope to make headway against the skilfully and successfully manipulated ideological pressure that is exercised by the historical forces to which individual freedom of decision is a thorn in the flesh. A society that agrees to examine the correctness of its own fundamental assumptions and changes those that do not stand up to examination is not immobilized thereby. It is not like a millipede brought to a standstill by thinking about the rhythm with which it moves its feet. It is when he does not think about his next step that man stumbles, in his personal as in his collective life. Old ideals of freedom will not protect us unless we retest them against reality. Freedom is a part of reality that we possess neither for certain nor for ever; to be able to defend it we must experience it anew, with a great deal of soul-searching and overcoming of fear.

But let us now return to the three aspects of education to show what each of them can contribute to the historical tasks that we have indicated.

### The acquisition of knowledge

It is not easy to distinguish specialist knowledge from specialist education. A man who knows all there is to be known about Shakespeare, or syphilis, or the benzene ring, may be fully equipped professionally, but that does not necessarily make him an educated man, for his specialist knowledge may be unrelated to any true self-knowledge and without formative influence on his social behaviour. The extent to which specialist education is harnessed to the search for truth and not predominantly to the practical purpose of making a living depends on the survival of curiosity, on emotional development, on the way in which individual talent is encouraged, on whether an individual succeeds, for instance, in keeping his mind open and is sensitive to interests apart from the immediate demands of his career. Successful specialist education undoubtedly contributes to mental development. It is not in itself mental development, but one of the conditions for it.

### Affective education

Affective education differs radically from this. An individual's degree of affective education is synonymous with his degree of 'civilization'.

He should be able to abide by the ways of behaviour prescribed by his culture and nevertheless achieve personal self-expression.

The degree of affective education attained by the individual is displayed at the moment of action. The individual should understand himself and his own behaviour under the influence of excitation; even in the latter condition he should preserve a feeling for himself as well as a feeling for his opposite number. In the affects we experience the interplay or clash of our inner drives with objects in the outside world, and this can help to relieve our tensions. We may be hungry, or angry, or may be demanding love; all states corresponding to unsatisfied inner urges that we may be experiencing at that moment. How do we help them to obtain satisfaction? In these situations there are no innate, characteristically human patterns of behaviour corresponding to those of the social animals; our behaviour is dictated by affective behaviour patterns specific to our human group. Our social environment tells us what we should or should not do, what is permissible and what is forbidden, how we should behave in general.

In the animal world, however, the whole of behaviour in mating, in establishing the 'pecking order', in seeking prey or defying enemies, is determined by a behaviour pattern peculiar to the species, from which there is no escape. In searching for food animals may make discoveries, but in their social behaviour they behave strictly according to unvarying behaviour patterns which they are unable to change. In Britain, for instance, blue tits have discovered that they can pierce the tops of milk bottles and drink the cream. They picked up this trick from each other, they have extended their field of knowledge, but no British tit or any other can change its behaviour to its fellows in any way whatever. There is no possibility of individual variation in mating behaviour, for instance, at any rate so far as we can observe.

The ways of behaviour specific to the cultures or groups in which human beings are brought up are in comparison far less assured and infinitely more short-lived. The social behaviour of cranes has not changed since the days of Ibycus, but there is no human law or commandment or taboo that is never infringed, no matter how severe the penalty. Behind such violations are inner drives which have not been absorbed by the learning processes of the social group, that is, have not been made usable inside the group and also are not controllable by the individual concerned; they are discharged through him, as in a short circuit, so to speak, in which his ego is more or less eliminated; neither his ego nor his conscience has been able to prevent it. It is here that the surplus inner drive comes into play that society has failed to divert to its own purposes.

In individual cases these processes may be exceedingly complicated, but they all derive from the fact that we have no adequate innate and hereditary behaviour controls. Each of us learns for himself the laws of behaviour prevalent in our social environment. But moral laws are not fixed and permanent. Social processes, for example, developments in methods of production, impose change on them. Also the desire for 'happiness', for a state of relaxed and unmenaced freedom, is a permanent force opposed to the yoke of socially dictated renunciations. Moral laws are defied. Their changeability and the desire, often the compulsion, to infringe them are structurally connected. Such compulsion may derive predominantly from the changed structure of a society whose moral code has not yet adapted itself, or from basic individual drives which have either remained untamed or have grown anarchical. The criminal who breaks the law is an extreme instance of this. But those of us who are not criminals also have numerous affects which cause us to act very much under the domination of inner drives, obtaining rapid satisfaction of an inner need without regard for the individuality of the other party, for instance, and at the same time finding arguments to embellish the situation. '"I did that," says my memory. "I cannot have done that," says my pride, and remains inexorable. Ultimately it is my memory that yields' (Friedrich Nietzsche[2]).

Nietzsche here describes two functions of the ego: its critical function in testing reality and the trace of it left in the memory when it says 'I did that', and the denial of reality, the repression that the same ego carries out when, in the interests of self-respect, social prestige, maintenance of the individual's social role, it says 'I cannot have done that'. The activity of this part of the ego takes place to a large extent, though not completely, outside the field of conscious reflection.

Under the Argus eyes of the social environment, and of the conscience as the internalized environment, our ego is obviously unable to face up to the naked truth, the reality of our instinctual behaviour; it is prevented by fear of clashing both with external judges and with the internal court of the conscience. The intellect – the conscious, rational, logical, critical ego – is obviously not the undisputed master of

the house. It tries to avoid coming into conflict with laws and commandments and, to state the situation in a simplified form, tends to invent
altruistic-sounding motives. Hence there arises an inner alienation in
ourselves, that is, between our rationalizing self-deception about the
motivation of our actions and the instinctual needs that in fact imposed
them. The extent of this inner alienation or split between our real impulses which have been driven to work unconsciously and the rationalizations that suffice to meet the demands of faith, ideology, or social
convention varies, but it can be very great. Also the alienation affects
only certain drives that are subject to particularly strong group devaluation or taboo.

Freud has drawn attention to two types of social behaviour. The
first is 'cultural hypocrisy',[3] in which merely superficial conformism is
attained; the individual behaves socially so long as he feels the eye of an
external judge to be upon him, but as soon as he feels that no one is
there to keep a check on him his egoistical drives gain the upper hand.
Opportunity makes the thief, in fact. The second form of behaviour is
more resistant to temptation; it is more firmly linked to the requirements of the social environment and represents a higher level of
'organized cultural adaptation'. A level-headedness that does not
collapse even in conditions of great stress points to a more firmly based
organization of the critical ego functions, which do not allow themselves to be misused for rationalization. Romain Rolland was one of
those who possessed to a high degree this *aequanimitas*, this impertur-
bability of a highly sensitive mind, and that is why his 1914–19
diaries[4] are a document of such great importance. Perhaps no one else
saw with such inexorable clarity the extent of the 1914 collapse of the
sense of reality that extended into the highest ranks of the intellectual
aristocracy of the belligerent nations on both sides.

Thus there is no such thing as biologically determined human social
behaviour anchored in the genes. Instead, man learns to control his
instincts in a manner specific to his group or culture. In order to be able
to live in a culturally acceptable way he has to find socially adapted
outlets for his drives. Only on these terms can his 'blind', asocial
aggressivity be turned to useful work and his purely sexual urges
develop into loving human relationships.

Another alternative to flagrant breach of the social code is overadaptation. The 'conscience' can develop into a force so menacing that

it can totally inhibit any finer individual distinctions in moral matters and cause the individual to act like a sheer automaton. The psychological situation of such a person is characterized by a reign of terror exercised by his conscience associated with intolerable guilt feelings and fears. Formal orthodoxy, self-righteousness, and conformity of this type are just as great an obstacle to humanization, that is, increased freedom of decision, as is subjection to the blind dictates of inner drives. Also closer analysis of the over-adapted often reveals secret 'excesses' or striking departures from the social norm, and still more often their self-righteousness is associated with the satisfaction of sadistic impulses in a way that inhibits any refinement of human relations. The sad situation of such 'moral judges' has a great deal in common with that of 'moral sinners'.

Thus the education of affect necessarily implies an alleviation of the conflicts between ineluctable inner impulses and social norms, the acquisition of tolerance in dealing with the inner conflicts with which we are faced, and securing the 'memory', in the sense of the word used by Nietzsche, against lapses that alienate us from ourselves. The civilization of the affects is the hardest task of education. Better knowledge of oneself, the truth about oneself as a creature of instinct, can be acquired only by painful experience. Nietzsche continues the passage quoted above with the following words: 'He has been a poor observer of life who has not seen a hand outstretched to spare – by killing.' And Pascal said: 'Evil is never done so thoroughly and so well as when it is done with a good conscience.'[5] We have often smiled a superior smile at the blind prejudice of the men who burnt witches, but we have to confess that similar events have taken place on a vastly greater scale under our own eyes in our own lifetime, and are still taking place.

We have now made some preliminary points about education. The term has manifold meanings, and its boundaries are often not clearly defined. An educated man is a man who has acquired knowledge, but he is also 'civilized' in his instinctual and emotional life, and he has 'manners', as our grandparents used to say, using the term in a wider sense than mere knowledge of etiquette. He should also be able to express fully his personality in the style prescribed by his culture. The Germans have the somewhat sentimental term *Herzensbildung* – 'education of the heart'; the 'heart' includes affect, feeling, passion, and is thus a pointer to the concept of affective education. A pure scholar need not be a truly educated man, and a gifted and successful specialist in any field need not be one at all. The perceptive among the so-called educated are often surprised at the amount of understanding, balanced judgement, internal poise possessed by the so-called uneducated. Thus the education of affect is no privilege of class or caste, but is attainable at the most varied levels of formal education. The reason why this tends to be so easily overlooked is that education is generally thought of in a very group-centred way; and only the marks of education peculiar to one's own group tend to be noticed.

A man is called uneducated, for instance, if he shows signs of having failed to pass through a definite system of education, and the term is applied to him even more carelessly if his social level is inferior to one's own. Education is associated with prestige, which one wants to preserve for oneself and one's likes – that is, one's own group. A feature of successful revolutions is the devaluation of the education of the previous ruling group and the establishment of a new type of education. This is an interesting pointer to the connection between education and the group, and it also shows that there is no necessary connection between it and the spirit of tolerance. Awareness of the relativity of one's own group standards rouses so much fear and guilt that the individual is generally incapable of it. Collective swings to new group standards are easier. In recent times there has been a radical change in the social distribution of expert knowledge; in this sphere a 'fundamental democratization'[6] has taken place. The privileges, based on magical ways of thought, that erected insurmountable barriers in caste societies even more than in class society, have been levelled out so far as the acquisition of knowledge is concerned. Affective educational contacts beyond the boundaries of one's own social or political province still present us with great difficulties. Ministers or economic leaders who are uneducated in this sense are no rarities, and travellers who understand little or nothing about the foreignness of the people they meet outside their familiar environment are the rule rather than the exception. It is easier to admire landscapes, go sightseeing, visit museums, etc., than to make contact with the inhabitants of foreign towns and landscapes. Language barriers illustrate the intractability of the problem. On the one hand groups as they developed historically are separated by language (and thus hampered in communication), and on the other their separate development is itself an expression of the completion of a process of formation of affective behaviour. True, the growth of world civilization involves a levelling out of this multiplicity into a few main styles of group education, in turn involving the sacrifice of a great deal of historical fulfilment (which would have been achievable in smaller groupings) among the masses. What new differentiations may take place in the development of mass man remain entirely obscure. Mass life demands no far-reaching affective involvement of the individual, but at present at all events it gives him little opportunity of living out his emotional tensions, above all the aggressive ones, in useful social activity.

*Social education*

So far we have discussed education as the acquisition of knowledge and as affective (or emotional) education. We shall now turn to social education, in which the affective ways of behaviour of individual members of a society are moulded by reciprocal influence. It is here that the social style of a group is determined, the conscience is formed, and prejudices of all sorts are rooted. The deliberate aim of moral education – the co-ordination of the learning process and above all the expression of affect with the style of the group – is here achieved as if of its own accord in the course of daily life.

In the chapters that follow we shall be continually occupied with the problem of social education. Here we shall merely draw attention to an easily observable phenomenon: the normally deep-rooted objection to critical analysis of human institutions such as schools and similar bodies and political organizations, above all, political parties and their bureaucracies. In industry psychological studies are relatively acceptable, because in this field economic factors are at work, though even here an anti-psychological bias still prevails and experience and common sense are regarded as sufficient to cope with the problems. Practical necessities rule the roost as if they were natural laws having nothing to do with the subjective processes that take place in the human beings who have to master the group environment; as if all that was required were discretion, common sense, tact, and good will in adapting oneself to the rules, and as if the only factors at play within the group were the 'realistic' qualities of dutifulness, conscientiousness, and subordination and personal aspirations played no part; as if there were no such things as ruthless ambition or anxiety, and as if disappointment and rebelliousness were not natural reactions but deviations worthy of punishment. These things are either denied outright or are authoritatively suppressed, like the bad habits of children or criminal tendencies. The picture presented to the public is of over-all conformist behaviour disturbed only by a regrettable minimum of maladjusted individuals.

To the teacher group psychology, if by that term is meant systematic investigation of his impact on his pupils, is still a non-existent science. In practice there is nothing whatever to prevent a group psychological self-analysis of teachers with a view to obtaining evidence of the real impact made by the teaching profession. Such study groups are a familiar feature of dynamic group psychology, but the teachers at any ordinary school would indignantly reject the idea of any such examination of the impact made on each other and on their pupils by their stereotyped values and attitudes. Academic curricula and publications seldom suggest that political science has anything to do with the laws of affective group behaviour, behaviour stereotypes, the roots of prejudice, or other psychological phenomena; or, if these things are mentioned, it is generally in the form of contemptuous references to the 'mass mind', etc. A politician's motives for entering one party rather than another, the factors that influenced his choice of means, his attitude to life as a living personality, the extent to which his choice was governed by emotion or by cold calculation of reality considerations, how far he was influenced by his education, social origins, or his own personality problems, are questions that seem to be taboo because, as we shall see in later chapters, they conflict with his professional prestige. Studying a teacher, a professor, minister, or industrialist at work with his group is regarded as a grossly improper idea, not as a project that might be helpful to society. It is felt that a man either has the stuff in him to fill a leading position or he has not; the fact that disturbing personal characteristics often have to be tolerated when they appear in an individual in authority while the best qualities in those in inferior positions are not mobilized is accepted fatalistically. E. H. Erikson's[7] observations that an outspokenly anti-psychological attitude always conceals a special psychology is true in general, but has a special relevance to the German situation, for in German social education the virtue of obedience holds a specially high place. This attitude is buttressed by the argument of practical necessity, which puts those in authority on far too lofty a plane for petty psychological consideration to be taken into account.

In societies in which stability of role prevails and power relationships are clearly defined and hardly questioned, social education is a process of habituation that inevitably leads to stagnation and repetition when the individual merges his personality with the definitive role allotted him. In spite of a distinct tendency to favour restorational and traditionalist trends, our social situation cannot be regarded as stable in comparison, for instance, with the social self-feeling of the bourgeoisie at the height of its sway. True, society functions in spite of an interdependence that has been vastly increased by the multiplication and complication of productive and administrative methods and, in spite of all the criticisms that can be made of it, its defects may not be greater than they have always been in view of the imperfection of human institutions. The real cause for anxiety lies in the competition offered to our fundamental values by new and aspiring rival social orders, all of which make use of the same scientific techniques. They will have the same material standards of living to offer, if not today, at any rate in the foreseeable future. When material conditions have been assimilated, what will be the generally accepted values by which our society will orient itself? What are the values which as a collective identity it will defend? 'Defend' in this context does not necessarily involve the use of force, either aggressively or defensively; it may just as well mean a process of inner consolidation, the attainment of a higher cultural level, that is, insistence on critical examination of reality and on the socially guaranteed freedom to do this. It can already be foreseen that many members of our society will not be prepared to mount the barricades for religious certitudes, and many others will not be prepared to mount them for existing property relations, particularly as the struggles for power we are here concerned with, contrary to what is generally believed, are not in reality decided by the threats or belligerency, but rather by assimilation of administrative practices, propaganda campaigns, and the corruption of words and symbols (the word 'freedom' or 'peace' or 'party' or 'democracy', for instance).

It would be unrealistic, not to say absurd, to expect the man in the street, who suffers neither from cold nor from hunger, has no cause for anxiety about his old age, does not feel that his capacities have been unused, and enjoys his share of mass prosperity, to say that black is black if his society insists on his calling it white. It takes a very determined champion of truth to oppose a convention at the cost of losing his position and his livelihood; and the convention has to be a very oppressive one if he is to inspire others with the courage to follow his example. But are conventions in affluent societies necessarily oppressive to the identity feeling of socially protected individuals? And what appetites remain unsatisfied nevertheless?

In attempting to answer questions stated in these terms, the social psychologist must restrict himself to dealing with the only constant in these unforeseeable developments, that is to say, human nature, with its unlimited, open-ended capacity for adaptation.

However important and indispensable may be the security given us by the system of values (and prejudices) of our own society, our critical consciousness tells us that all human systems are transitory, and that natural human drives have again and again undermined existing systems and at the same time contributed to the creation of new ones. We most certainly are not using the term 'critical consciousness' as the equivalent of 'consciousness of doom', but we cannot avoid the conclusion that the achievements that led to the development of consciousness in history are no better assured against the undermining process than were systems that originated predominantly in magical ways of thought. We are aware of the paradox, to which psycho-analytical experience has accustomed us, that both individually and socially a high degree of technical skill and ingenuity – that is, specialist knowledge, perhaps even specialist education – can coexist with magical ways of thought. A state organized on Orwellian lines – highly rational and at the same time highly illusory – is no Utopia, but a very realistic vision, with a multitude of historical echoes and a high probability of one or many recurrences.

However, in spite of all our awareness of the relativity of social values, these considerations have brought us a gain that is not to be despised. The historical choice with which men are faced is another constant, itself closely associated with human existence. The vital question is not whether this or that system is 'better' – 'better' or 'more useful' to whom? – but whether and in what way it is nearer the truth. By truth we mean, not a permanent, supra-historical possession that can be acquired once and for all, but a symbol, a standard, by which the critical ego measures itself. Does society demand of its members a critical search for truth, countering magic, fantasies of omnipotence, and their own affects, or does it use these things to instil fear into them, keep them under control and ensure their obedience? The choice between these alternatives will decide the level of civilization even in affluent societies. Let us repeat: Where is the impetus to come from that will make the so anaclitic member of these mammoth societies of ours raise this question of truth? Where is he to get the strength to ask it if his society does not do so, or does so only in certain restricted fields? Where lies the difference between the cult of the personality in openly totalitarian régimes and others which side by side with totalitarian areas have cults in which critical freedom prevails? The difference is certainly only of degree. But such degrees disappear quickly in history.

The purpose of this book is to oppose anti-psychological affect in our social education. Our premise is that only the strengthening of alert, critical thought can prevent the extinction of the European tradition. Since the beginnings of the Enlightenment this tradition has called for individual responsibility in addition to collective obedience – the irreverent questioning of taboos that buttress questionable claims. Here lies the individual's chance to be more than a 'knot or relatively distinguished point in a supra-individual network' (Gardner Murphy).[8] It may be a rare situation that calls for it, but it must be possible and legitimate to oppose prevailing opinion without being threatened with ostracism or death. Behind the great ideological conflicts of our time we foresee a struggle for this freedom.

## Composite nature of education

Thus education is a sum-total of processes of entirely different kinds. In the first place, at the level of the intelligence, there is the mere acquisition of knowledge. We rightly feel this to be insufficient and incomplete. The other requirement, that if a man is to be considered truly educated his knowledge must be associated with the development of his critical faculties, points to a second process through which we pass: the formation of our affects and affective behaviour in accordance with a pattern specific to our group and civilization. A great deal of the knowledge we accumulate, in particular historical knowledge, is closely associated with judgements of value. These are the result of affective reaction to processes in the outside world, and they again kindle affect.

Thus affective prejudices and the pseudo-knowledge contained in them have always acted as successful barriers to demonstrable truth, as is obvious enough in everyday life. Thus 'the shrewdest people will all of a sudden behave without insight as soon as the necessary insight is confronted by an emotional resistance, but that they will completely regain their understanding once that resistance has been overcome'.[9]

Emotional impulses that threaten the *status quo* generally appear in the guise of prejudice. The process of subjecting a prejudice to critical examination threatens the *status quo* and undermines some of our social assumptions, for the alien ideas that threaten to demolish prejudice share the fascinating certainty characteristic of the latter. The intrusion of knowledge and understanding into an area previously not understood may involve a very painful threat of self-devaluation, which we fight off almost as if by a reflex action even before the pain or unpleasure associated with it is experienced; for that is the economic function of prejudice. We never produce so many rationalizations as when we rush to defend the values associated with our ego feelings against the intrusion of 'alien' values.

Even in the field of science the evaluation of a phenomenon can be affected by unconscious affective ties. An example of this is provided by schizophrenia, which for a long time was held to be an organic psychosis – a process uninfluenced by conflict with the social environment – and that is what a considerable number of psychiatrists still hold it to be. In the first place, however, schizophrenia is now known to be a general term, a descriptive label applied to a whole series of psychopathological phenomena, different processes of development that culminate in the symptoms so referred to. In some cases the predominant factor may be constitutional, that is, an exceptionally low toleration for the inevitable disappointments of life, while in others, as has been shown by Lidz, specific psychical deprivations in infancy may have been responsible. In between the two extremes of psychosomatic susceptibility on the one hand and extreme psychical deprivation on the other there lies a whole range of intermediary cases. This situation is, however, denied, on the ground that schizophrenia is primarily of organic origin, even if the organic cause is unknown. The stubbornness with which this assumption has been defended for years originates, not in an unprejudiced scientific approach, but in the unconscious defence mechanisms of those dealing with the mentally ill. If the patient's condition is unconnected with our social reality, if it is not the reflection of a conflict with which the patient cannot deal except by an illusory denial of reality, the physician, like people at large, can regard this highly disturbing illness as a meaningless collapse of the personality, as insanity pure and simple, and thus maintain his detachment from it with a clear conscience.

Thus defence mechanisms play their part in those who have fallen out with our social environment (a category that also includes many criminals). These mechanisms buttress the psychical equilibrium of those who have to maintain social contact with them, but they are able to do so only so long as this defence function remains unrecognized. The belief that schizophrenia is a disease of purely organic origin unconnected with the social environment is defended with such affective violence that it provides unexpected evidence of the unconscious context in which a scientific theory can fulfil a function going beyond all rational evidence.[10] But even in the case of less disturbing illnesses it goes against the grain – with patients as well as with physicians – to recognize any causal connection between them and the patient's personal life.[11] The resistances that stand in the way of calm consideration of this possibility by many doctors, and apparently the majority of patients too, are irrational in nature. An investigation at an American psychiatric clinic showed a definite correlation between a psychiatrist's school of thought and the proportion of cases of schizophrenia or psychoneurosis (mental illness precipitated by events in the patient's life) diagnosed by him.[12]

The example here quoted from the world of medicine could be supplemented by many similar examples from other scientific fields, as well as from politics and elsewhere, both past and present.

Tried judgement, a sure appraisal of the values of one's own culture, a breadth of vision for things that enjoy high esteem in other cultures, are characteristics of maturity, that is, of a degree of education that enables the affects to take a back seat and not disturb and distort our picture of the world at the very moment of perception. The function of the affects at that moment is to ward off the alien and unknown, which is felt to be dangerous, disturbs equilibrium, and awakens fear.

Thus prejudices fuse with affect for the purpose of maintaining equilibrium. This is a complex process, to which we shall frequently revert in the pages that follow. In general, the ability to control affect and detach oneself from the emotion that automatically sets in when values are touched on is not easy to develop, and is therefore rare. But it is important in an age of mass societies which have in their own hands the power to decide whether or not to annihilate themselves, and in the future it will be even more important.

*Affects and defence against the alien*

A glance at history shows that affects serve two purposes in the life of a group. On the one hand they serve to unite it, and on the other they defend it against the alien. Over long periods they stifle intellectual curiosity about other groups or societies. It generally takes generations for different social groups to get to know one another. The reader is reminded of the hereditary enmity between neighbouring family groups as well as between nations. A hundred years ago a war between Bavaria and Prussia was still a possibility, though belligerence of that kind on that scale in western Europe seems hardly conceivable today. But a price has been paid for this pacification, which in any case seems to have been achievable only as a result of a shift of aggressivity to other objects. The idea of proximity is a very relative one. Mutual tolerance is slowly arising between the social values of the French and the Germans; the differences are no longer regarded as threatening. But at the same time new polarizations of power have arisen, between the western world and Russia or China, for instance. Once more we see two groups each feeling the other to be hostile and unintelligible and each perceiving repellent characteristics in the other, and these perceptions are emotionally charged to the highest degree. These tensions step into the place of the old as the latter fade away, demonstrating how unsatisfied surplus drives arising in one's own cultural unit are diverted against the enemy of the moment. This is of course far from being the whole explanation of such hostile attitudes, but it explains their persistent, irrational nature. They arise, not only from real conflicts of interest, but also from the emotional needs of human social groups, and in particular from the deficiencies of one's own group. The affective reactions to these seek an outlet and are diverted to scapegoats specific to the group.

If man were completely adapted to his environment, there would be no systems of value and no conflict between his impulses and the standards of behaviour prescribed by his group; also there would be no group deficiencies resulting in the need to find a culprit outside it, that is, adapt him to this purpose by projection. Common to all fantasies about the goal of human history is a society imagined as being free of conflict, but society has never been like that; civilization is an ideal we struggle for but never attain. The slightest temptation is sufficient to shatter the good intentions of many individuals, their adaptation to the standards of their society. Let us take a commonplace example. A soldier travelling by train discovers on returning from the toilet that he has left his wallet there, with all his papers and money. He hurries back, but it has vanished. The conductor accompanies him from compartment to compartment, but in vain. Opportunity makes the thief, as the saying is. In psychological terms what has happened is this. Finding the wallet presented the finder with a temptation. His cultural standards told him to respect the property of others, but his egoistical impulses were obviously in instantly rousable conflict with this precept, by ignoring which he was able to obtain easy satisfaction for them. His conscience, the internal representative of the social code, was unable to prevail against the emotional tension provoked by the temptation, and by yielding to it he showed himself to be a cultural hypocrite.

This warns us not to overestimate the degree of organized cultural assimilation achieved by the forms of education we have so far developed. There is much in our education that is remote from reality and reflects the wishful thinking of the educator rather than his ability to cope with the situation. As Freud put it, 'students of human nature and philosophers have long taught us that we are mistaken in regarding our intelligence as an independent force, and in overlooking its dependence on emotional life. Our intellect, they teach us, can function reliably only when it is removed from the influence of strong emotional impulses; otherwise it behaves merely as an instrument of the will and delivers the inference which the will requires. Thus, in their view, logical arguments are impotent against affective interests, and that is why disputes backed by reasons, which in Falstaff's phrase are "as plenty as blackberries", are so unfruitful in the world of interests.'[13]

The thief in our story had an appropriate maxim ready to hand. 'This'll teach him to be more careful next time,' he no doubt said to himself as he pocketed the wallet. Such are the specious arguments by which the intellect protects itself against the conscience; and the speed with which the incident took place serves to show how precarious is cultural behaviour always and everywhere, and how quickly conflict can arise between selfish drives and the restrictions placed on them by a group's moral code.

Hence the most important characteristic of an educated man is that in affect-rousing situations he remains in more or less permanent control of his own impulses. The greatest offence against our social code, the crime that is most vigorously pursued and punished by the law, is killing our fellow-men, and yet in our periodical wars killing ceases to be a crime. 'But what no human soul desires stands in no need of prohibition; it is excluded automatically. The very emphasis laid on the commandment "thou shalt not kill" makes it certain that we spring from an endless series of generations of murderers, who have the lust for killing in their blood, as, perhaps, we ourselves have today,' Freud says, and he continues: 'Mankind's ethical strivings, whose strength and significance we need not in the least depreciate, were acquired in the course of man's history.'[14] The painful struggle to achieve adaptation, to create a society that will permit some outlet to insatiable impulses and yet make them tolerable to others, is like building on shifting sand.

### Historical change and the drive for knowledge

The first outcome of our reflections on adaptation in relation to education is that it is brought about in us by two forms of organization described by Adolf Portmann as the fixed, hereditary behaviour structure and the adjustment structure. Adjustment is a characteristic of all forms of life, and it always depends on the interaction between relatively invariable hereditary factors and others that are variable. Portmann quotes a simple example to illustrate the contrast between 'fixed' and 'open' behaviour. Migratory birds that fly by day orient themselves in their great spring and autumn flights by the position of the sun. 'At every hour of the day they fly at a definite angle to it and thus "take into account" the sun's movement.' Man can navigate by exactly the same system, but the background is entirely different in each case. Both use 'a complicated system of intercontinental orientation', but in one case it is 'completely hereditary, while in ours it has been painfully acquired by generations of individual intellectual effort'.[15] It is not only our capacity for orientation in space that depends on our 'open hereditary structure'; the same also applies to nearly all the difficult tasks of orientation with which we are faced, and in particular those that confront us in relation to our social environment. The powerful instinctual component in our nature seeks the satisfaction of our basic needs. The vital restlessness of our basic impulses is not captured and ritualized in relation to the outside world by hereditary factors. The rituals, ceremonies, laws, and customs that govern our everyday behaviour are established by collective consent and have to be learned individually. The hardest part of this learning process lies in abiding by what has been learned.

Our rituals are historical and are subject to change. The agency that forms and co-ordinates our attitude to our human environment and the world in general is in psychological terminology the ego. Let us reiterate. This ego, which is the regulative agency that governs our behaviour, that says yes or no, is a new function of life characteristic of man. Thus his actions can be said to depend on the drive for information to an incomparably greater extent than applies in the animal (P. Brückner). Curiosity about the unknown, the inquisitiveness that is very marked in animals, particularly young animals, has to survive much longer among human beings if they are to avoid mistakes, sometimes fatal mistakes. As man has such a wide area of ignorance about himself, he falls back on prejudices of all sorts for support. A theoretically not insoluble conflict lies in the function of these prejudices. Which are reliable and which erroneous, though comforting? There is no end to the ego's task.

## Aspects of the ego

In view of the difficulty of coming to grips with its subject, the danger of reification, oversimplification of its concepts, looms large in psychology and is hard to avoid. The term 'ego' that we used a moment ago inevitably has associations for us, but it must be emphasized that it is by no means identical with what we are aware of as our conscious self. The reactions of our partner in a conversation sometimes show us that there is a great deal about ourselves of which we are unaware, that there are, for instance, a great many affective overtones in our behaviour that are obvious to others. When Freud points out that a great deal of the ego, 'and notably what we may describe as its nucleus',[16] is unconscious, he draws our attention to mental processes that resemble hereditary behaviour in their effect and, though they have been acquired rather than inherited, cannot be critically influenced by the individual, who cannot, except at the cost of great effort, even become aware of them; it is truer to say that they just happen.[17] And yet there is an important difference. Unlike the animals, we can learn; we can examine our social behaviour critically and reflectively, and we can change it.

The ego developed genetically out of the id, the sum-total of mental processes associated with organic life the role of which – from the evolutionary standpoint – is to regulate behaviour in order to ensure the survival of the species. The ego's function of criticizing reality and itself, being associated with the appearance of the human species, is comparatively of very recent origin. The lack of fixed, hereditary behaviour patterns specific to the species is made up for in man by acquired behaviour patterns specific to groups. The fact that cultural differences have no taxonomic significance in the biological sense, but play a merely chance or 'provincial' role, means that trying to understand and orient oneself among behaviour patterns that differ so profoundly makes heavy demands on the ego. In societies such as ours, in which environmental conditions and the social structure itself are liable to such rapid change, the extent of the conscious as a prerequisite for the critical examination of reality is of ever growing importance and is perhaps vital to the survival of the species.

We do not know the causes of, though we do know some of the conditions associated with, the 'still mysterious features of our openness' to self-perception and the moulding of our behaviour, that is, ego functions. The most important difference, compared with the higher mammals, lies in the shortness of the period of human gestation. In comparison with the young in the animal kingdom, the child, as we have pointed out, is born immature, both physically and in functional behaviour. According to Bolk,[18] Portmann, and others, a period of human gestation equivalent to that of other mammals would be from twenty to twenty-two months. Portmann therefore calls the first year of a human life the 'social uterus period', in which the place of the womb is taken by the social group. This is the period of maturation of the capacities for 'the upright stance, speech, and understanding behaviour in relation to the environment', that is, the physical and mental characteristics of human life. To quote Portmann again: 'The division

34

into two of our all-important early period of development is no mere chance. The formation of the specifically human characteristics we have just mentioned contrasts sharply with the development of all the higher mammals. While all the characteristic traits of the latter develop *pari passu* with the maturation of fixed hereditary characteristics in the monotonous shelter of the womb, with us the development of the essential traits takes place in a very marked combination of maturation and learning processes. . . . The uniqueness of this extra-uterine infancy . . . is the counterpart of the uniqueness of the human relationship to the world, which we may describe as intelligent or open to the world.'[19]

The consequence of these biological conditions is that from earliest infancy we can be educated only in interaction with our human environment. Learning to understand other selves is the foundation of our so limited self-understanding, and is therefore a primary human task. Thus maturation into an individual able to attain awareness of himself as a human entity distinct from other human entities presupposes a high degree of adaptability. Not till I understand how to adjust myself to others in a continuous learning process, a continuous give-and-take, do I attain self-awareness. The real yardstick of the degree of humanity attained by the individual is whether and to what extent this process remains open in the course of the emotional experiences associated with it, and whether it is performed willingly or avoided.

We shall now go on to consider the biologically anchored and socially transmitted components of human behaviour in relationship to each other. In particular we shall concern ourselves with understanding and misunderstanding of the phenomenon of our social roles. The dialectics that control our social behaviour will stand out more plainly; we learn roles and are guided by them. But in these circumstances are we really individuals in the full meaning of the word implied by our moral principles? Or is something further required of us of which we are capable – ascertainment of our own true nature, critical detachment, appraisal of our own role, and drive-dictated behaviour?

# III

# Insufficiency of Instinct

## Evolution of the conscious

The problem of human freedom raised at the end of the last chapter seemed in the past to be a philosophical or ethical one. For all the traditional respect paid to philosophy, however, in many fields of social life more powerful influences were at work, and it was ignored; things took their course unhampered by ivory tower reflections. In recent years, however, the problem has suddenly become topical and more difficult to ignore. Scientific developments directly connected with questions of life or death have assumed a leading role in our society and make a far more immediate impact on our social consciousness; or, to state it more cautiously, they are more alarming to the latter, because the problems involved are manifestly connected with survival.

From the scientific viewpoint, and that of the theory of evolution in particular, the ability to exercise conscious choice about his way of living that developed in man is so significant because it marks a new stage in evolution. It seems no exaggeration to say that old theological descriptions of man as made in God's image have been reformulated within the framework of scientific theories in which questions of freedom and responsibility are also involved. The picture has changed greatly since the days of the drab, mechanistic interpretations of evolutionary theory characteristic of the turn of the century. Biological modifications having made possible a conscious orientation to life accompanied by release from genetically fixed behaviour patterns, the consequence is that a great burden of responsibility, that of guiding and controlling human behaviour, has devolved upon that conscious orientation. Looking at the situation more closely, it can be seen that a consistent, historically traceable process has been at work in which responsibility has developed into a consciousness of responsibility dependent on itself alone. It is legitimate to talk of increased responsibility, because the theory of evolution as part of an analytical science is hardly reconcilable with the idea of a personal God as handed down by the traditional religions. It must be emphasized that in the present socio-psychological context we are not concerned with theological or philosophical subtleties, but only with the form in which religious ideas affect the general social consciousness. What we are concerned with here, that is to say, is the religious feelings of the man in the street, the extent to which these are genuinely felt by him and how they affect his behaviour; and in this context it can hardly be doubted that the God he is taught to believe in is a personal God.

## Mythology v. science

If scientific evidence and scientific theories about the development of life up to the moment when it became conscious of itself are taken seriously, it is impossible, except at the cost of a split personality, simultaneously to believe in a mythological theory of creation. The dilemma is faced with admirable courage by theologians of the type of Teilhard de Chardin. The psychological difficulty with which science confronts us lies in the impossibility of projecting responsibility upon an anthropomorphic God. For all the emphasis laid by theologians on the absolute and on the absolute otherness of God, the psychological reality remained that God was a being who could be spoken to, that is, was in some way similar to ourselves. The approach to Him by way of speech – chiefly in the form of prayer – and with it the delegation of responsibility on the pattern of the child-father or child-parent relationship has become impossible, and the disillusionment has not been compensated for by the appearance of new precepts for behaviour on which total reliance can be placed. To the majority this is such an oppressive situation that they seek to evade it regressively – in a word, irrationally. They resign themselves to the dilemma, on the one hand accepting the benefits derived from the untheological scientific outlook, the achievements of which in some cases they actively promote, while on the other they acquiesce apparently uncritically in a moral code and in beliefs that cannot be confirmed by rational experience.

Now, *credo quia absurdum* is certainly no modern paradox; the sense of humility in the face of the vastness of the universe is increased rather than diminished by our increased knowledge of it. It is not to that that the paradox applies, but to a complex claim to social authority, the duty of believing in a doctrine of salvation that forms an essential part of the dominant system.

## The conscious and social integration

Two consequences follow from this situation. In the first place, rationalism is continually invading new fields, and even the nature of man, his social institutions and values, turn out to be accessible to rational analysis. The knowledge thus acquired has permanently affected our attitude to the world in which we live. Implicit in all statements based on the rationalist principle is that they can be tested and corrected by observation. The process of rational discovery is dynamic and never-ending. The critical method takes the ground from under the feet of the social authoritarianism that claims an absolute validity that must not be submitted to examination. In accordance with the claim to represent truths immune from criticism, authoritarian institutions resting on this principle have always tended to trace their genealogy back to divine actions. Criticism of them has been treated as sacrilege, and to anticipate conflict in this field educational practice has sought to impose inhibitions on the freedom of thought.

The second consequence concerns affective behaviour. Rational criticism is not, as neo-mythologists have claimed, hostile to affect. Understanding is not an enemy of the 'feelings', but it does stand in the way of emotional logic. Metaphysically based authoritarianism uses this emotional logic; in other words, it admits rationalization to the service of its own interests.

Critical rationalism has no metaphysical certitudes to offer, but it is capable of striving for understanding in fields in which powerful instinctual wishes or guilty fears are at work and behaviour that – in the general view – may seem natural, even though crude and repellent, may be near the point of discharge. Its potentialities for exercising such control should not be underrated as a factor in social security.

What all this leads to is the question of how man will manage without projecting his group-specific social organizations – the family structure based on undisputed paternal authority, for instance – on a world scale. What will a society that in this sense will be fatherless, that is, not controlled by a mythical father and his terrestrial representatives, look like?

The question could be more confidently left for the future if in the long history of paternalist societies so much instinctual life had not been treated repressively; instinctual wishes thus removed from the influence of the critical ego periodically broke through the social framework with varying degrees of murderousness and destructivity. This method of socialization, associated with present-day technical aids, may cost the life of the whole human species. That is why the split-mindedness mentioned above is now a major source of danger. To deny this would be a neurotic response to the situation rather than an attitude worthy of the critical conscious. Thus everything depends on whether the forces of consciousness developed by the evolutionary process can reach full development before the simultaneously produced release of instinctual drives results in catastrophe.

In a less repressive society, less subject to magical modes of thought, better integrated, and with a more fully developed conscious, the authority of the code of behaviour will have a form and function different from any that we can yet imagine. We, however, are con-concerned with the social order, not just from the point of view of the historical process in the narrower sense, but from that of the development of life as a whole. The authority of the mythical traditions is no longer sufficient to bring about a social integration of mass society; its ultimate outcome is always dictatorship.

*Evolution becomes conscious of itself*

Let us therefore spend a little more time seeing what evolutionary theory has to suggest on the subject. First of all it must be borne in mind that 'the notion of evolution is by now not solely a theory about certain processes which may go on in the living world, but is one of the essential dimensions within which biological thought must take place'.[1] Julian Huxley considers that there have been 'two critical points in the past of evolution . . . the first was marked by the passage from the inorganic phase to the biological, the second by that from the biological to the psycho-social'. First, in the sub-human sphere, there took place the formation of patterns of behaviour innate and specific to the species – what used to be called instincts – and then man appeared with his conscious and his individual learning of a social pattern of behaviour. 'Today, in the twentieth century, the evolutionary process is at last becoming conscious of itself, and is beginning to study itself with a view to directing its future course.'[2] This stage is plainly marked by consciously purposive tendencies, while the finality of development of the non-human evolutionary processes remains subject to dispute. If human evolution becomes conscious and within limits controllable, scepticism about teleological thinking, at any rate so far as this sphere of life is concerned, loses its justification. On the contrary, full attention must be paid to its aims. Responsibility grows with increased awareness of the consequences involved.

Heredity, like education, can be regarded functionally as an information transmission system. 'In the sub-human world this transmission of what we may call, in a general sense, "information", is carried out by the passing on of hereditary units or genes contained in the germ cells. . . . Man, alone among animals, has developed this extra-genetic mode of transmission to a state where it rivals and indeed exceeds the genetic mode in importance.'[3] Waddington, like Portmann, uses the ability to fly to illustrate the transition from one method to the other. 'Man acquired the ability to fly not by any noteworthy change in the store of genes available to the species, but by the transmission of information through the cumulative mechanism of social teaching and learning.' Consequently he 'developed a socio-genetic or psycho-social mechanism of evolution which overlies, and often overrides, the biological mechanism depending solely on genes. Man is not merely an animal which reasons and talks, and has therefore developed a rational mentality which other animals lack. His faculty for conceptual thinking and communication has provided him with what amounts to a completely new mechanism for the most fundamental process of all, that of evolution.' Thus release from genetically anchored information and development of 'socio-genetic transmission of information by teaching and learning'[4] mark a third critical phase in the evolutionary process.

In other words, the solution of this truly vital problem is associated with the process of civilization, that is, progressively conscious control of socio-genetic behaviour.

*The converging sciences*

It is interesting to note how findings in different scientific fields are beginning to converge. Freud's dynamic psychology fits in admirably with the views of the evolutionists. His view that the ego developed out of the id is a statement about evolution. The id, the whole field of unconscious mental activity, belongs historically to the sub-human phase of psycho-social development, in which behaviour is determined by genetically transmitted information of an instinctual nature. But the appearance of the ego, the supervention of the conscious mind, did not take place at one blow, nor did the new method of transmitting information eliminate its historical predecessor. The ego functions superimposed themselves upon the existing systems very slowly, and partially changed them in the process. In this connection Freud's observation that the nucleus of the ego remains unconscious is of great importance. The social learning processes take place to a great extent below the threshold of consciousness; above all, they begin in infancy, when the conscious critical faculties are still very weak. On top of that it must be borne in mind that the factors we have summarized under the heading of affective and social education have an inherent tendency to fall into stereotyped patterns, to automatization. Thus they relapse into the preconscious or completely unconscious field and are to a greater or lesser degree beyond the influence of the critical conscious. The super-ego, or ego ideal, which Freud once called a stage towards the ego,[5] is a kind of precipitate of the experience of social authority and a centre of behavioural integration which receives and transmits information to a large extent unconsciously. This preliminary stage of the ego is also very difficult to influence consciously.

Opposite forces are at work at two levels. The intellectual achievements of the ego have created powerful aids for humanity. For the first time in history technology has made it possible for men to live in increasing freedom from material want. This creates conditions that allow the critical ego to bind an increasing proportion of instinctual energy and subject it to its aims. On the other hand, the technical aids themselves become powerful allies of impulses alien to the ego. This is all too evident in the political methods of threat and deterrence.

The same opposite tendencies reappear at the level of the super-ego; here too impulses are bound and directed to social aims and behaviour patterns. Without inner guidance the promptings of which seem patently right we should hardly be able to orient ourselves among our fellow-men. But the patent rightness of this guidance hobbles us when it succeeds in enlisting us for destructive trends when these arise in our society, and our sense of adherence to the community (the result of the influence of the super-ego) turns us into dangerous aids of impulses alien to the ego. The outcome of all this is that we have to accept as a fact the coexistence of levels of organization in our behaviour and self-feeling that derive from different stages of evolution. But we must try to admit this to ourselves as plainly as possible.

## The protestant line

Nevertheless we must not overlook the fact that our historical period confronts us with special tasks. One of them is facing on a reality basis new situations for which there is either no historical precedent or – just as important – for which traditional solutions are inapplicable if immeasurable disaster is not to ensue. Thus the extension of our critical conscious is our most urgent need. A larger proportion of our behaviour must be determined by insight and reflection than has hitherto been the case in social life as a whole.

This can be brought about only by education. The striking feature of the situation is that the great obstacle in the path of an extension of our conscious is traditional education – its deficiencies in the affective field in comparison with its high development in that of imparting knowledge. Social education is to a large extent dominated by archaic models. This involves the ascendancy of stereotyped values and expressions of affect in the very field in which examination of the facts and of the self are becoming increasingly indispensable. The highly respected institutions that transmit such systems of orientation bar the way to awareness of the altered situation. The historical form that they took has – like an inherited behaviour pattern anchored in the genes – proved to be incapable of adapting itself to new conditions; and this is another instance in which a return to a condition of greater plasticity and a fresh start seem impossible. Like a sense organ that has lost the capacity to adapt itself to a new kind of stimulus, their sensibility is blind to the substance of the new conflicts. Just as the eye reacts only to a limited range of light waves, so the historically developed organs of society perceive only a limited range of the factors and combinations of factors that govern human behaviour in the social field and in relation to themselves.

Ever increasing density of population imposes functional conformities in everyday life. But at the level of decision that goes beyond (though it reacts on) everyday life the cultivation of a protestant spirit among the majority is required in order to counteract the inertia of social institutions. A protestant spirit in this context means the determination to defend a newly acquired scrap of critical freedom of thought against external pressure to conform and internal fear. That was the distinguishing feature of Protestantism when the word and the the thing entered history, and there is no reason why the same term should not be applied to later stages of the development of the conscious. As in the age of the great religious Protestants, we are concerned with enlightenment – the words *post tenebras lux* are inscribed over the tiny window of the ruined Protestant chapel at Les Baux – and with the incursion of personal responsibility into spheres previously left to authority, whether that of a personal deity, a divinely approved social system, or a father or father-figure who is above criticism.

After a brief revaluation during the fifties, two words have again acquired distinctly derogatory associations in our country; these are 'liberal' and 'rational', and this applies particularly when the function of reason is being discussed and the word 'rational' is used. The levels of the personality that are older in the evolutionary scale gladly take their stand on 'brains' in so far as the individual's career and personal prestige are concerned, but they do not take kindly to thought. It is, however, to these older levels of experience that the formation of social character is left; individuals come to terms with each other, and society comes to terms with them, at a level of simpler psychical processes, a level of fantasy. The critical testing of reality is neglected, consciously by-passed, or for unconscious reasons avoided. It is rational to apply the critical conscious to information communicated by dream or faith; it is irrational, and dangerously misleading, to fail to see that the nonrational attitude to life is a fact of the greatest importance in man's historical development. At this point liberalism comes into play. There are obviously many and various beliefs that man acquired nonrationally. To be tolerant of them is liberal; to adopt a critical attitude towards them, or at any rate to claim the right to do so, is rational. In the critical phase of evolution through which we are passing it is hard to see what other attitude to adopt to the multiplicity of demands on our belief and the survival and coexistence of many different outlooks.

The often individual, often institutional, and in the recent past socially imposed discrimination against liberalism and the rational examination of reality (including self-examination) will not deter us from applying both to the field of social psychology.

### Lack of sharp outline of human roles

From the long-range view of evolution let us now return to the immediate social environment. The picture as seen by the participant is often bewilderingly complicated and at the same time monotonous. It is bewildering because of the continual surprise effects of actual situations. On the one hand, widespread freedom from obligatory behaviour patterns allows divergencies of impulse, interest, belief, feelings, opinion, and prejudice to arise in inexhaustible variety. On the other, the extent to which the actors are bound to their roles contributes to the monotony; they are bound to them to a far greater extent than their self-esteem relishes.

The interest of both theoretical and empirical sociologists has in recent years to a large extent been concentrated on the roles, role stereotypes, role status, and other aspects of behaviour arising from imitation, identification, or, as it is often called in the latest literature, introjection. Our purpose is to try to understand the ontogenetic processes involved in assuming roles, that is, to analyse the part played by them in human life. We shall be able to look at a few examples only, and it will be left to the reader to supplement them from his own experience; also to a certain extent we shall inevitably be steering a zigzag course between human and animal role behaviour.

The lack of definition of human role behaviour will be reflected in our survey. It is tempting to say that fixity of role is in inverse proportion to humanity; that the more human behaviour is, the less it consists of mere role fulfilment. But that would be a misleading generalization, and would not lead to the heart of the problem. For even the human freedom to attain critical detachment is not absolute; it has to be attained from the standpoint of some role. Maturity of the ego presupposes adaptation.

*Roles as signals*

This will be shown by our first example. The individual may gain a distinct sense of freedom from the decisions and choices he makes in the course of his work or in satisfying his consumer needs. In politics people show much less freedom; they are less flexible, and their opinions are more tied to their environment, while, so far as religion is concerned, in the great majority of cases the individual remains in the religion into which he was born. But, apart from the objective limitations of his income, there may be restrictions on his freedom of choice even among the wealth of consumer goods at his disposal. The head of a big hospital, for instance, for many years drove a car in the middle price range, while his assistants drove cheaper models. When he at last decided to buy a car that accorded with the consumption standards of his social status, his subordinates sighed with relief, because they were at last able to buy the cars in the middle price range that seemed appropriate to them. In the United States, where a secularized industrial society is still characterized by a strict Puritan class hierarchy, it is taken for granted that directors' secretaries buy their clothes from the best store in town, while the secretaries of heads of departments buy theirs from the next best, and so on. Thus the new status levels are strictly reflected in the field of prestige consumption goods. This goes much deeper than is implied by the saying that 'clothes make the man'; cars, clubs, restaurants, residential neighbourhoods, are not only amenities but also essential elements in the individual's self-regard. They define his status in his own eyes as well as in those of others.

It is not easy in the course of everyday life to tell where individual freedom and independence begins and role-dictated behaviour ends; it depends on what is meant by freedom and independence. Our definition is that it is the ability before deciding and acting to detach oneself from role demands, demarcations, valuations, etc., even under the pressure of affect. It should be added that detachment is also required in relation to our own feelings; we must, for instance, be able to admit the anxiety that divergent behaviour is capable of rousing in us.

In the choices we make in the course of everyday life we seldom or never have a simple, one-dimensional relationship to the environment. The head of the hospital who came to the reasonable conclusion that a cheap car was good enough for him may at the same time have established another status privilege for himself by way of 'non-verbal communication', indicating that it would be inappropriate for his subordinate colleagues to own cars more expensive than his, for this would have disturbed the ranking order. Alternatively, if cars were not associated in his mind with prestige and seniority and the whole thing was a matter of total indifference to him, his colleagues were unable to claim the same scrap of freedom for themselves by choosing cars that accorded with their tastes and income.

## Possessions as signals

The world of consumer goods is new territory that is being perpetually extended. It is evident enough that the libidinal cathexis of these goods is high and that they are felt to be an enrichment of the individual's self-regard. It is also evident that to the ego this new territory plays the same part as historically older forms of possession, that is, is associated with the individual's status and ranking order. Whether his extracting their full practical value from these new possessions makes him freer is at least open to question. The domestic use of electric light, for instance, being available to everybody at a cost well within his means, has lost its status-signalling value and has become purely a matter of convenience. But that cannot be said of innumerable other so-called consumer goods (cars, carpets, one's residential neighbourhood, etc.); and it seems Utopian to look forward to a technical Elysium in which the libidinal cathexis of such things will have been so reduced that all the products of industry will provide a similarly unnoticed background.

The development of industrial society in fact shows a trend in the opposite direction. Powerful social forces take hold of these new goods and superimpose on their utilitarian value a symbolic meaning indicating status and social role. There are, of course, natural differences between men, their natural abilities vary, and in particular their capacity to develop. The latter means making an advance in freedom, and advice or instruction on how to achieve or practise that can hardly be given (though it cannot be achieved except against the background of the social context). But there seems no doubt that even the idea of individuality is extremely rare. Most men's view of their own identity is completely governed by their role; freed of the attributes of their role and their prestige possessions, their concept of themselves turns out to be very vague indeed. The significance of role behaviour and of the external attributes of roles as guiding lines for the formation of self-feeling can hardly be exaggerated.

## The individual as role

This problem, strangely enough, tends to be evaded by social psychology. The only conclusion to which examination of it leads is that the sense of individuality cultivated by our culture is a highly idealized and actually hollow one. The key question is: What is the social function of this idealization? The answer is that it is to reassure the individual by suborning him into acceptance of group standards, saturating him, often corrupting him, with the possessions or power that give status and prestige within the group. The mere fact that those who live lives relatively independent of the group tend to be dismissed as oddities, outsiders, Bohemians, ascetics, etc., in other words persons of doubtful conformity, points to the difficulty of solutions adequate to the ego.

Individuals who become heroes are in the last resort invariably stylized as servants of society, even though they suffered painfully under it during their lifetime. Hofstätter[6] paraphrases as follows the previously mentioned observation by Gardner Murphy[7]: 'We might perhaps arrive at a definition of individuality within the framework of social connections; the individual would then be a knot or relatively outstanding point in a supra-individual network. But such an attitude is remote from our present cultural inclinations.' Science can hardly allow itself to be guided by what is pleasing to our 'inclinations', that is, our group habits of mind. If the question is subjected to closer examination, as it has been, and very effectively, by industrial psychologists, for instance, the proposition that Hofstätter and Murphy cautiously stated in the conditional is confirmed. The 'man in the street' is very remote indeed from the ideal of himself projected by bourgeois individualism. He is group-guided in every facet of his affective attitudes, is satisfied with his role as agent of various group requirements, and has neither inclination for nor understanding of making independent decisions.[8] The reason why social psychologists are so hesitant to advance into this field may lie chiefly in the fact that the artificiality of the ideal superstructure (the individual has normally been exhaustively described when all the groups to which he belongs are known) points inevitably to its lack of substance; and this ideal superstructure is also specific to the group. No one willingly exposes himself to the charge of making such 'destructive' criticism, because ostracism has lost none of its terrors in modern times. Nevertheless the situation is that the fragile achievements of the ego are possible in the last resort only in a relatively free society in which it is permissible to criticize not only objective situations but also the taboos that aspire to no less than prescribing the self's own attitude to the self.

### Roles as the enemy of understanding

It follows from what we have said about the third critical phase of evolution, the step from the sub-human socio-genetic mechanism of behaviour control to the conscious level, that the identification with our roles to which we are all more or less subject indicates the survival of ties with older forms of organization. But for the possibility of conscious orientation, the challenge arising from the development of life itself, human society would not be what it is. Nevertheless role-ridden individual life leaves open a gap in communication. A striking instance of this, illustrating what we mean better than any abstract description, is provided by typical conversation between adults and children.

The child is not yet familiar with social roles, and is therefore far more individual than the adults surrounding it. The fashion in which the latter bend down and talk to it often shows a shattering lack of capacity for intuitive understanding, empathy. They project upon the living creature confronting them a role image of the child as transmitted by society. The artificial tone of voice, the demonstrative display of affection, the false identification with the child's interests and its play world, are all intended to overcome the actual inability to communicate; and the negative look in the child's eyes, its non-comprehension, is misinterpreted also.

At the same time the child, who has to learn social forms in order to bridge the gap in understanding between it and its environment, is thrown back on these models. It *has* to identify itself with them, and thus increasingly loses its spirit of free quest.

At the same time, over and above its inner struggles with its introjected behaviour patterns, there remains a sense of frustration, a feeling that something is lacking. Adults in speaking of their youth often say they never really knew their father or their mother, or both. Even in the intimacy of the home, role behaviour often stands in the way of understanding the child's more individual characteristics, the searching, uncertain, immature, or sometimes selfish and rebellious behaviour by which it seeks to establish itself in relation both to itself and to others. These outbursts are either all too quickly dovetailed into role stereotypes, or suppressed, or – which is just as bad – passively and impotently accepted by the parents, or not noticed by them. The possibilities of misunderstanding range all the way from brutal repression to unobservant indifference. The father may represent stern or mild authority to the child, but his ideas, anxieties or failures, the temptations he succumbs to or resists, are practically never discussed between parents and children, because such subjects are 'unsuitable' for the latter, and their discussion is regarded as inconsistent with the parental role. Instead the model held out for the fallible individual to follow is of a mythical, idealized father, immune to error, temptation, anxiety, etc., with a resultant loss of contact, or at any rate silence where there should be speech, and loss of knowledge which the individual badly needs for his self-orientation, as is made only too plain from his retrospective regret.

There is, however, also another factor which is lost sight of, namely, that the lack of hereditary co-ordinated behaviour inevitably leads to misunderstandings. The tendency to assume social roles, like the learning tendency, compensates for the lack of innate behaviour patterns. As we have mentioned, in the animal world these patterns, in so far as they relate to social behaviour, are genetically fixed. The animal's learning capacity does not extend into the social sphere, and misunderstandings are rare, though they occur; the male and female common raven, for instance, have identical plumage, and sometimes a male makes advances to another male by mistake. Conversely, in the human world many roles have become ossified for the purpose of preventing intuitive understanding in situations in which this might lead to confusion and disarray. This applies to all rigidly disciplined organizations, and also in diplomacy. The incumbent of the role is expected to experience the actual situation schematically. He reacts to any diversion from the prescribed pattern of behaviour by others in accordance with the prescribed ritual, imposes conformity, hands out punishments, makes *démarches*, etc., etc. Thus in these fields the learning process ends by abolishing itself.

### Precariousness of learnt role behaviour

If the word 'instinct' is used in the vague sense of ordinary speech ('my instinct tells me that . . .'), it can be stated that this instinct imposes upon men the direction of their object choice, but is not geared to that of the other party. Sometimes we read in the newspaper of a child beaten to death by its parent or parents, or left to starve or die, and indignantly we ask ourselves how such things can be possible. Such extreme cases are of course rare, and it is hard to understand how a mother – even more than a father – can offend so deeply against her 'natural' feelings or be so lacking in them as to be untouched by her child's plight and not rush to its protection. But, if we consider the innumerable situations in which children are harshly told to keep quiet, or have obedience imposed on them by threats or blows, or are subjected to adults' irritable moods, and if we also consider that hardly any adults are completely innocent of this abuse of their power, it becomes clear that there is a whole range of affective outbursts leading up to such extremes. The latter are singled out by the penal code, but they have much in common with the ordinary experiences of a large number of children. And it must be added in this connection that lack of guidance for the child, parental indifference or passive non-understanding, leads to just as pathological a condition, to the development of the same asocial characteristics, as does authoritarian intimidation. The attitude of parents is a permanent source of danger to the child far exceeding that of chance external accident. Violence or unobservant self-absorption on the part of the adult disturbs the equable, protective, emotional relationship on which human beings depend during their prolonged childhood. The remnants of the innate nursing instinct that manifest themselves in love of the child can, as experience demonstrates, easily be overpowered by other drives, which may turn the child into an object of unbridled hate or cause it to be neglected in a spirit of deep indifference. To appreciate the chaos of contradictory impulses to which man is subject we need only recall Rousseau, the prophet of the Enlightenment and of the return to nature, who is said to have handed over six of his children to a foundling hospital.[9]

Those who have frequent occasion to listen to people talking of their childhood see how the experiences of that time are reflected in them. They frequently have to listen, for instance, to stories of fearful paternal punishments for minor misdemeanours, many of which enter the victims' memory like brutal execution scenes. In its impotence the child experiences the punishment as overwhelming proof of its guilt and shame; it feels expelled, robbed of its parents' love and protection. The parent who inflicts the punishment – if it is the mother, the effect on the young child is even greater – assumes in the child's mind a violent, inhuman, demonic form. If one learns this from the child and later has the opportunity of discussing the incident with the parents, it is easy to decide that the real picture was far more innocuous. But that would be a mistake. The child cannot feel its way into the adult world, for it lacks the experience; the adult, though generally only with difficulty, can feel his way back into the world of the child. The latter is still ignorant of the grown-up world and its motivations, all it experiences is the immediate situation, the enormous disparity between its own and adult strength, which indeed, as we know, can in extreme cases lead to the death of the weaker. In the brutal process of punishment the child feels a direct and immediate fear of death which the angry parents totally fail to take into account; alternatively they soothe their conscience by saying that that was the last thing they intended. But their true intentions are undiscoverable to a child confronted with a grown-up who is 'beside himself'; all he is aware of is the state of 'being beside oneself', and a parent in this state is no longer the known, familiar figure, but a demonic stranger who strikes terror, the terror of death; and the terror is further intensified by the fact that the child's natural refuge when it is afraid, its parents, have now been suddenly transformed into this alien shape.

The effect on the child of this alienation in affective excitation is that the familiar role identification is split; the familiar individual has been suddenly transformed into a terrifying stranger. The child is still far from secure in his role identifications; one has only to recall the simple measures needed to disguise oneself from a child and become unrecognizable to it.

This affective alienation is a highly important basic social experience for the child, who for its normal development requires constancy of aspect in the individuals in close contact with it. If they periodically become alien under the influence of certain stimuli, the child will introject the split as part of the identification process – another instance of how tradition can be unconsciously passed on. The consequences are grave. The child will be no less terrified by the suddenness and strangeness of its own impulses and physical experiences (of pain, for instance) than by affective storms from without. The process of fitting the former into a 'body ego' (like that of adaptation to the rules of the group) has not yet been completed; the limited experience appropriate to its age makes them seem just as terrifying and uncanny as many of the non-understood events in the outside world. The introjects of its inconstant models associate themselves in its unconscious with its own frightening physical experiences. Thus the adult who 'loses control of himself' becomes the model for the primitive role behaviour by which the child tries to discharge its own impulses. But there is another social rule which says *quod licet Jovi non licet bovi*, and the child is punished for this assimilation.

## Roles and masks

A role, in short, is a pattern of behaviour in relation to others. Every role is to an extent a mask, a prefabricated one, that the individual either actively assimilates or passively adapts himself to. There are circumstances of two different kinds in which he may drop the mask: (i) when he is overcome by affect, or impulses representing it; and (ii) in a conflict situation when his conscience and individual ego attainments, that is, his critical conscious, cause him to step out from behind it and respond to a situation in a spontaneous and improvised fashion, whether mastering it or being mastered by it. In the first case the controls (which we attribute to the ego) vanish and impulses previously fought off upset the role pattern of behaviour, while in the second case the ego succeeds in bringing about a change in preconscious and unconscious patterns of stimulation and response, both in values and in action.

An important place in all the conceivable combinations and forms of assimilation between individual characteristics and pre-existing role patterns is occupied by the accuracy of the information-processing of which the individual is capable – that is to say, the firmness of his sense of identity in the environment to which he belongs. We must be careful, however, not to oversimplify the picture. Firmness of identity can be bought at the cost of great sacrifice of the individual's inner organization. This is always the case when he has to defend his identity, his self, against violent impulses (and their organization by primitive introjects). In this event adherence to 'roles' must be regarded as an equally primitive form of defence; the role patterns then used generally include the judgements of value, the prejudices, needed by the ego to keep down the unruly impulses disapproved of by convention, and the forces of the ego are completely used up in the task of stabilizing such compulsive role behaviour. Compulsive behaviour (even when inwardly directed in the form of obsessional ideas and fantasies) is a caricature of the kind of role behaviour that succeeds both in warding off and satisfying inner drives. A functional unity of anxiety and repetition-compulsion is a distortion of the latter. True, it is the deepest motivation of any role, but it is also that of the innumerable pathological obsessional features encountered in daily life, ranging all the way to obsessional illness.

On the other hand, unreliability and outbursts of affect point to weak ego control, and thus to a fragmentary identity. The reality-testing ego is easily submerged in a 'pleasure ego', which in a stimulus situation yields to impulses regardless of social considerations.

Compulsive role playing in the service of an (unconscious) super-ego and compulsive drives practically unhampered by consideration for others often coexist in the same person. Abrupt transitions from one to the other (from behaviour guided by the super-ego to that guided by the id) endanger the smooth development of the ego during the natural crises of the phases of growth; and the danger is increased when this coexistence achieves social recognition and general approval as a respected type of role. The imago of the authoritarian personality, the perverted form of authority that is so widespread, is marked by this alternation between compulsive behaviour and outbursts of affect; and when the two characteristics are idealized by society, one as just severity and the other as strength, a most unfavourable climate has been established for development of the capacities of the ego. Looking back at the stages of evolution, it can be said that patterns of behaviour were encouraged that became structuralized unconsciously. Regressions to this state and survivals of such archaic regulation of social behaviour are numerous both in individual and in collective history. The character development that takes in these circumstances is only partially or not at all ego-syntonic; strictly speaking, it is role-syntonic.

We cannot here digress to the extent of giving a full picture of the processes of mental development that take place under the influence of an authoritarian environment. Psycho-analysis has shown that in these circumstances infantile paranoid anxieties receive a strong charge of affect from alienating models and enter the character as fixed attitudes to life. The consequence of this is that infantile defence measures against an alien and threatening inner and outer world cannot be given up, perhaps for a whole lifetime. An important method of getting rid of these anxieties is similarly infantile, namely, projecting disturbing or dangerous feelings into the outside world. Here lie the roots of prejudice.

### Transfiguration of the past

An ideal relationship between child and adults would thus be free from excessively abrupt changes of mood and affective action on the one hand and from strained rigidity of attitude on the other. It is an ideal which can never be completely attained. Fortunately, the child has plenty of toleration for variations in the affective climate, though these are not helpful to the establishment of the atmosphere of intimacy and confidence which is indispensable to the development of what Erik Erikson calls the 'basic trust'[10] which the child needs as the background of all its future ventures into the world.

There is one symptom of a disturbance of this basic trust that can readily be perceived. Many people speak of their childhood as of a golden age. There are, of course, plenty of people who really had a predominantly happy childhood, which invariably means that their parents felt their way into their world, interests, needs, and anxieties, and treated them understandingly. But those who propagate the myth of their conflict-free childhood are often persons of striking rigidity of character who have all sorts of difficulties in life and suffer from anxieties and physical complaints – in short, are unhappy and discontented. Their story does not ring true and, if one probes deeper, quite a different picture emerges, often very slowly and accompanied by great anxiety and guilt, and it appears that in their childhood they suffered from severity, lack of understanding, and loneliness. Such was their plight that in retrospect it had to be repudiated, denied, idealized, transfigured.

The child and later the adult sought to obtain relief by thus distorting reality, identifying himself in his helplessness with the hostile and infinitely stronger punishing agency. In this situation the child feels himself to be worthless and bad and his severe parents to be good. They tell him innumerable times that their intentions are for the best and, indeed, according to their lights that may be true, and the child ends by rejecting all memory of the times when he was alone and his parents filled him with mortal fear instead of coming to his aid. He feels himself to be bad, to have deserved his parents' severity. If they punished him, it was because he was bad, disobedient, lazy, careless. They were right. In the next phase of memory distortion, the child has become the good child his parents wanted him to be, with the result that they had no need ever to be angry with him.

This enforced harmony does the child no good. Of course his conflicts seem to have been resolved; if one had good parents and was oneself good and obedient, one's childhood must have been happy. All memory of suffering fades from the mind, or is repressed. But the reality of those early experiences, which make an impact the magnitude of which it is almost impossible to exaggerate, continues to exercise its baneful effect. It remains as a memory-trace behind the 'identification with the aggressor',[11] and determines, not only the psychical defence mechanisms which enable the growing personality to conceal from itself the anxiety and impotent hate feelings of its childhood, but also and above all its pattern of expectation. Whenever in later life the individual is confronted with superiors or inferiors, his old, now hidden experiences, the fears he never overcame, his disturbing wishes, will seek to emerge. Thus history repeats itself. It is truly a vicious circle. For the adult who was so treated in childhood will, without being conscious of it – and it is not so easy for him to become conscious of it – 'avenge himself' on his own children for his childhood sufferings, which is precisely what his own parents did to him. Once again we are brought face to face with the traditional nature of affective patterns of behaviour. Having been imposed too early in the child's development, subsequently they cling too firmly, and in many circumstances are unshakable. The ego has learnt to submit to them.

## The overburdened mother

Thus the relative underdevelopment of hereditary patterns of social behaviour in man makes it possible for misunderstandings to occur even in the primary relationship between mother and child. When there is a clash between the maternal and other, particularly narcissistic, impulses, the conflict is especially deep. The idealization of the maternal role in society's taboos indicates that in the interest of the survival of the species the mother-child relationship has to be buttressed by social regulation, and also that this is often not sufficient, and that deficiencies have therefore to be covered up by idealization.

There is also the consideration that the mother-child relationship is being loosened by social developments. The continually increasing employment of women in industry and mounting standards of living are not the only factors. This process has long since been motivated not only by practical considerations but also to a large extent by conformist pressures to establish status; the signalling of this by the possession of prestige-giving consumer goods is thus a contributory factor. The shift of emphasis from the possession of land to the possession of mobile consumer goods throughout the population has been accompanied by the transformation of family relationships under the influence of industrial production and urbanization. A small family, consisting of parents and children only, normally lives in a confined, relatively isolated, cell-like space, side by side with similar families in similar accommodation. This means that members of the family are more closely penned up together than in the past, which puts a greater strain on emotional relations between mother and child. In comparison with village conditions, which (without showing them in an unduly favourable light) can be said to have offered a relatively constant environment for thousands of years, the area of the known and emotionally familiar has notably shrunk so far as the town child is concerned. Opportunities of escape to other members of the family are more restricted. In other words, the whole ambivalent emotional tension of the child is predominantly concentrated on the mother, who often feels overburdened by this and feels more ambivalently towards the child in consequence. Also having children involves giving up work, reduces the family earning power, puts the mother back into a position of greater financial dependence, and subjects her to ties which, in view of the social trend to freedom of choice (in consumption and use of leisure), she feels to be a great and often unfair sacrifice. To a greater or lesser extent the child becomes the object on which she discharges her unpleasure tensions. Making light of the overcharging of the mother-child relationship inherent in our social development, or putting on a Madonna-like pedestal the often impatient, irritable mother who feels chained to her duties, may suffice for the aims of idealism and wishful thinking, but makes life easier neither for mothers nor for children. True, it saves society the feeling that it should change itself.

It would, however, be oversimplifying matters to relate the tensions between mother or parents and child only to present environmental changes, though these are no doubt becoming more acute. In relation to the child's insatiable demands, failures of parental response are inevitable, and the best and the most unselfish parents must be expected to be endowed with some 'bad' aspects in the child's fantasy world. The overpermissiveness with which some parents treat their children in order to reassure themselves hampers the process of social maturation no less than does neglect.

### Animals and men

Let us return to the observation with which we began this chapter. In the field of sub-human evolution the fixed regulatory mechanisms of instinctual behaviour are related to a relatively constant environment, or rather they developed in such an environment. With man the capacity actively to transform the environment appeared on the scene. In recent years this has been making advances with explosive speed. Unstable regulation of inner drives, conscious understanding of reality, the 'tool brain' and with it the ability to bring about controlled change of the environment, all interact. Experiments with animals make shatteringly clear the disturbances of biophysical equilibrium which are henceforward inevitable. Cultural patterns of behaviour provide safeguards against excessive dissociation between individuals with insecure drives and their environment. When an experimenter arbitrarily changes an animal's environment, which the animal is not capable of doing itself, he artificially establishes such dissociation; in other words, he establishes a situation of the human type; and it is astonishing to see primates, for instance, producing reactions familiar to us from human psychopathology, that is to say, demonstrating abnormal mental behaviour which can be regarded as an attempt to cope with intolerable psychical stress. When a human child is overwhelmed by fear and despair at a stage at which its cerebral maturation and hence the approach to higher levels of mental development are still in a fluid state, its reactions are very similar to those of animals at a comparable stage of development. In the animal kingdom this occurs only when a human experimenter disturbs the natural environment, while in human development it occurs naturally, that is to say, inevitably, as the result of cultural conditions.

The experiments with rhesus monkeys carried out by the American psychologist Harry F. Harlow[12] have shown this in most interesting fashion. He demonstrated the basic drive that sends the young animal to its mother when it feels in danger, but his experiments went far beyond that familiar fact. He either completely separated young monkeys from their mother at birth or gave them surrogate mothers. The latter were 'welded wire cylindrical forms with the nipple of the feeding-bottle protruding from its "breast" and with a wooden head surmounting it'. Some of the surrogate mothers were 'cosier', covered with terry towelling. The infants developed a strong attachment to the cloth mothers, and took no notice of the wire mothers as long as the former had milk. When it ran out, they would go to the wire mothers to feed, but soon returned. They also always returned to the cloth mothers after expeditions round the cage, especially when something happened to startle them. It could also be shown that the permanent tie was the warm, fur-like feel of the cloth, not the feeding experience, because, when the monkeys were frightened after the cloth mother had been removed from the cage, they never ran to the wire mother, but simply froze in a crouching position. These observations, Harlow says, suggest that man too cannot live on milk alone. In fact, monkeys reared with wire mothers alone never fled to them and their nipples in moments of fear, but threw themselves on the ground, hid their faces in their arms, and shrieked with despair. The warmth and protection of the 'social womb' is essential for normal development.

Harlow's experiments went further, however. Rhesus monkeys reared without mothers or mother-surrogates until they were eight months old did not react to a cloth mother when one was offered to them. This leads to the conclusion that the possibility of the development of the specific affective social contact that we call 'mother love' exists only in a limited, definite period of time. For rhesus monkeys, according to Harlow, the critical period is between the third and the sixth month, and the corresponding period in the human infant is between the sixth and the twelfth month. Subsequently this kind of 'imprinting', as was first demonstrated by Konrad Lorenz in his experiments with ducks, is no longer possible. 'If the child has not learnt to love in this period, it will never learn.'

This correspondence of affective needs in the human and animal infant world is supported by observations made by René Spitz[13] before Harlow's experiments. He observed infants under the age of one brought up in a foundling hospital (in a country which for reasons of discretion we shall not specify). So far as dietetic and hygienic conditions were concerned, there could be no criticism of their treatment, but there were no mothers or mother-surrogates. Each nurse had twenty babies to look after, so that she had no time to establish 'affective contact' with them. They were never picked up, carried out, or rocked, and no one talked to them soothingly and lovingly before and after feedings.

It seems hardly possible to doubt that there was a causal connection between this state of affairs and the shockingly high death rate, the incidence of reactive (anaclitic) depression and of general retardation of development that were to be noted. It seems evident that during the period of what Portmann calls the 'extra-uterine spring' no problem of 'spoiling' exists. During this period the infant is entitled to ask for everything and need do nothing in return. Premature training routines on the reward-and-punishment principle do harm at this stage. By reason of its exceptionally early birth the human infant needs care and attention that quickly gets rid of unpleasure tensions by many routes. The human mother, like the rhesus mother, must always be available as a refuge when the infant experiences unpleasure, otherwise the consequence is mistrust. Only by the satisfaction of its needs in the 'primary love'[14] relationship between mother and child does the latter acquire the fundamental experience of social 'basic trust' as the deepest foundation for its experience of life.

Erik Erikson[15] regards dealing with this 'conflict between basic trust and basic mistrust' as a task with which man in his struggle with his environment is confronted throughout his life. Only when a secure foundation of basic trust enables him to resolve the conflict can his affective relationships, in psycho-analytic terminology his object relationships, be firm and stable; and it provides the most favourable conditions for an unhampered development of the intelligence and the ego and for an attitude of curiosity that will persist in adult life. However, 'the sum of the trust derived from the child's earliest experiences does not seem to depend only on the quantity of food and love, but also on the quality of the bond with the mother. A trustful attitude will be aroused by care which combines sympathetic satisfaction of the baby's individual needs with a strong sense of the mother's personal dependability within the tried and tested framework of her environment. The basis of a feeling of identity forms here.'[16] Those who have not had this experience of dependability clearly have great difficulty in gaining a growing understanding of their own identity through the turbulent years of development.

Harlow's and Spitz's observations make it plain that deprivations of social and emotional exchange in infancy not only create a real danger of collapse of the psychosomatic regulators, of emotional death by starvation, but also, even when this extreme situation does not ensue, cause irreparable damage to the capacity for making human contact. Monkeys that grew up under quasi-human conditions to the extent that they survived the loss of their mother (which in their natural environment would not occur), or were thrown back on an artificial mother-surrogate, which can be regarded as the equivalent of a human mother alienated from her child, subsequently developed defective reactions exactly equivalent to those of their human counterparts. It should be added that in human beings these defects cannot be remedied by specifically ego attainments, for instance, intelligence and understanding. Intelligence and understanding are impotent against such damage.

Harlow's further observations supply direct experimental confirmation of the psycho-analytic theories that postulate the formative significance of early emotional experiences for the whole of subsequent mental development. This was of course for long regarded as absurd, the more so the more the regulative force of unconscious mental processes was denied. But since Harlow's experiments scepticism about the psycho-analytic theory of infantile traumatization as the foundation of subsequent psychic and psychosomatic disturbance can hardly be maintained.

Meanwhile Harlow's rhesus monkeys, as he has reported,[17] have grown into mature animals in the best of physical condition. In spite of that, they show no inclination whatever to normal mating behaviour. Even when introduced into a larger group of animals that grew up in normal conditions, their attitude of total uninterest remains unchanged. They neither show any spontaneous sexual interest of their own, nor do they respond adequately to the advances of other animals. Harlow's theory that the child must learn to love in early infancy in order to be capable of love in later life is confirmed by the consistent absence of sexual excitability in the sexually mature animal. Harlow assumes this to be a consequence of its motherlessness. He states that the mother must have some subtle way of communicating the ability to indulge in normal sexual behaviour.[18]

And that is not all. It appears from a preliminary communication by Harlow (1961) that a female monkey brought up in a wire cage without a mother and several brought up with surrogate mothers were finally induced to mate, though their behaviour did not resemble that of wild monkeys. So far two of them had produced offspring. But both the motherless female and the female brought up with the surrogate mother responded abnormally; their reactions ranged from 'indifference to outright abuse', or they 'reacted not at all to their newborn infant, though the latter reacted normally to them'. They never looked at it, but 'stared into space'. The motherless female removed the child from her belly or back with the same indifference with which she would remove a fly, and her behaviour displayed a striking resemblance to that of a completely affect-free human schizophrenic.

Thus, as we have said, Harlow artificially reproduced the process of dissociation that follows interference with instinctive behaviour patterns, here that between mother and child. In the animal kingdom this dissociation does not occur naturally. In the human field it is natural, and is corrected by the social pattern of behaviour, but not in a fashion so unambiguous that misunderstandings are excluded, and also not in any consistent fashion. The standards of infant care change from place to place and from time to time. Bearing in mind Harlow's experiments and Spitz's observations, it must again be emphasized that innate regulatory patterns are sufficient in the case of animals, but

SOCIETY WITHOUT THE FATHER

not of man. A glance at the multiplicity of disturbances, ranging all the way to the perversions, to which the human capacity for love is subject, at the outbreaks of aggressive anti-social behaviour and the devious paths taken by it, in short, at the amount of neurotic and psychotic illness, reveals how exposed to danger is the human condition in the situation into which it has manœuvred itself. The challenge of self-awareness thus includes comprehension of the earliest stages of human life, when only one of the parties concerned, the adult, is capable of acting with understanding and insight.

### 'Re-education'

Individuals who have suffered the disaster of early deprivation – for instance, neurotic mothers who, because of what went wrong with their own 'imprinting', are unable to understand their own child – by no means constitute the whole of the problem. Standards of behaviour specific to a culture can lead to neurotic distortions *en masse*. If these make a great impact on the very first social contacts – as by insistence on premature training in cleanliness and punishment in the event of failure – the imprinting effect is practically ineradicable. In the absence of the experience of tenderness the sublimation of aggressive and sexual trends can be attained only with difficulty in later years. Sometimes a person is said, for instance, not to have been granted the gift of tenderness; it was withheld, however, not by nature, but by the human environment.

It is this that so often leads to the failure of later missionary attempts at re-education, whether individual or collective. Rationally it is intelligible enough that it should have been desired to convert a nation that had been capable of the most appalling excesses to a less blind living out of the obviously insatiable urges of its internal cultural tensions. But when one considers the condescension and contempt with which the re-education attempted in Germany some twenty years ago is nowadays referred to, both in public and in private, the truly tragic impotence of mind against non-mind is borne in upon one. In this arrogance which is again springing up everywhere there is no sign of any insight into the motives of the collective trance of those earlier years, which is made the more puzzling by the fact that it so successfully harnessed technical intelligence to its murderous aims.

People simply say that no one has any right to teach us anything, they would do better to look to their own middens. It probably cannot even be claimed that this pride is a psychological reaction-formation to the humiliation of total defeat. As in the case of Harlow's motherless monkeys, there seem to be collective character imprints that make people totally unfeeling and insensitive to wide areas of social reality. The individual is inaccessible to the affective appeal coming from groups that have been ideologically damned; he simply remains blind to their plight. Yet we talk of hard-heartedness when we recall the horrors of the early stages of the industrial revolution, when no objection was taken, for instance, to ten-year-olds being made to work for ten or twelve hours a day.[19] But in the course of time such defects in the social system have been corrected. Slavery, and what is similar to it, the exploitation of women in many patriarchal societies, are receding into the past, though in large areas of the world they still survive. Though the enslavement of the ideologically damned has frequently taken the place of formal slavery, it is to be expected that this kind of social disregard for the plight of others will not continue to be rationalized and defended for long. True, the key factor in the growth of humanitarianism towards the weak has been not so much increased sensibility on the part of ruling groups as economic and social developments. Housemaids enjoyed little consideration so long as there was a country proletariat from which they could be drawn, but when the demand for domestic help exceeded the supply a change came about in their pay and conditions; in this instance the new attitude was enforced before any subjective need was felt to treat the individuals concerned more heedfully. The question indeed arises whether real changes in attitude to the underdog do not always first arise from an improvement in the latter's power position. If one does not conceal from oneself such phenomena in one's own society, one begins properly to appreciate the difficulties of any far-reaching re-education. We know from psycho-analysis the amount of patience, time, experience, and therapeutic skill that are necessary to bring about changes in the character structure of a single individual, and indeed it would all be labour in vain if the patient's suffering did not provide him with a powerful motive to seek a cure. But in a community a painful symptom, an agonizing sense of irremediable failure, can be warded off if its members identify themselves with their defects and elevate them into virtues.

We have already cited the instance of the authoritarian personality whose uncontrolled affect and obsessional cruelty are misinterpreted as signs of strength of character and ability to rule. Another was the complacency with which we Germans rejected the attempts to re-educate us made by the victorious powers. In doing so we forget (i) that their reality calculations were better than ours, otherwise they would not have been victorious; (ii) that their social conscience was more developed than ours, or they would not have been able to resist the impulse to exterminate us as we set about exterminating Jewish and Slavonic 'sub-men'; and (iii) that we were the oppressors, and the victim has a longer memory than his oppressor. The reason for this last phenomenon is that the oppressor, so long as he is able to preserve his position, is confirmed in his identity, while that of his victim suffers a cruel blow.

Since the failure of re-education the old identity has sprung up again from the ruins. Nothing seems able to shake the traditional way of feeling and the ways in which it manifests itself. We select a few nationally widespread traits: *naïveté* in relation to the self, cringingness in defeat, energy and practical efficiency, anxiety in the face of ridicule because of a lack of irony in relation to the self, sentimentality, deadly earnestness in convictions (roles), fascination by naked power. Leaving aside the practical efficiency, these tendencies make it plain that the predominant moods and feelings are infantile, that is, are not affected by the conscious, by cool criticism, by sober realization of the relativity of one's own abilities. Self-feeling and feeling about the outside world easily merge into fantasies of omnipotence, and only the extreme sensitivity to criticism (as exemplified by the reaction to the attempted re-education) shows the weakness of an identity that is more an aspiration than an attainment.

All attempts to pinpoint 'national characteristics' are of course crude oversimplifications. We are not here attempting a full description of a culture. We are trying to find clues to the constancy of certain reactions that have shown themselves to be dangerous, or at least disturbing in everyday life and in international contacts, and obviously cannot be influenced by learning processes.

Before we go any further, let us quote an example to show that there are collective attitudes that have been susceptible to easier and more rapid change; perhaps the contrast will be helpful to understanding.

The Victorian age was dominated by a prudishness that to us today seems as hard to understand as does the wholesale massacre of defence-less people carried out in our lifetime by our own countrymen, the Germans. The collective sensibility was moulded to react with as much repugnance to anything reminiscent of sensuality as it was recently in our country to 'sub-men'; so much was this the case that most individuals felt these reactions to be completely natural and self-evident. 'The Victorians . . . regarded themselves as more civilized than the men of the preceding century',[20] and they based this opinion on their contempt for sex. Thus we are confronted with the paradox of a high degree of self-feeling with a crude condemnation of sexual intercourse, which was deprived of all possibility of intimacy, affection, and human understanding. 'Animals must rut, but man – noble, brave, rational – should be able to procreate without descending to such uncivilized contortions. In short, the Victorian saw sex not so much as something sinful, but as something bestial, something disgusting.'[21] This attitude has passed away. The reaction came in the hectic sexual anarchy of the 'roaring twenties', and has now subsided partly into a petty bourgeois morality and partly into a state of mind in which sexual pleasure rates rather like that to be obtained from other consumer goods, neither poetically transfigured nor associated with a guilty conscience, but merely boring. The picture as a whole does not suggest a very high culture of sexual relations, but in the course of a few decades it has changed completely. G. Rattray Taylor is no doubt correct in connecting this with changes in the paternalist structure of society. The Victorian bourgeois, in accordance with the role imposed on him, identified himself with his father. This involved him in the conflict with his mother that Freud described as the Oedipus complex. 'He feels that she has betrayed him sexually by her relationship with his father. The mediaeval paternalist met this by postulating a com-pletely pure, ideal mother who never had sexual relations and urged all other women to a like purity. He wanted them to be virgins, but suspected them of being witches. The Victorian paternalist felt the same conflict. But, as he was no longer disposed to solve it by postulat-ing a divine virgin, he was forced to divide the female sex into two categories: "good" women, who had no sexual feelings, and "bad" women, who had them.'[22] Taylor produces a quotation from medical literature that illustrates how so-called scientific objectivity can be riddled with collective prejudice. In his book on the functions and disturbances of the organs of reproduction W. Acton stated that it was a 'vile calumny' to suggest that women were capable of sexual feeling.

What are we to conclude from this example of a rigid collective attitude that so demonstratively turned out to be subject to change? The Victorians denied the evidence of genital sexuality; reaction-formations prevented them from seeing a reality that belongs to a full experience of life. It was the unresolved conflict with the father for possession of the mother that led to that odd state of mind. This conflict, arising out of the individual's relations with his first love objects, is ever-present, but trends must have been at work in society that greatly intensified it at that time. Perhaps the explanation is to be sought in the anarchical intensification of competition brought about by industrial development and the anxiety associated with it, which made the son-father rivalry unconsciously seem especially dangerous, with the result that the libidinally cathected object of the rivalry, the mother and wife, was subjected to taboo. By this compromise the conflict was superficially resolved, but no progress in understanding was brought about. The tabooing of the love object was the more necessary as with puberty and the attainment of genital maturity the fixation reappeared, and with it a whole chain of neurotic defence mechanisms dating from infancy. The Victorian repudiation of sex was essentially a collective sexual neurosis of the hysterical type. The disappointment of infantile sexual wishes turned into fixed attitudes and expectations with which later experiences of a sexual nature were met.

Apart from the symptoms of hysteria, there is no doubt that the whole social structure also showed signs of pregenital (anal) neurosis. It can be observed that under stress refuge was sought by retreating from one neurotic attitude to the other. The neurotic suffering of the age lay in its preoccupation with money and sex. The desire for money compensated for the repudiation of sex, and the acquisition of money made it possible to enjoy the possession of 'bad' women.

The national characteristic of covering up callousness with sentiment which we mentioned above must have other, older, and more direct roots in unconscious processes that cannot be so easily modified by history; in other words, the traumatic influences must lie in the period preceding the age of five or six, the heyday of the Oedipal conflict. We do not claim to have any certain evidence of this, but psycho-analytic experience gives us good reason to seek the explanation in very early experiences which recur with relative uniformity among a large number of individuals in our national social culture. These must be considered in relation to patterns of behaviour that are so much taken for granted that they have hitherto escaped critical examination. Let us recall Harlow's observation that rhesus monkeys brought up without parents later do not assume the maternal role; in other words, that any affective exchange, even the primary relationship between mother and child, has to be learnt, and that deprivation of maternal care makes the young animal subsequently incapable of responding and reacting to sex, and actually insensitive to the approaches, even the existence, of its own young. From this it seems reasonable to assume that human patterns of behaviour that later turn out to be unmodifiable are the results of missed learning experiences that can take place only at a definite stage of development and cannot be compensated for later.

As we have said, we are here drawing conclusions about collective patterns of behaviour from animal experiments and experience with individual human patients. We cannot produce convincing evidence to satisfy the critic who rejects these theories as speculation. As Freud said with characteristic caution, 'these are only analogies, by the help of which we endeavour to understand a social phenomenon; the pathology of the individual does not supply us with a fully valid counterpart'.[23]

The experiment – if one wants to call it an experiment – that we suggest is a change in early upbringing in the direction of constancy of affective approach. That would amount to a humanization – increased awareness of the individuality of the other party, in this case the child – in affectively guided behaviour. There must be no rationalizing of deviations from this course, for all we know for certain is that no abruptly or carelessly or casually taken affective decision is without consequences, perhaps permanent consequences.

The anthropologists have made us acquainted with euphoric and depressive, open-handed and paranoiacally mistrustful cultures, and our psychological knowledge suggests that these variations of social environment are the result, apart from material conditions, of the customs prevalent in those cultures, particularly those connected with the upbringing of children. We have mentioned the dissociation of subject and object in conscious life. Though the nursing instinct is relatively one of the strongest in human nature, it is not adequately secured against the influence of the social atmosphere and conflicts with other emotional drives. In cultures with a strong community life the relationship between mother and child, and between the child and other members of the family unit, predominantly accords with the community pattern. In these circumstances the individual can hardly avoid traumatizing factors inherent in the social pattern. With the increasing fragmentation of the family there is no protection against individual neurotic influences, because the security provided by collectively practised methods is lacking. The corrective against isolation is increasingly becoming the dissemination of scientific knowledge; nowadays the young mother is told how to handle her baby, not by other members of the family, but by a book or a counselling centre. But scientific views are subject to rapid change, and in the anthropological field are certainly not free of status prejudices, as can be shown by many instances besides William Acton's statement about the sexual feelings of women which we quoted above.

As it is a mistake to identify the fragmentation of our society with individualism, meaning by that a strengthening of the ego functions in relation to the emotional drives, the situation is more critical than it was in the days of closed family, clan, or provincial cultures. David Riesman[24] applies the term 'other-directedness' to the tendency of modern communities to be guided by fashionable emotional trends. The uncertainty of orientation expressed in continual adaptation to rapid changes of convention seems an inevitable form of cultural transition. In a rapidly changing environment stability can be found only in genuine individualization, that is, stabilization of the critical ego faculties. If our theory of the guiding evolutionary role that henceforth devolves upon the conscious is correct, the latter must learn to see and judge what it does to itself in the educative process at a stage when it is present only as a potentiality in early childhood.

The embryonic organization of the psyche seems as susceptible to toxic influences as is the embryonic physical organism. Many kinds of upbringing obviously have toxic influences. Man's instinctual behaviour is not sufficient to guide him through life, and the large amount of social behaviour he acquires does not protect him from disastrous acts of folly. When it is borne in mind that the imprinting that takes place in the 'extra-uterine spring' determines the basic inhibitions and imperatives that continue to work in all subsequent stages of development, and that human destiny is thus settled at this very early stage, it is evident that any attempt at adult re-education is doomed to failure, however humanitarian in intention it may be. It is also evident that collective standards and prejudices in general, in so far as these are related to the early genesis of character development, are exceedingly hard to correct. The choice now before us is whether revolutions bearing the stamp of the mythical parricide – processes, that is to say, that make a deep mark on the psychical life of the community – can result in a strengthening of the ego functions, or whether the level of consciousness so far attained is sufficient to assure a gradual, progressive development of the integrating reason – before an increase in radioactivity brought about by *Homo sapiens* either exterminates him or does irreparable damage to his genetic substance. It is a race with time.

Whether the partial socialization of humanity that the patriarchal age achieved will be strong enough to neutralize the surplus aggression that present forms of culture generate is impossible to foresee.

# IV

# The Precariousness of Moralities

## *The creation of identity*

The strengthening of the ego capacities to which we have just referred implies a process of maturation. With it the individual's identity feeling develops, and the consequence is that his memory of himself is not so easily overborne by external stimuli and the eruption of powerful impulses in himself. We have described this acquisition of control over our impulses in the buffetings of social life as affective education. The less our affects succeed in evading the ego and thus directly influencing our actions, the greater is our self-knowledge. To the extent that the integrative power of the ego prevails, one does not lose one's head; that is, one is able to remain true to oneself in one's behaviour, no matter how different or stimulating or disturbing may be the situation in which one finds oneself. Identity is thus stability both of social behaviour and of self-knowledge.

All attempts at clarification such as this, however, remain incomplete and abstract in the absence of yardsticks enabling us to distinguish between genuine identity and its spurious forms. It is not always easy in ordinary life to differentiate between blind and non-understanding consistency, that is, inflexibility, born of the fear of being driven into an unknown darkness by internal pressures and external seductions, and consistent, considered behaviour that does not have to shut its eyes and stop up its ears to be able to decide which course to follow. Thus identity also implies a capacity for adaptation by the integration of new experiences.

Earlier[1] we briefly mentioned man's perpetual restlessness due to the permanent threat to his stability caused by his inner urges. Instincts, we said, quoting Freud, have their vicissitudes. What happens to them at turning-points in individual development is especially important. The attainment of genital maturity, for instance, calls for new modes of control by the ego, to which there correspond new demands for adaptation on the part of the environment. One of the necessary conditions for the formation of identity is that, as Erik Erikson puts it, the young person should feel 'responded to, and that society is attributing a function and station to him as a person whose gradual growth has meaning – and this above all in the eyes of the people who are beginning to have meaning for him'.[2]

The rapid dispelling of unpleasure characteristic of infancy remains unforgotten. Slowly, often not slowly enough, the environment exerts its pressure, calling on the child to learn to tolerate unpleasure, to conceive of non-immediate aims that promise satisfaction and adhere to them even when quicker but prohibited pleasure-gain beckons.

Such training in the postponement of instinctual satisfactions, in asceticism of varying degrees of severity – for that is what civilization is – would be inconceivable, because unnecessary, for an individual living in solitude. Renunciation is called for solely by the necessity of living with others. But renunciation can have meaning, can itself be a source of satisfaction, only if his environment has meaning to the individual or, to put it bluntly, if he has had reason to love someone. The concrete foundations of an experience in which so many deep contradictions are united cannot be argued or idealized away. Your truly civilized man is not exclusively in love with humanity or a party or some other abstraction, or with the Virgin Mary or some other numinous figure, but has first of all been able to love one other human being, in spite of all the tensions of ambivalent experience inevitably involved.

*Satisfying renunciation*

The vicissitudes of the instincts we have just described throw light on one aspect of human nature. I am able to attain relief from tension in spite of the renunciation of selfish instinctual satisfaction, but only by the route of sharing with a person whom I love. I am able to feel by identification and yet with detachment what the latter gains from my renunciation, and that is the only kind of renunciation that yields satisfaction. It may indeed be the key experience in any real love. Love can, however, be described the other way about; it can be said that I fall in love with someone who seems to fulfil an ideal pre-existent in my fantasy. In so far as I succeed in securing co-operation from the love object within the sphere of my experience, the latter only strengthens me in my fantasy and becomes the means and object of my satisfaction. But if my partner begins making independent demands on me, the feeling of being in love often vanishes quickly enough.

## Unsatisfying renunciation

It is as well, however, to be tolerant about these distinctions and differences. Even in a mature individual who is capable of love there is a mixture of primary, selfish aims and subsequently acquired ones; a natural and proper tendency to seek satisfaction for his own wishes works in tolerable harmony with respect for the wishes of the other. It is excessive altruism that is suspect, as well as obvious narcissism. In the instinct-regulated animal kingdom the problem of instinctual control does not arise. Apart from the ritualized behaviour in caring for the young, opportunities for gaining satisfaction are governed by the individual's ranking order in the group. The regulative agency is strength; the weaker have to wait their turn.

It can hardly be denied that, in spite of the revolutionary advance to consciousness, human group behaviour continues to be riddled with the powerful inheritance of this regulatory principle of sub-human social organization. Civilization has succeeded only to a limited extent in enforcing instinctual renunciation and endowing it with a sense of social purpose. Moralities on the one hand call for a great deal of masochistic perversion, and on the other yield considerable gains of sadistic satisfaction wherever prevailing precepts impose the duty of loving, respecting, honouring, obeying, and so on and so forth, implying the right to impose obedience by force, for instance. But if I have never felt that anyone has ever renounced anything because of a sympathetic understanding of me that was at the same time meaningful to himself, I am unable to feel as much respect for him as the moral code tells me I should. So I am thrown back on learning the painful consequences of defying the power principle, and this I respect, out of fear. I refrain from stealing or destroying only because I fear the threat of being destroyed myself. The fact that the penal law is still governed by the retributive principle shows the strength of sub-human instinctive urges in law-breakers and guardians of the law alike. It also shows how poor in love is the human environment as a whole, that is, society.

Renunciation imposed by force cannot give satisfaction; it produces temporary compliance, and that is all. The proposition we are trying to establish is that deprivation of love on this scale should not be accepted as a fact of life as unalterable as a natural law. On the contrary, the predominance of loveless force belongs rather to an environment in which a shortage of vital necessities prevails and the great majority live periodically or permanently in a state of material want. Poverty is the product of partial cultural development.

*Collective structural changes in self-awareness*

The continuous social revolutions of our time are connected with the technical possibility of doing away with want; they are also directed against privileges of rank that date from times of poverty and emerged in the social order as the result of force. On closer inspection the processes involved in the structural change in collective self-awareness characteristic of our age turn out to be much more complicated than mere struggles for primacy between old power groups and new aspiring ones. The technical, affluent society needs a new moral orientation. The necessities that led to archaic moral codes have to a large extent been superseded. Freedom from hunger, epidemics, back-breaking labour, and the pressure the higher classes used to exercise on the lower certainly have a euphoric effect, but the frequent appearance in one and the same person of the wild behaviour characteristic of puberty, but in a permanent form, combined with a tendency to make anarchical demands and anxious adaptation to new status habits, appears to indicate, not just the decline in moral standards that is the subject of ever-recurring complaint, but that things are in a state of flux at a deep level underlying that of the existing moralities. In view of the relatively loose association between 'instinct' and ('satisfaction'-promising) object in human nature, any disturbance of customs can be met only by trial and error on a broad front before there can be any assurance in new ones. For even the socially overadapted individual at the height of his self-satisfaction is not able to decide 'so clearly and so free of doubt'[3] as our moral guardians proclaim.

73

The burden imposed on societies that leap from purely agrarian forms of social organization to the possession of modern technical aids – that is, entirely without historical preparation – can hardly be overestimated. Their unreadiness for this drastic change means that the danger of irrational reactions mounts with the expansion of rational techniques. Hence the increasing political concern of the leading technical powers with the periphery of their spheres of influence. The European has had centuries in which to habituate himself to the spread of rational processes in his social field (and his landscapes); in an irrational pattern of living he was given a sense of security by magical certitudes which he has now lost, but he has had time to come to terms with the loss. Max Weber accurately observed this habituation to rational processes. But to the individual they are becoming ever stranger and more bewildering. Max Weber wrote: 'No ordinary consumer has the slightest knowledge of the techniques by which his everyday consumption goods are produced; generally he does not even know of what materials they are made or which industry produced them. All he is interested in is the performance of these artifacts' – whether, for instance, the engine of his car is likely to fail on a motor-way. 'The "savage" knows infinitely more than the ordinary "civilized" man about the economic and social conditions that govern his existence.'[4] More recently, however, tendencies have appeared that help to overcome anxiety about the mysterious products of civilization. The consumer is beginning to demand information about the raw materials and manufacturing processes of the goods he buys.

The technological and scientific society has set in train a dialectical process. On the one hand, constant advances are made in the rationalization of every field of commerce and industry, administration and research, and on the other the resulting rationalized productive, administrative, legislative, etc., structures become increasingly 'alienated' from the individual's field of experience. He obeys the instructions, and wonders whether there is anyone who really understands the processes at work. (This state of mind is very evident in the attitude to the traffic problem, for instance.) Probably, indeed, such understanding is possible only to a limited extent, for the processes of our civilization take place on a scale of anonymous self-regulation, rather like those of nature.

*Problems of size*

This over dimensional scale creates the basic problem for the socialization of man in rational society. After the passage quoted above, Max Weber continues: 'And it is by no means always true that the actions of the "civilized" man are subjectively rational. This varies in different spheres of activity, a problem in itself.'

In societies that depend on magical modes of thought the instinctual element in behaviour is caught up and ritualized by tradition, and the processes of adaptation to these take place within a relatively stable framework. But what happens in a technological, rationalized mass society sharply divided between a working life, the tools of which behave with total predictability, and a 'private life' of emotionally determined decisions, which are also supposed to take place within a framework of predictability but the meaning of which is hard to see? The contents of the latter have to a large extent been taken over from magically oriented historical conditions.

To illustrate the conflicting calls made on the individual, let us compare two injunctions both of which he is supposed to follow. In the first place, there is the virtue of thrift. This could become a collective virtue only when as a consequence of economic developments a relatively broad section of society had been assured of the essentials for the maintenance and reproduction of life, that is, in 'classical' bourgeois society. Whatever may be the motivation of thrift in individual cases, it always includes a desire to provide for a 'rainy day'; it is, so to speak, a premium paid to ensure the independence that has been so painfully acquired. In middle-income groups money was also saved for the purpose of acquiring durable goods, involving renunciation of the satisfaction of minor, immediate needs; and employers saved to accumulate capital for expansion, that is, the production of more goods. Thus a vital interest in acquiring and multiplying possessions led to the traditional bourgeois trinity of virtues, namely, respect for acquisition, respect for property, and the precept of thrift. On top of this there was the bourgeois 'anal preoccupation' with property (preceded of course by the aspiration for it). The precept of thrift still survives as part of the bourgeois tradition, and it is used to teach the growing child renunciation of immediate instinctual satisfaction. But the greater the emphasis placed on renunciation, the more the idea of saving is overlaid by that of self-sacrifice, and it ends by being totally repressed by it.

The attitude described here and the thrift precept, though obviously still valuable to the individual, run counter to the interests of the economy and thus of present-day society. It is a primary factor retarding the welfare state and the principle of full employment, which necessarily require a high rate of personal expenditure. Saving is selfish and against the general interest – or so at any rate it seems. If the investment made possible by savings contributes to increasing productivity, the rate of increase of production calls for the exact opposite of saving. This points in the direction of making a virtue of extravagance, because only rapid consumption can keep pace with production, and it is production that provides mass society with its livelihood.

Thus surrender to consumption in all its aspects not only satisfies the individual's worldly appetites but is also considered to be moral, since it promotes the general prosperity. The possibility of adequate food, housing, and education for the masses is inseparably connected with their prosperity, that is, the production of non-essential goods. Thus security of livelihood for the masses comes into sharp conflict with the individual's moral salvation – at any rate, according to his world-denying religious code.

This brings us to one aspect of the personality splitting, schizophrenic trend, inherent in the coexistence of new and traditional codes. No less disquieting is the fact that the spheres of action related to the individual's picture of himself and the fulfilment of his ego ideal are to a large extent still occupied by much older, sub-human fantasies of violence and omnipotence. The new field in which this inner constitution finds expression in a social role is that of the technicians of the great administrative structures, the 'managers'.

### Rationalization or fatalism?

Such fantasies do not, of course, rise to the conscious level; should the individual by any chance catch a fleeting glimpse of them in the twilight background of his self-awareness, rationalization, in the psychoanalytic sense of the term, steps in. It simply means embellishment. Apparently conclusive arguments in harmony with the traditional moral code are promptly found to justify what is in reality action based on an inner drive. A man who uses doubtful methods to secure an advantage over his competitors excuses himself to his conscience by appealing to the Darwinian principle of the survival of the fittest; alternatively he may fall back on the Puritan principle that success is a sign of God's grace. In either case it is merely camouflage for the power principle of the horde adapted to a society organized on bureaucratic lines. The pseudo-rational superstructure of such behaviour puts the critical conscious in a position of impotence which idealistic assurances do little to help, because they serve only as a deodorant.

Prevalent morality is deeply imbued with the (largely unconscious) purpose of lending an appearance of justice to existing power privileges. Looked at from the point of view of the critical reason, morality in action behaves very atavistically. The questionable actions committed by the individual find him well prepared, for he has an effective defensive routine to protect him against a bad conscience, and he can always appeal to the double standards that are widely current. The only rational reaction to this, and the only one open to those with deeper understanding, may often be the stoical one expressed in the saying: Do not be angry, only surprised.

This capacity to tolerate, not fatalistically but calmly, is one of the ascetic characteristics of the more civilized man. He does not deny the existence of the deeper drives and their demands, and he does not idealize them into aesthetic innocence, but he doubts whether existing forms of social organization offer them the best possible outlets for obtaining satisfaction. It is only in appearance that his attitude is fatalistic, and his aspiration for more human, that is, more conscious, control of forms of association in the affective field are not Utopian. Also the implications of his asceticism must be made clear. He does not extol renunciation for the sake of fulfilment in the next world, but is concerned with the renunciation of cheap satisfactions in this world obtained at the cost of the rights of others, and also at the cost of discriminating self-knowledge.

If the 'civilized' man accepts an often hardly tolerable impotence in order to avoid more brutal and disreputable alternatives, he can of course do so in obedience to religious principles. But in this connection a concomitant phenomenon of religion must be recalled. Those of other faiths, non-believers, etc., are presented to the masses as sub-standard human beings, in relation to whom the precept to respect one's fellow-men does not fully apply. The question arises whether a form of organization based on obedience, original sin, and fear of outlawry does not inherently require a scapegoat, because of the unattainable degree of instinctual renunciation called for and imposed, particularly in the sexual sphere, and because of the down-grading of the deeper, instinctual side of man's nature into something essentially dirty and evil. In this connection we must again recall that, though it would be easy to quote theological trends running counter to this 'excommunication' of the deeper instincts, these are irrelevant in the present context. What we are concerned with is that at any rate in recent centuries such milder views have made little impact on the broad social consciousness. In response to the dirty drive the dirty 'object' duly makes its appearance, the scapegoat, the culturally despised minority, the uncivilized 'savage', the 'bad woman', etc., etc. In this connection an example that is slowly passing into history may be recalled – that of the lazy worker. He had to be lazy and stupid, otherwise he could not so easily have been exploited without a twinge of conscience. Also there was no alternative for him but to be 'lazy', that is, uninterested, because it was his only defence against exploitation.

## Cultural pressure to evil

Thus a first step towards a contemporary morality would lie in education in restraint from cheap instinctual satisfactions. This could be achieved only if the human instinctual constitution were regarded with less prejudice in the collective mind, and if the methods of force and humiliation were not regarded as the primary methods of civilizing it. Such a new morality should also try to overcome the traditional and paradoxical fear of prosperity, the belief that 'poverty ennobles'. It should show the way to deal rationally with affluence, because (always assuming that the world's population increase does not over-take its food production capacity) technology has made it possible to provide everyone with essentials without depriving anyone else. The new morality will no longer be able to justify renunciation either on the ground of other people's poverty or on the devaluation of instinctual urges. As no one has any experience of a society that has carried out the changes in living conditions that technology has brought within our reach, the morality of such a society is hard to foresee. Presumably it will be based more strongly than in the past on the recognition of the individuality of one's fellow-men. In other words, a higher degree of self-awareness will be a guiding factor, side by side with awareness of role.

The more obscure the rationale of the processes of civilization are, the less helpful are taboos and moral injunctions that condemn man's instinctual nature and impute to him little capacity for self-responsibility. Such taboos were practicable in small and supervisable groups in which they could be enforced. The only way of making meaningful the renunciations necessary in relation to one's fellow-men in conditions of affluence, in the 'city jungle', is the direct appeal to the principle of humanity. Such humanity is attainable, but it presupposes the ability to learn to see things and oneself differently, and depends chiefly on the education of the ego in the understanding of man's instinctual nature, on man's being on a better footing with himself as a creature of instinctual needs and being able to recognize that others are the same.

It is of course easy to preach mildness, gentleness, which is obviously more peaceable than its opposite. But is it known how it is attainable? And what of all the rewards for aggressivity that are simultaneously and alluringly displayed? Since the days of the Amphictyones, the early Greek semi-religious, semi-political bands who swore to observe chivalry in battle and spare the lives of defeated enemies, attempts to fuse the erotic and the aggressive drives have always been broken down by processes of dissociation which have destroyed whole societies or made social life a torment. Gentleness, tenderness, is an early, pre-genital form of sexuality, which must be taught and learnt in earliest infancy. It is the very first form of sexual expression, and is thus associated in the process of development with primitive aggression; the two together make possible the further satisfactory development of the child. The subsequent capacity to attain a proper understanding of the world instead of merely learning conditioned reflexes depends on the combination, experience of which constitutes the basis without which there can be no future stable link or combination between the two. The stability of this link is always threatened; it has to be rediscovered and re-established at every phase of development.

The dissociation of inner drives is always a sign of disturbed maturation, which implies a growing ability to integrate both fundamental components into an increasing number of behaviour patterns and the beliefs and attitudes and judgements underlying them. If in the individual's ordinary living conditions one of the two components has to be renounced, it cannot be lived and experienced and has to be fended off, repressed. But society itself uses similarly anonymous compensatory mechanisms to create situations which permit the repressed to be lived out. Aggression against the authority of the group is always severely penalized, but similar aggression against the authority of alien, hostile groups is, if it is successful, applauded and acclaimed. Such situations are inevitable if society imposes excessive repression and thus deprives the ego of the possibility of guiding its deeper impulses. Thus, if these drives were insufficiently associated in the first place or if they become dissociated under the influence of strong excitation, the phenomenon is in either case to be regarded, not as a sign of man's natural, innate wickedness, but as a result of disturbance of maturation under the influence of social usages.

The number of persons constitutionally incapable of adapting themselves to the demands of society seems incomparably smaller than that of those who would be incapable of living outside their social framework. In the affective field the possibility of learning – gentleness, for instance, and the choice of that way of behaviour in dealing with objects – is obviously restricted to certain definite early periods of life. As is amply shown by our own experiences, if these imprinting periods are allowed to pass unused, there are many things that cannot be learnt later. Expectations in relation to the objects of the outside world have then been so thoroughly established that fundamental character changes are almost impossible. Above all, they are not desired by the individual himself, because he has identified himself with his adaptation to the world, even if he is not in every respect satisfied with his adaptation.

The development of these preliminary stages to identity-formation is by no means clear in detail, but we have obtained some insight into the process. The vital experience of tenderness is certainly first experienced through the skin. In infancy the skin is a highly cathected organ of communication (Freud calls it the erogenous zone *par excellence*).[5] By means of it the infant feels the pleasure and unpleasure that to a large extent constitute its knowledge of the world. Additional confirmation of this biological function of the skin is provided by Harlow's experiments with monkeys. It is through the skin that the infant acquires its basic experience of being soothed, warmed, protected; and its experiences of unpleasure and pain, and of loneliness when neglected or approached unfeelingly, come to it by the same channel. If the infant experiences more painful unpleasure than pleasurable protection in this way, the experience of reality imprinted on it will grossly affect later calls on it to develop gentle, considerate, social behaviour. At best it will be possible to impose on the individual a façade of instinctual fusion which in situations of conflict will easily collapse.

Moral codes provide the framework for instinctual behaviour. When they crudely ignore the biological phases of development, they are necessarily disobeyed. Not only that; deficiencies in the early satisfactions deprive the mental processes that set in later – the development of the conscious ego capacities – of the vital foundation of experience of a situation in which conflicting instinctual impulses can be satisfactorily fused. To regard the discord thus brought about in human beings as an innate defect is fatalism based on false premises; the argument that because of their innate violence men can be kept in order only by force is based on this fallacy.

It follows that man's identity feeling is not constitutional or innate; it develops in the cultural context. When the group or the social order strongly disparages the senses and displays this attitude towards the pregenital phase of instinctual expression, because it regards aggression and libido as permissible only in connection with definite role privileges and most definitely impermissible in the child, who must be sexless and pure if he is not to grow up spoilt and uncontrolled, the adult has great difficulty in associating his drives with his identity feelings; and he has difficulty in attaining any lasting memory of his real instinctual conduct. For from the beginning of his life, that is, his phase of pregenital sexuality, he will have received no proper guidance to socially approved behaviour enabling him to find a satisfactory and acceptable outlet for his instinctual trends.

True unification of the personality depends on incorporation of instinctual experiences into the identity feelings; it is this alone that makes it possible among the temptations of everyday life to prevent behaviour from ending in real guilt, contempt, callousness, anti-social behaviour, or 'killing with a good conscience'. It is guilt and fear of tabooed instinctual drives that prepare the way for these destructive trends, for denying the essential drives brings about not integration but disintegration of the identity, and forces them to seek satisfaction by circuitous routes; some of these circuitous routes may be valuable, but others are inevitably the violent and fearful ones from which humanity suffers. Denial of the instinctual drives permits only a partial civilization of man, and – to reiterate it yet again – the unsocialized part, so far from being his 'real nature', is the part distorted by cultural pressures.

Also the denial of instinctual urges that is to a large extent imposed by our morality is not identical with the renunciation of urges necessary to civilization. It is infantile to deny something on the ground that 'what ought not to be, cannot be'. The impact of the moral codes as they are broadly experienced is to keep man psychically infantile in order to make renunciation easier for him. It is more than doubtful whether humanity will be able to master the crises of the future on this basis, for it is too tightly chained to the compulsion to do evil. Thus our task is to show that the socio-genetic process of evolution requires a moral code directed to the growth of ego responsibility instead of adherence to the demands of the super-ego.

### Hope as part of man's 'openness'

To the sceptic who rejects this train of thought on the ground that the only tried and tested means of maintaining social order is force, and that it is Utopian to believe in the possibility of a civilization more conscious both of love and of violence, the only possible reply is the principle of hope.[6] For hope is the psychical counterpart to the biological openness of human nature. Hope too must be subject to doubt, for it is an open question whether the voice of reason is capable of exercising a formative influence on self-activating social processes (such as the increasing division of labour, for instance, and the concomitant diminution of the sense of individual responsibility). Only if we hold fast to our original idea that it is possible to combine a rational order with understanding of its meaning are we protected against the pseudo-rationalism that would dismiss the purpose of life as being obedient service to some political system. The driving force of history has always been the association of the powerless under the principle of hope. Only enforced emotional perversion can transfigure impotence and hopelessness into a destiny ennobling to its victims, though that is a line of argument that appeals to those who have received a harsh early imprint and are tempted to react to it by simply regarding force with contempt. The paradox that ideas move the world, but that force totally devoid of ideas does the same, cannot be resolved by withdrawing from the world into any kind of cloister. 'Though it certainly conflicts with many deep-seated assumptions in Germany, the sociologist cannot avoid feeling that ideas in themselves have little chance. They need men for their dissemination, to help them to impose themselves, and again to co-ordinate their impact. The purely literary activities of writing and reading have only secondary significance. Notions such as that the ideas of Rousseau or Voltaire "spread in France" and finally "led to the revolution" are alien to reality and support the fallacy, as if the real motive forces of history were writers. One must always look for the actual groups of men who propagated, imposed, and demonstrated the ideas.'[7]

The approach to the problems of human association based on the principle of rational insight into the constitution of the human psyche is a late-comer in the field, and not a little patience is called for in consequence. In our analysis we constantly come across psychical defence mechanisms against infantile lesions which continue to exercise their effect; inhibitions of thought which have become automatic, for instance, and fixed prejudices (particularly when the individual feels moral certitude) which are totally immune to argument. Like neurotic developments in the individual, the fixed patterns of taboo and prejudice imposed by society are to be regarded as collective attempts to compensate for the traumatic damage inflicted by society on its members at the very beginning of their lives. Under these compulsions the ego, if it does not develop a consummate mastery in completely denying or totally misunderstanding its own instinctual impulses, brings them to consciousness in the most complexly distorted fashion. This diminishes tensions neither in society nor in the individual, but more or less suffices to complete the process of learning the contents and the behaviour patterns of the social code. Of all the possible ways of rational approach in this field, only those that serve socially predetermined ends are socially recognized.

The many beliefs that society imposes are taboo to rational criticism; they are expected to be apprehended by other psychical faculties, such as the heart, the soul, or racial, national, or class feeling, and so on and so forth. My racial or national or religious feeling dictates to me how I am to see, interpret, and judge both myself and others, and that with absolute certainty and finality. This state of being closed to divergent experiences is a sign of the survival of infantile defence attitudes against reality. The original insensitivity of children to racial characteristics is well known. An unfavourable cultural influence that associates racial differences with differences of value and links these with revulsion, fear, or hatred can easily cause the child to see what had hitherto been friendly relations with members of a different race only through the distorting lens of this evaluation, and the change can take place overnight. The change of attitude must be regarded as a surrender to social pressure. Its disastrous permanence can be established only where the instinctual life has been subjected to severe and non-understanding repressions, in other words, when close human intimacy has been either unknown or evanescent. When such experiences fall within the 'imprinting period' we have described, their effects are permanent; credulity and superstition, prejudices and many other ineradicable character traits stem from that time. They are the psychical response to external pressure, the typical reactions of a psychical apparatus that has not yet achieved complete differentiation but seeks equilibrium between demands from within and demands from without with the means available to it. If the situation is unfavourable, the 'openness' of human nature of which we have spoken fails to develop, the 'principle of hope' remains restricted to vain and unreal fantasies, and only a limited sector of reality is available to help in the orientation of behaviour. It is limited to the perception of what is collectively prescribed, and hope too is then tamed and domesticated and not binding.

# V

# Dynamics of the Drive

*Drives and guilt*

The word 'drive' is an almost indispensable tool for the understanding of many phenomena of life, or at any rate it has not yet been displaced by a better. It is an intellectual short-cut, like zero or other mathematical symbols which avoid a great deal of beating about the bush. The same applies to other concepts we shall use.

Like most of our organic processes, the drives are not accessible to our self-awareness. Freud has described a series of characteristics of instinctual life that are of such basic importance for the understanding of human behaviour that we shall briefly describe those most relevant to our purpose.

We differentiate between the source, the object, and the aim of drives. The source is to be sought in biological processes in the organism. A series of somatic processes reach the mind in the form of a stimulus. This psychical representation of a biological event is described in psycho-analytic theory as a drive. It is characterized by its origin in the sources of stimulus within the organism and by its appearance as a constant force; it is from this that it derives its unmanageability by flight reaction[1] on the part of the individual. The compulsive nature of drives, the impossibility of evading them, or rather the necessity of living under their pressure, is thus the most important characteristic of their dynamics.

Now, there is no such thing as the 'blind' instinct of popular speech. The adjective 'blind' applies only to the desperate, compulsive search for an appropriate object in the external world which will make possible the attainment of satisfaction: 'the end of the state of excitation at the instinctual source'. Thus a drive, which manifests itself psychically as a sense of want, of unpleasure, is inconceivable without an object to satisfy the want; it can no more exist without an object than can a wish. In the course of psychical development the proper object of a drive can of course be lost from consciousness; it can, for instance, be repressed or denied. 'There are drives that subjectively express a need but do not include consciousness of the objects appropriate to satisfy them.'[2]

Animal behaviour is more or less object-fixated and ritualized. The compulsion of an organic need – that expressed by the sensation of hunger, for instance – sets in train a search for an object to satisfy it, and the animal behaves in a manner specific to its species; it searches for objects its innate knowledge tells it will satisfy its hunger. Thus the strictest object ties and pre-established behaviour prevail. The animal's vision of the world is governed by its innate recognition of signals, which thus become its environment. Certain colours (of the mother bird's open beak, for instance), or acoustic signals, or definite shapes (as of the feathers of the parent bird's head), or movements (in the case of rutting behaviour) serve as trigger mechanisms; that is to say, they set in train specific behaviour, characteristic of the species, by which the animal relieves its instinctual tension in dealing with the object. In social contact it is mutual recognition of signals that indicates to both parties the presence of an object that will bring satisfaction.

However complex in many cases this process in man may be, in whatever elevated forms instinctual tension or satisfaction or disappointment may manifest themselves, primitive expressions of social contact, such as the use of a sexual partner without respect for the latter's personality, for instance, show that structurally the same laws apply to man as to other living organisms. The peculiarity of the human constitution is in the first place the loosening of object ties – surrogate objects, for instance, can take the place of the original; and in the second place the far-reaching recession of social behaviour patterns specific to the species and their replacement by variable behaviour patterns specific to cultures; and finally there is the extraordinary expansion of man's learning capacity. This situation reminds one of the chicken and the egg; it is impossible to say which step in development came first. The learning process goes on; human cultures in their present form require the subjection and adaptation of biologically anonymous instinctual life to an environment that has grown very dissimilar to the original human environment.

The object of the instinctual drive is satisfaction by the relief of tension. However, the biological pressure to obtain diminution of tension as rapidly as possible meets with competition from other psychical mechanisms, the ego mechanism, and the demands of the super-ego, which again compete with each other. They are subject to a different rhythm, and counteract the primary urges in the regulation of instinctual life. Without the critical strength of the ego, adaptation to the many levels of our social life is possible only to a very limited extent, and this involves an ever-increasing danger both to the individual and to the group. The long memory that cultures have for their great lovers, heroes, and sages and the high valuation put upon their character and their story in national literature is striking evidence of the difficulty of combining instinctually guided behaviour – which is selfish in nature – with behaviour that satisfies others and meets the ideals of the culture concerned.

As a cultural area increasingly succeeds in safeguarding itself against natural dangers, so does the regulator of instinctual trends cease to be 'real' fear; it increasingly becomes fear of guilt – of infringing established cultural standards. The factors that rouse this guilt have been very varied in the course of history. In early cultures (and traces of this survive in our own culture to the present day) it took the form of fear of the gods and demons that governed the forces of nature; rituals and taboos were acts of propitiation for offences against the gods, who punished them with natural calamities. Guilty anxiety and magical modes of thought as a whole are connected with a magical conception of the universe. The guilty anxiety of modern man is concerned with a far wider range of disapproval by his fellows and their withdrawal of love and respect; it is only remotely concerned with divine punishment. 'When the ego is forced to acknowledge its weakness, it breaks out into anxiety; reality anxiety in the face of the external world, moral anxiety in the face of super-ego, and neurotic anxiety in the face of the strength of the passions in the id.'[3] The proximity of moral to neurotic anxiety is the consequence of the desire of both to prevent a break-through of instinctual forces apparently bound to have a destructive impact in the social field; for neurotic anxiety holds fast to the contrasts of infantile experience. On the one hand the child is oppressively small and helpless in relation to grown-ups and the outside world, and on the other its fantasies of omnipotence are reflected in a tremendous overrating of the power of its own drives, to which the sense of guilt attributes positively world-shattering strength.

Guilty anxiety poses a social problem of the first magnitude. The question is whether the arousal of guilt in a given society should be treated as an intermediate or definitive principle of socialization. In any case insight into the real necessities of the situation diminishes anxiety. The relationship between anxiety and anxiety-free insight shows the state of development of members of a society, the amount of progress they have made from subjection to demands of the super-ego alien to the ego (and passive acceptance of authoritarianism) towards understanding behaviour in relation to their own instinctual demands as well as unsatisfactory social conditions; it is true that the latter are now the subject of uninhibited questioning.

### Forms of fossilization

The biological processes are permanent sources of stimulation. They survive the phase of satisfaction and become active again. Only when these organic processes cease, in the cycle of hormone distribution, for instance, does the process of inner stimulation and corresponding object search disappear.

The intensity of the urge is manifested in the restlessness it can create in the individual, which is directed towards eliminating the state of stimulation at the instinctual source'.[4] Man's behaviour clearly demonstrates the loosening of the fixation of the drive, its 'especially close link to its object', that has taken place in him. This puts him in the position of being able to find satisfaction in objects very remote from the original objects of the drive. He does this with the aid of the ego functions (curiosity attitudes organized in the form of learning). They enable him to find his way about in the world of cultural symbols. The 'mobility' attainable by instinctually governed behaviour is the functional prerequisite of all higher intellectual attainments.

But if, as the consequence of individual traumatic experiences, there is an early and all too strong fixation on an object of instinctual behaviour, all further advances in learning in this field of experience are cut off. Easily recognizable examples are the fetishist, and the monomaniac whose aggressivity is concentrated in the belief that the

Jews, for instance, are the source of all evil. Repetition takes the place of the continual quest for new objects of satisfaction and the dropping of old ones that is culturally desirable during the period of maturation. The absence of such quest indicates a neurotic miscarriage of development, a deviation into a gratifying cul-de-sac.

It is not difficult to find examples in the cultures of the present day of this fixation on gratifying objects by which development is blocked. The group style, for instance, may imprint on the individual a life-long attitude to authority corresponding to the childish view of a physically and intellectually vastly superior father, and the conformism of the majority makes this attitude exceedingly difficult to correct. Such fixations are characteristic of the multiplicity of the forms of social organization; from inside the group they are felt to be normal, natural, and self-evident. Only where real superiority in any field is recognized as between equals, and does not trigger off infantile behaviour patterns such as submission or rebellion, is there reason to assume that this fixation in the style of a group on an infantile pattern of authority is capable of being avoided.

A widespread educational ideal is the consolidation of social behaviour patterns in childhood, so that they remain fixed and permanent. The educators who pursue this aim argue that most people are not intelligent enough for independent orientation. The conclusion is invalid, because it is based on existing circumstances. In the first place, the origin of the pattern of behaviour that is held up needs to be examined, and the question asked whether the process of instilling it leaves open to the individual a pathway by which, without its making heroic demands on him, he will be able to achieve independence and maturity of judgement, or whether the educational system based on this principle rests on the maxim that authority is an institution that the ego is not qualified to question. If the latter is the immanent principle of the social order, as certain ideological rationalizations would have us believe, there is no occasion for surprise if naturally inquisitive children develop into unintelligent adults.

It is not necessary that men should automatically make a subterranean link between outstanding attainments and the contents of ancient fantasies. They should be able to appreciate an outstanding individual on his merits, and at the same time bear in mind that distinction in one particular field is not and cannot be accompanied by distinction in everything, and in any case does not call for blind hero worship; and, last but not least, they should realize that the occupation of a socially superior position by an individual who is no way superior is a questionable phenomenon. All this relative cutting down to size of authority implies the very reverse of a disrespectful levelling process. Two developments – the evolutionary step represented by the loosening of instinctual object ties and the advance in maturity by which infantile models are not allowed to continue functioning inaccessibly in the super-ego but are subjected to examination by the critical, understanding ego – combine to bring about a release from old fetters and to create the necessity of developing appropriate social forms and obligations. From the psychological point of view, the achievements of the intelligence to which we owe our cultural inventory are incomparably more developed than those directed to the socialization of affective man, the creation of his affective or emotional social constitution. The terrifying encounter with his instinctual nature has far more lasting effects in paralysing his ego potentialities than all the terrors of the real world.

Defence against this terror has taken the form of the inculcation of custom, which is the business of education; and custom generally buries the question, and in particular the question of the origin of the custom itself. But self-understanding based on habituation is deceptive, because the unpleasure of its origin is concealed. The sparing of this unpleasure is its economic function, and sometimes also the explanation of its disastrous unintelligence. Analysis of ritual going all the way to neurotic obsession shows the system of equilibrium established by it between aggressive and libidinal trends on the one hand and the integrative forces of the psyche (the super-ego and the ego) on the other; or, to put it more crudely, at what a high cost the custom is established.

Collective customs of social regulation are the counterpart to innate, instinctive patterns of behaviour. To the social psychologist it is important to discover what practices and concomitant circumstances cause these learnt object relationships to harden into incorrigible habits. At the end of his maturation the individual, after giving up temporary object ties in the course of his development, in any case settles down to permanent object ties and repetition in many fields of behaviour. The aim must therefore be to make the degree of mobility more elastic and keep the equilibrium between instinctual drive and reality testing open to new experiences. Hence the necessity of submitting to scientific examination the 'tried and tested' methods of education and the early educational indoctrination practised in the spheres of influence of the oldest social institutions, the churches, in so far as these are educational institutions, and the schools, in so far as the latter have not overcome tendencies to train the young to be subjects rather than free citizens. For these institutions do not transmit tradition primarily in the form of objective knowledge, but tacitly carry out the affective training of human beings in the use of that knowledge. Institutions such as the Catholic Church, and the Russian educational system, which resembles it so greatly in its methods, know that children must be brought under their influence as early as possible, that is, in the best period for imprinting, in order to bring about complete emotional obedience, an unbreakable tie, to the knowledge they transmit. An education aiming at genuine insight, on the other hand, will pursue the precisely opposite aim of avoiding, as far as possible, the arousal of guilty fear in the guidance of the child. The affective aim will be, not to take possession of the child, but to leave freedom for the child's initiative. Enlightenment – application of the critical intelligence to man himself – can certainly claim that its work on the sources of anxiety has not been without influence on these institutions, but the cultural task with which our epoch is faced will for a long time continue to be marked by this contention.

## Confluence of instincts

Our next step in this outline of a general theory of the instincts is to mention a process which, following Alfred Adler, we shall call confluence of instincts. The same object can simultaneously be the aim of several instinctual trends. Similar processes are to be observed in the animal kingdom, in the parent bird's search for food for its young, for instance. Here the instinct of self-preservation manifested in the search for food is combined with the nurturing instincts and put in their service. Instinctive actions directed to the preservation of the species (feeding the young) converge for a time with the individual's impulse for self-preservation. The parent bird looking for food is impelled by hunger, but satisfaction of the impulse is partially inhibited by another impulse; instead of swallowing the food, it takes a large part of it to its young. It is the latter impulse that in practice predominates.

In the human race a large number of learnt cultural behaviour patterns similarly inhibit direct instinctual satisfaction. But in this instance the conflicts we observe are not concerned merely with the direction to be taken by an instinctual activity, but are between more or less differentiated areas of psychical organization in which instinctual energies are organized. The mother who feeds her child though she is hungry herself is not actuated by a compulsive behaviour pattern that does not reach the level of consciousness and therefore allows her no alternative, but deals with a conflict between her own needs and the prompting of her conscience. The latter is certainly linked with residues of innate behaviour patterns, but had to be consolidated by the learning process. But, as human childhood is so prolonged and so full of situations to which the conscience does not provide automatic answers, there are many decisions which have to be made in subjective freedom. In one instance (when 'basic trust' predominates over 'basic mistrust') it may be perfectly tolerable to a child to be left by its parents for a few hours, while in another the fear of abandonment provoked may leave traumatic traces behind. The underlying conflict between the parent's own instinctual needs and those related to the child, and the lack of confluence between them, are thus very plain. Over-anxiety about the child's needs on the one hand and insensitivity to them on the other are the two extremes that show us how difficult confluence of instinct is to achieve.

### Hostility to instinct

One of the most important contributions of psycho-analysis to the theory of instincts was the discovery of the instinctual development that is concomitant with biological maturation. When we think of instinctual satisfaction, we must do so in relation to the degree of maturity attained. There is a striking difference in the degree of clarity we have so far succeeded in gaining about the processes of libidinal and aggressive maturation respectively.

At present theory can offer a differentiated development pattern only for the stages of maturation of sexuality, with its pregenital phases, characterized respectively by oral, anal, and phallic predominance, finally emerging into genital sexuality. Concepts such as orality are to a large extent technical terms which cannot be explained here. They refer to forms of libidinal satisfaction each characteristic of a definite phase of development; at each of these phases one particular organ is the chief transmitter of this satisfaction, the part acting for the whole. Thus the oral phase indicates, not that pleasurable satisfaction is experienced only through the mouth, but that it is experienced predominantly through that channel. The whole psychology of the first year of life belongs to the oral phase, the high sensitivity of the skin as an organ of communication, the importance of olfactory signals and auditory impressions, the fluid, or at any rate not yet sharply defined, body sense, the total, undifferentiated motoric participation in the expression of affect, and a great deal more besides.

A similarly differentiated pattern of development for the aggressive drive does not yet exist. It seems by definition to be associated with the voluntary muscular system, but its development proceeds progressively without any stages of emphasis on particular parts of the body comparable with that of the erogenous zones. The most important differentiation that can be made is that between archaic, that is to say blind, activity that hits out heedlessly at its object and consciously guided activity.

It should be borne in mind that this pattern is presented, not as a description of reality, but as an aid to understanding. In practice the two drives appear together and are blended in behaviour. The libidinal drive can (and must) make use of aggression, and aggressive impulses must similarly make use of libido.

The theoretical differentiation is important above all in relation to the feelings. We can detect which is the leading impulse both from the individual's self-feeling in a human situation and from the feeling his behaviour rouses in us.

It is these perceptions and feelings that provide the point of departure for our further reflections. Educational practice is based on them and not on any abstract conception of 'instinct'; experience of and contact with the environment take place by way of the erogenous zones and the motor impulses. It is the powerful impact made by these that creates the individual's picture of his own body and of his social environment. However far his development and his knowledge and ability may remove him from the scenes of his earliest experience, it is

93

the latter that once and for all determine his attitude of expectation towards new experiences and encounters, his basic mood, his quasi-physical self-valuation or non-valuation. The development of the ego, the organizing element in the psyche, is continually influenced by events during the process of instinctual maturation.

Where, for instance, tenderness (a matter to which we shall return later) is culturally despised, a form of instinctual satisfaction in which aggressivity is modified by libido and assumes a quite specific form of expression is missed.[5] Thus an ego experience that can act as a brake on aggressive and sexual impulses and combine them into a new form of behaviour, namely, tenderness, is also missed. Because of the absence of any memory traces of this, there can be no recourse to them later in situations that call for such behaviour. The more repressed these tendencies are in childhood, the stronger the reaction-formation against them (contempt for 'softness', for instance), the less possible is it for tenderness to be learnt or felt, not to say manifested, later. It is a common fallacy to assume that there is a close connection between feeling and the expression of feeling; that first there is a feeling and that then it is expressed. The link is much deeper than that. In the absence of a previously imprinted behaviour pattern, an inner blue-print for action, many of the most highly differentiated human feelings cannot be felt in their full subtlety at all. Feeling is always at the same time also behaviour, or at any rate an inwardly imagined living-out of the feeling.

The moulding of the feelings associated with the instinctual impulses in social behaviour has to take place early, so that the process can be completed later. Primary identifications provide the foundation on which instinctual demands come increasingly within the sphere of influence of psychic forces closer to the conscious and are modified by them. New kinds of outlet for them come into being which permit ego satisfaction in addition to direct instinctual satisfaction. This applies, of course, not only to pleasurable experiences, but also to the 'Spartan virtues' of mastering pain and fear, when the ego prevents the natural reaction of flight from the unpleasure-causing situation. It would, however, be overestimating the ego to regard it as the master of instinctual life, able to impose itself with complete freedom on the latter. That is the fallacy of those who idealize humanity, using the defence mechanism of denial in the process. We can adapt Kant's remark that concepts without first-hand knowledge are empty by saying that an ego devoid of experience of the libidinal and aggressive trends actually at work in the self would be empty too; it is the instinctual urges that first establish contact with the world and at the same time enable the ego to become aware of itself. The taming of instinctual demands by the ego is a process involving a continual struggle for primacy between the different agencies of the psyche. Only rarely is 'every instinct brought completely into the harmony of the ego . . . accessible to all the influences of the other trends in the ego and no longer [seeking] to go its own independent way'.[6] Much more frequently the ego, as we see from our examples, has to defend itself against instinctual wishes by excluding them; to make a political comparison, it suppresses minority wishes or uses tactical adroitness to outmanœuvre powerful trends; and conversely, of course, selfish primary trends can assume the mantle of idealism.

In our culture the defence tactics of the ego are greatly encouraged. This may be connected with a long history of hostility to libidinal and in particular genital sexual impulses. Its last peak was reached in the sexual morality of the Victorian-bourgeois age, which survived until the First World War. With the collapse of the social predominance of the bourgeoisie, this code, which oscillated between denial of sexuality and crudeness in obtaining satisfaction for it, collapsed. This led to a liberation from taboos that let fresh air into a lot of stuffy places. But what followed was not conscious control of a specific instinct; the first consequences were deep bewilderment and a retreat from object cathexes that manifested itself in fleetingness and unselectivity in erotic contacts. The effects of the survival of 'fragments of the super-ego' belonging to the old tradition were, however, more far-reaching; these identified sexual pleasure with a bad conscience and a sense of sin. The latter implied that sex was the root of all evil, represented the devilish element in man, and was therefore to be shunned. Such taboos prevent a whole area of the personality from being experienced as close to the ego, and all signs of sexual distress or aberration are met with horror and alarm. It is interesting to note that our culture does not react with anything approaching the same degree of horror to the greatest perversions of the aggressive instinct. The severity with which society is prepared to treat sexual perversions has only to be compared with the excuses that are made and accepted on political and ideological grounds for aggressive crimes of the greatest magnitude.

The term 'hostility to instinct' should not, however, be used indiscriminately wherever civilization calls for its restriction, for it can offer the way out of sublimation. As Freud says in his study of Leonardo, 'We are obliged to look for the tendency to repression and the capacity for sublimation in the organic foundations of character on which the mental structure is only afterwards erected'.[7] The capacity for sublimation means that under the influence of the ego functions we are able to divert instinctual trends to objects alien to their primary aim but from which satisfaction can be obtained thanks to the intervention of the ego. This feat of harmonization of the ego and the id enables us to talk of 'ego satisfaction'. It is thanks to the processes of repression and sublimation that human civilization has developed so differently from all the social organizations that exist in the animal kingdom. 'Observation of men's daily lives shows us that most people succeed in directing very considerable portions of their sexual instinctual forces to their professional activity. The sexual instinct is particularly well fitted to make contributions of this kind since it is endowed with capacity for sublimation: that is, it has the power to replace its immediate aim by other aims which may be valued more highly and which are not sexual.'[8] Thus all cultures, and highly specialized cultures in particular, are bound to require their members to exchange original satisfactions for satisfactions specific to them, though this is not sufficient in itself to enable them to be described as hostile to the instincts. The renunciations of instinctual satisfactions are different from those demanded by a society hostile to instinctual satisfaction. This hostility is to be observed where a whole field of instinctual activity is subject to a negative valuation and the heart and essence of an instinctual trend – such as that for sexual pleasure – is affected by this valuation, with the result that even the act of reproduction can be carried out only with a bad conscience.

## Conservatisms

Sublimation is essentially an achievement of the ego organization. It is a defence against the claim of the id to sole control of behaviour, but it is not a mere suppressive measure, as are repression and denial. A collective hostility to instinct can be said to exist only where an almost complete suppression of sexual life – or of aggressivity – is called for, and hence forms of defence are imposed on the individual which (in contrast to the processes of sublimation) permit instinctual activity no share in behaviour and try to keep it away from its primary objects and aims. Such overstrained ideals, such an imaginary picture of a humanity separated from its instinctual base, do not exactly provide 'the most favourable conditions for the exercise of sublimated sexual trends',[9] because in these conditions the ego organization has to expend a great deal of energy in suppressing, excluding, etc., instead of making integrative use of the forces of the instinctual base. However, the extent to which men are ready to martyr themselves in the service of such instinct-denying doctrines is very striking. The only possible conclusion is that such renunciation must enjoy special prestige in their groups. The loss of self-esteem that follows disapproval by the group or the conscience represents a greater evil than the renunciation of pleasure, which they are therefore prepared to tolerate.

Like all other abilities, that 'organic foundation of the character', the ability to sublimate, varies very greatly. The group style or code is obviously capable of stimulating abilities in the individual which would develop only against the specific cultural background. We have already mentioned the Mundugumor people, who believe that children born with the umbilical cord wound round their neck are destined to be artists and therefore systematically encourage the assumed gift in such children. Parallel phenomena occur in all cultures. They enable individuals to do things that in a different environment would seem alien to them and not even worth trying.

The saint, who achieves a high degree of transformation of his sexual and aggressive impulses, is – if he is truly entitled to claim wisdom – freer from the value judgements of his group. An example of this is the life of the hermit – provided, of course, that society recognizes his cell as still belonging to its territory. The danger that threatens him is the strengthening of his secondary narcissism. What is meant by this is that the libido that has been withdrawn from objects in the external world in pursuit of an ascetic ideal may be shifted to the ego itself. The ego then becomes the object of libidinal cathexis; object libido is transformed into ego libido.[10] This takes place in a pathologically extreme form in the total separation from the outside world that occurs in schizophrenia, but neurotically milder examples are to be seen in the many individuals who have every opportunity of obtaining sexual satisfaction but, for reasons that we have just indicated, are unable to love. The saint's renunciation of instinct – demonstrated in its highest form in the life of the Buddha – is a forswearing of the world that yet keeps his own salvation in view. Consideration of the destiny of these instincts again reveals the openness of human nature to adaptation to the most heterogeneous environments, as well as the impossibility of shaking off instinctual nature and the long practice in favourable social conditions that is required if instinctual life is to be successfully brought within the sphere of influence of the ego. Superficially it always looks as if it is instinctual life that pays the price of civilization, but it is only necessary to recall the whole range of individual and group pathological phenomena to see that untamed instinctual trend imposes self-alienation on the ego. The ego too sometimes has to pay the price of civilization.

A high degree of conservatism attaches to instinctual trends, and to character habits also. The explanation is the long period of evolution during which there was a firm link between instinctual trend and instinctual object, and this is reflected in human instinctual behaviour. When an instinctual trend has once found a satisfying object, it tries to keep it. In this connection one recalls children's preferences for certain foods, games, or toys, for instance, or the habit of smoking. The child seeks by repetition to obtain the same pleasurable sensations that it previously experienced, and it avoids the unpleasure of new experiences; it cannot be certain that they will produce the pleasure it had before. Education tries to exploit this tendency to cling to an object that is cathected with interest. Sometimes a fixation, 'a specially close tie of the instinct to the object', is established that is subsequently not easily dissolved in the course of further development, but attains a secondary reflex autonomy. Violent reactions intended to frighten the child away from a desired instinctual satisfaction sometimes do so with such lasting effect that not only is the original instinctual object abandoned and a substitute sought, but all experiences in that instinctual field are henceforth shunned. In these circumstances an interdependence that is in the truest sense of the word involuntary is established between ego and instinctual trend. The trend remains, but the ego unremittingly wards it off. The defence process becomes habitual, and henceforth betrays itself in rigid character traits in which fear of the warded off object is avoided while the surrogate object is held fast.

### Terminological

When we use Freud's terminology and talk of object cathexis, and of object libido which supplies the energy for it, we are using abbreviations of a type commonly to be met with in science. Strictly, of course, as Calvin S. Hall pertinently points out,[11] an object cannot be cathected, but only the perception, memory, or impression of it. He goes on to observe that similarly it is only the perception, memory or idea that one has of oneself and not the self that can be cathected. Therefore, when Freud talks of object or ego cathexis, or of object choice and narcissism, what he means is the activation of a perception, memory, or idea related to an external object or the self. Thus identification, for instance, is the transformation of a cathexis of a perception of an object into such a cathexis of the self. Concepts are always intelligible only in the context of the ideas from which they sprang. Psychology requires a conceptual language that does justice both to the immaterial nature of our experience and to the fact that this experience arises out of material organic processes and the instinctual trends arising from them and also from the artificiality of the outside world, particularly the social world. We see both our own experiences and the outside world 'with our own eyes', that is, with all the assumptions transmitted to us by our culture and worked up by us from our own situation in life.

Organic processes result in instinctual trends which are variously reflected in our experience as fantasies, moods, compulsive experiences, etc. Psychological concepts are meaningful only when what to our reason seems to be the unbridgeable gap between mental experience and somatic processes is borne in mind, as well as the fact that both alike are events in the life of the organism. They are attempts to establish working connections in a field which as a whole has an infinity of aspects. We often succumb to the danger of measuring and evaluating by each other aspects which do not belong together though they are not mutually exclusive. The explanation of this is that discussion is often directed not so much to the establishment of truth as to the defence of 'objects' that a particular investigator has cathected and values highly. Hence many who have once arrived at a fixed view of a concept which is offered to them – this, though it alienates them, provides an outlet for their libidinal or aggressive trends – make no further effort to understand it. Freud wrote: 'But I know . . . that qualifications and exact particularization are of little use with the general public; there is very little room for them in the memory of the multitude; it only retains the bare gist of any thesis and fabricates an extreme version which is easy to remember.'[12]

### Identification and moral injunctions

Close ties to the earliest objects that provide satisfaction, protection, and security, that is, the parents and other relevant individuals in the environment, arise quite naturally out of the intensity of these contacts. The process of identification and the slow development of a super-ego, a conscience, out of these identifications are the consequence. Ties of varying degrees of intensity with other model figures follow; each of these contributes by means of identification to the fixation of object cathexis in the developing personality, and the fashion in which instinctual trends attain their direct or provisional aims is thus stabilized.

Thus instinctual objects and the manner in which instinctual satisfactions are obtained present themselves differently or are tabooed in accordance with the style prevailing in the cultural group. Even in the most natural and closest of human relationships, that between parents and child, there is no such thing as a fixed, hereditary pattern of behaviour. Both parties contribute to a harmonious atmosphere between them, and to attain this the parents must be able to identify with the child instead of projecting on it their own narcissistic trends; only if this condition is satisfied can they be constant models to the child through all the stormy phases of love and revulsion. The significance of the reciprocity of the relationship is often concealed by adult self-righteousness, a failing which is itself the outcome of childhood deprivations. We shall deal later, in the chapter on obedience, with the question of one-way communication between the strong giver of orders and the weak on whom obedience is imposed. When this form of social contact prevails, education is a mere process of training by reward and punishment. Identification processes play their part here too, of course. Parents see in their child an object intended to fulfil their own disappointed wishes and ideals; thus a part of their moral super-ego is embodied in the obedient child, and only if it is obedient are they able to love it.[13] For its part, the child submits, in order not to incur the loss of its parents' love, and it identifies with them and builds up its own self-ideal sadistically-masochistically, on the strength-impotence principle. Active and passive adaptation to the world within and the world without take place in extreme forms. The sharp ambivalence of feelings that is natural to the child apparently disappears; as it is not tolerated, the child expends a great deal of psychical energy in repressing it and keeping it repressed. It finds this very difficult, because 'in the state of immaturity and unestablished identity the affects have strong sadistic or masochistic trends'.[14] Under the pressure of excessive discipline or pampering the child may become 'good, quiet, and well-behaved' or rebellious and destructive. If either of these trends prevails to the extent of becoming a dominant, fixed pattern of behaviour, it is obvious that the socialization of the child has failed. The rebellious child is the more disturbing, but not necessarily the more disturbed. In such circumstances the primary aggressive impulse against the forbidding or weak-seeming parents is dissipated hardly at all, or only with great difficulty. Both trends of development are reaction-formations to conflicts of identification with which the child cannot cope; it therefore retreats into overadaptation or into reactively fanned destructivity. Both are compulsive, and restrict the field of decision of the ego even before it has properly established itself.

We have spoken of the almost unlimited human capacity for choosing objects of instinctual satisfaction and cathecting them with libido and also for withdrawing from objects which it is natural to love. This wide range of choice makes it possible for libidinal affection to be lacking even in the parent-child relationship that is so necessary to the maintenance of the species. The social code bears witness to this. The commandment does not say: 'Thou shalt love thy father and thy mother' but bids one 'honour' them; in other words, love of one's parents may develop or it may not, depending on the parents' ability to love. The commandment therefore calls on the individual to acknowledge their authority; it calls specifically for behaviour that has to be learnt, not to reactions from spontaneously developing behaviour. But honour should develop naturally, like love. This commandment again demonstrates the precarious basis of social standards. On the one hand social life is impossible without them, while on the other real behaviour (of the parents, for instance) may be such that they can be honoured only at the price of dishonesty. Freud's observation that the most variable thing about an instinct is its object, there being no original connection between the two, could be used to deduce dogmatic injunctions not only for children but also for parents; at all events 'thou shalt honour thy children' would be a very valuable one. But it runs counter to the basic assumptions of a paternalist social order. Thus the tendency is rather to a fatherless malformation of development rather than to a proper differentiation of the stereotyped role of authority. If roles were more properly understood, recognition of freedom depending on the individual's level of development would make substantial demands on paternal (and maternal) authority.

We do not know nearly enough about the circumstances that release or inhibit the feeling of love, why unsuitable or disappointing love objects are often so obstinately clung to while easily accessible objects ready to respond are overlooked. As expressions of like and dislike are so noticeably associated with sense perceptions (one cannot stand the sight or smell of an individual or the sound of his voice, the idea of contact with him makes one shudder, etc.), it is to be assumed that the affective pattern that later awakens feelings of like or dislike is established at a very early stage, that of the first experiences of other human beings, at a period of exceedingly vivid sense impressions when the ego capacities are still unformed and the interpretation of experiences is subject to magical modes of thought.

Encounters that are felt to be supremely significant – and the encounter with one's own child is one of the most outstanding of these – thus awaken earlier experiences originating in unconscious memory. True, the sight of a baby (K. Lorenz's 'baby pattern') triggers off a series of obviously innate behaviour responses – protectiveness, tenderness, the desire to nurse it, and so on. These spontaneous reactions and feelings are familiar to everyone. But, as we pointed out in discussing lack of tenderness, they do not govern behaviour continuously, and we know that, even when there are no spectacular conflicts between parents and children, the latter can be hated from the moment of conception. When that occurs, it is generally the 'imago' of the unloved sexual partner that is transferred to them. Women who are unhappy about being pregnant are often told to wait until the child is born, when everything will be all right, and indeed this sometimes turns out to be the case, for the 'baby pattern' imposes itself. But sometimes it does not, and the child is rejected by the mother or father, or both. There is a manifest conflict between the missing libidinal cathexis and the demands of society, for the latter expects the child to be loved by its parents and encourages this. But the child sees through the quasi-loving behaviour that develops under this imperative, for loving contact cannot be simulated. At the same time a great deal of surplus aggression – aggression, that is to say, which is free of ties and is therefore still searching for an object – can be satisfied at the child's expense in the name of such social values as strictness, discipline, cleanliness, and tidiness. Alternatively a reaction-formation against their own basic aggressive feelings, which conflict with social standards, may take place in the parents, rousing their sense of guilt. Unconscious guilty anxiety may cause them to spoil the child.

### Ambivalence and discord

As E. H. Erikson has shown, the feeling of 'basic trust' in the child can be roused only in the relationship with its parents, and the same relationship can in unlucky cases lead to 'basic mistrust'. As one continually encounters the idealistic and sentimental idea that discord between parents and children is unnatural, we shall point to some of the circumstances from which it can arise.

What is natural is that every affective human relationship is fed from both instinctual trends, that is, is inherently ambivalent. Thus the feeling that predominates at any particular moment – especially in the case of the child – can switch rapidly into its opposite. The extent to which aid is offered in mediating between conflicting libidinal and aggressive forces is socially determined. A constitutional characteristic of our mental life is the dialectic of 'both . . . and'. The accentuation of experience in relation to objects, above all the extent to which an 'either or' emotional attitude is enforced, is linked with the group attitude at any particular time. The conflict between the parents' innate nurturing trend and their selfish tendencies is universal. Renouncing their own satisfactions for the sake of the child is capable of rousing great hostility and aggressive irritability in them. In other words, a struggle takes place between the narcissistic, libidinal cathexis of their own individuality and the partial sacrifice of this demanded by nurturing behaviour. The social behaviour pattern seeks to damp down this conflict and bring about a confluence of instinct. The many educational practices known to anthropology – and the more familiar practices of our own culture – are often very crude, and make it very evident that the 'conflict of ambivalence' is inevitable and that collective behaviour patterns have not succeeded in moderating it. Because of the authority that clings to custom, as Pascal saw, there is resistance to saying so, but if we are to avoid idealizing the human race it must be stated that a great deal of collective ritual, a great many socially supported opinions and behaviour patterns, are symptoms of ill health as great as that from which individuals can suffer. The advantage of understanding instinctual dynamics is that we no longer have simply to accept these crippling, paralysing, tormenting, but sanctioned practices as absurdities, oddities in the historical peep-show (chiefly of course when they are other people's and not one's own), but are slowly acquiring knowledge enabling us to understand them.

Further material for conflict between parents and children arises when the children are hated (whether this is admitted or not or is unconscious or not) because they are a physical embodiment of a rejected part of the parents' own personality, of which their behaviour is a constant reminder. Their attitude and appearance embody weaknesses and defects from which their mother or father suffered and to which they later blinded themselves. Unexpectedly encountering them again in their own children causes them to react with hatred. This is apparently the most frequent factor of disturbance. It greatly restricts the possibility of a positive identification with one's own child; the child conflicts with the ego ideal set up inside oneself as a reaction-formation against one's own weaknesses.

A counterpart to this disturbance of the parental relationship by hatred is that which can be caused by excessive doting. We have already indicated that love of one's own child can be strongly marked by the characteristics of narcissistic self-love. This is the 'overpowering' love of one or both parents that imposes upon the child the realization of a parental ego ideal and unduly prolongs the originally organic symbiosis into stages of development when the latter should be superseded by the child's trend to independence.

Finally, in addition to psychological processes, it would be wrong to overlook trends deriving from changed economic traditions and conditions of production that exercise an influence on affective feeling between the generations. In predominantly peasant cultures children represent capital, a natural source of cheap additional labour, security for the parents' old age. In modern industrial society prolongation of the period of education represents a using up of capital, and the task of providing for old age has to a large extent been shifted to institutions; each generation has to look after itself.[15] This has resulted on the one hand in greater freedom for the individual (in choice of occupation, for instance), but on the other hand it calls for greater altruism and sacrifice, which human beings do not unresistingly accept. The fact of alienation between the generations has many sources, but among them is certainly the primitive one that less material advantage is nowadays to be gained from one's children, for parents and children each go their own way.

The question whether aggression is to be understood as a primary, cyclical phenomenon or a reactive, regulative one has been much discussed.[16] The reason why it is so hard to decide is that we can measure human expressions of aggression only at a stage at which they appear in co-ordinated form – when the child has acquired some control over his motor reactions. At this stage it is far from being a release of 'pure' instinct, but always takes the form of a reaction to the environment. Freud's observations led him to the conclusion that a primary aggressivity was to be assumed. His postulation of a death instinct roused much criticism. We accept Freud's view. But we need not concern ourselves here with theoretical matters.[17] What matters is that we find aggression in all forms of human civilization, which have had very different degrees of success in moderating it.

In the present situation the vital question is that of the extent to which aggressivity (the destructive trend) is linked with libido, enabling it to develop into productive activity – and how much either primary or above all secondarily roused surplus aggression and destructiveness overflow into human activity. Thinking in terms of models, it can be assumed that severe sexual frustrations must lead to an increase of aggressivity and destructiveness, because the aggressive component always contained in the libidinal trend has not been released. Finally a situation arises in which the aggressively tinged

actions in the social field which have to compensate for libidinal deprivation are themselves charged with secondary libido, and thus gain in
aggressive strength. Reverting to our theoretical models, they do so
only to the extent that mixed forms of both instinctual trends occur in
all expressions of life fed from instinctual sources.

Let us return to our previous example of a mother's reaction to her
crying child. Different mothers, we said, respond differently in these
circumstances. We can now restate the situation in greater detail. The
different responses of different mothers depend on their different
points of departure. These are determined by the following factors,
among others: the strength or weakness of their innate instinctual
trends and their socially encouraged or discouraged readiness for
libidinal object cathexes in general and in nurturing behaviour in
particular; the proportions in which their libido (primary or secondary)
is narcissistically fixed or available for the cathexis of objects; and the
degree of security of the link between their libidinal and destructive
trends, which may or may not be sufficient to ensure that no disproportionate surplus of unsatisfied destructive trends endangers the
libidinal tie to the object. It is the strength of this tie that determines
how the nurturing trend, which originated in new instinctual sources
(the organic processes of pregnancy and suckling), will establish itself
in relation to and in competition with other instinctual trends. But the
extent to which the mother's reaction to the 'crying' signal is stereotyped or spontaneous will also depend on the nature of her character-
formation preceding her pregnancy and the birth of her child, on
whether her adaptation is predominantly assimilative or actively
integratory; and her innate capacity for ego development will play its
part in addition to environmental influences. This again is connected
with the defence mechanisms used by the ego and the amount of
energy it has had to expend on counter-cathexis. By this we mean the
cathexis of the reaction-formations the purpose of which is to prevent
the return of that which was repressed. If, for instance, in her own
childhood she was not allowed to show her need for affection (desire for
skin contact, loving attention, spoiling, and so on) because this was
held in low esteem by the group as weak and 'feminine', she can
obtain the social recognition she needs only by being active and
vigorous. In that case she will tend to merge this reaction-formation
into the whole of her behaviour, developing it into a marked character

trait. Her rejection of the opposite kind of behaviour shows the strength of the counter-cathexis.

This restriction of maternal freedom of choice brings us back to the mutual relationship between the amount of object libido available and the narcissistic libido required for the maintenance of the equilibrium of the individual's character. It is this relationship that determines whether the individual will be able to make choices in life based on a reasonably unprejudiced view of reality or whether he will be able to see the latter only through ideological spectacles. In many respects the latter themselves represent a collective reaction-formation. The shelter provided by conformity with accepted prejudices prevents the distortion of reality involved from being critically questioned, and the distortion is unreflectingly accepted as reality.

Even the oversimplification involved in the theoretical model we have taken shows how complex are the conditions at work in the mother-child relationship, which is much more powerfully determined than others by a natural instinctual object and residues of innate instinctual behaviour. Our analysis has shown at how many points and by what instinctual conflicts even a relationship so closely linked with the preservation of the species can be disturbed, and how easily the meaning of social injunctions can be distorted and converted into their opposite by unconscious instinctual trends. Our purpose was merely to show how easily ambivalence of feeling can lead to rifts between human beings.

*Inner objects*

Let us now return to the concept of fixation, which we described as an especially close tie between an instinct and an object. It should be added that there are internal objects that can be even more strongly and permanently cathected than objects in the external world. There are grounds for assuming that the specific characteristics of the external object that 'releases' animal behaviour correspond to the content of innate inner objects which are represented in fantasy and in turn represent the external object sought under the influence of instinctual tension. Such imagos, or archetypes, are assumed to exist in human beings also. It should be borne in mind, however, that this is a speculation, a possibility, not a necessary assumption. What we are able to observe is the assimilation of interior objects in the processes of identification or introjection. Reverting again to a theoretical model, we can regard such introjects as stimuli for the shaping of affective behaviour in relation to objects. Applied to the situation of the child, the process is as follows. The child is drawn into a social field in which it encounters feelings, and its wishes are met with varying degrees of completeness. Inevitably it will also have to accept denials and refusals. There will also be a greater or lesser readiness, depending on the culture, to impose obedience on the child by physical punishment or the withdrawal of love. It will consequently encounter the same people in very different affective situations. It gradually introjects this complicated pattern of experience, which can be regarded as a primitive, preliminary stage of identification. Unconsciously the child moulds its behaviour on the pattern of these first objects in all their contradictoriness.

In the later process of identification a much larger amount of deliberate imitation is contained, but this too extends far beyond the field of conscious intention and is by no means a pure act of will. Use of the word 'imitation' is justified only if it is borne in mind that its roots lie in unconscious processes and are influenced by the original processes of introjection and their results, the introjects. The introject begins by being an externally experienced pattern of action; it ends by imposing from within an identity of action and valuation with the model. The earlier the introject is formed, the more stubbornly it maintains its influence. Detachment from action taken in consequence generally remains minimal. As no development of ego capacities has taken place in infancy, the introjects act as organizers of instinctual behaviour. They work compulsively, for good as well as for evil. The relationship between introject and ego reflects the real power relations between adult and child. The often so heterogeneously introjected objects end by forming the inner command-post of the super-ego. In conformity with the early roots of these formative processes, there is a great predominance of experiences and imprintings that remain unconscious. To make clear the archaic structure of these beginnings of the super-ego, it should be explained that the introjected objects are of course not complete persons as we later experience them, but 'part-objects' – reactions or command signals that are organized as complete objects in a way that is not yet understood.

Normal development then leads from these part-objects to the perception of complete objects and identification with them. If, however, we observe inter-human relations more closely, we note that, though the parties to them are intellectually capable of regarding each other as whole persons, many of their reactions reveal the extent to which they have remained emotionally at the phase of development of part-object relations. They are unable in fact 'to bear the sight' or 'the smell' of someone, or regard that person only as a partner who ought to spoil him orally or satisfy him sexually; apart from these aspects, they are hardly capable of forming an idea of the individual as a whole.

This shows that the subsequently established ego capacities have succeeded in bringing about an ability to function socially; in a more superficial, practical sense, the social techniques essential to living have been mastered, but emotional experiences have not been freed from the predominance of primitive levels of organization. The principal factor – leaving aside the great variety of constitutional aptitudes – which determines whether this is achieved or not is the intensity with which the introjection process was imposed from outside and associated with fear. The greater the fear, the less the possibility of later critically examining or changing these character traits and automatic reactions.

Introjection and identification are the earliest ways in which social ties are established. Identification processes take place throughout youth and well into maturity. Their importance to society can be deduced from the fate of those individuals who are deprived of sufficient emotional contact in early childhood and of sufficient opportunities for the forming of introjects, with the result that they later have great difficulty in establishing lasting identifications. They turn into lone wolves or enemies of society. Leaving aside imbeciles and some very deviant characters in whom, perhaps because of innate constitutional characteristics, no binding of instinctual trends takes place, closer investigation sometimes shows that a super-ego has indeed been established among antisocial individuals in the broader sense of the term, but has assumed an especially archaic form that is inadequate for coping with instinctual trends in a differentiated social world.

A question that arises is that of the economic cost to society of the task of primary socialization of its members. What is the failure rate of the process of adaptation, that is, what is the proportion of ill-adapted individuals? Looked at from the point of view of the interests of the society as a whole, what groups are there that are a source of disturbance and what is their importance? Closer examination of social reality is required if the process of social adaptation is to be understood. In a relatively enclosed group whose economic conditions and techniques of making a living are relatively constant, the social style will be what D. Riesman calls tradition-directed. The number of ritual formative processes that accompany the path to maturity in these circumstances is very striking. In this respect our own culture is deficient. In a tradition-directed society there are few occasions on which tried and tested standards for action and judgement are not available for the individual's guidance. In these conditions ego development is of course overshadowed by powerful, collectively controlled customs and the inner authority of the collectively shaped super-ego that reflects them. That does not mean that ego and super-ego cannot coexist in a harmonious character structure. The individual is held firmly by the bonds of his culture, he shares its typical pleasures and pains with his fellows, knowing that his forefathers lived in exactly the same way. In such cultures the formation of individual behaviour by internal objects of collective validity is especially plain. There is no conflict between social behaviour and a greater or lesser area of private life with its own private standards. Stagnation of socio-economic development seems to involve a stabilization and quieting down in the socio-cultural sphere also. All the members of the group share the same views in relation to most of the situations arising in their lives, and act on them. Individuals with more subtle affective nuances do occur, but the tone is set by the average.

The greater the territory covered by different groups united into a single state, the greater can be the differences between the sub-cultures within it. The state need not further affect the style of life of these sub-cultures; the extent to which it is able to refrain from interfering with their traditional style depends, indeed, on its wisdom or short-sightedness. But when a division occurs in a society in the sphere in which the most powerful taboos prevail, that of religion (as in the Reformation, for instance), the most alarming alienations from the traditional way of life set in. The fusion of instinctual trends consolidated by tradition in familiar and universal patterns of behaviour breaks down and makes way for new dynamic processes. Things previously familiar suddenly become alien and hostile.

Unfamiliar and powerful excitations disrupt the familiar guidance by the inner objects united in the super-ego. Cultures normally provide intermediate aims for unsatisfied instinctual trends, particularly the aggressive trends. They offer, for instance, as Malinowski[18] has described, a phase of promiscuity before marriage, or ritualized war games. In so far as the group fails to provide outlets for surplus instinctual trends within itself, it seeks to divert them outside, away from the affective links within the group. The most usual outlets for aggressive trends outside the group are hunting and feuds, and in so far as these are practised collectively they strengthen both identifications and libidinal ties within the group. But if some members of the group suddenly turn into 'non-conformists', the previously diverted aggressive potential within the society is discharged between the conflicting parties with exceptional violence, being reinforced by the fear of the alien that has suddenly come so close. Religious wars, civil wars, the persecution of heretics, are the result.

The aggression that breaks out so uninhibitedly against a different, alien system of values is by no means natural and obvious. There is no reason why the attitude to such a system should not be one of friendly interest or total indifference. When this is not the attitude, it is because tensions within the society have caused the imago of the alien to be projectively cathected; the projection makes an unprejudiced look at the alien impossible. The unconscious psychical processes that take place in these conditions are quicker than the critical functioning of the ego. As projection is always defence against repressed and denied impulses within the self, it is not real fear that is involved when an alien or an alien system of values is immediately felt to be hostile, but defence against intolerable feelings of worthlessness in relation to our own standards that have arisen in the interior world of our own experience in contact with persons well known to us. The persecution of heretics, for instance, is always also the persecution of one's own heresy, one's own offences against one's code, flight from one's own guilt feelings – just as not loving one's own child is a symptom of the rejection of one's own ego by one's own super-ego.

The history of the persecution of heretics shows us all the nuances of what happens when aggression is released from the ties of convention. The fertility of invention shown by the torturers shows the nature of the fantasies that take control when the restraints of the super-ego and the ego are lifted. The tortures inflicted on the enemy, whether alien or alienated, disclose part of the nature of the 'primary processes' – the name given by Freud to the psychical processes that take place 'under the dominance of the unconscious laws of thought'.[19] In the course of maturation to reality-related super-ego and later ego functioning, these primary processes are inhibited by secondary ones that block their path to action. But they reappear in the most terrifying fashion when society agrees on a scapegoat, in relation to whom all checks on release of affect by the secondary work of civilization are put out of action.

But this again, though it is by no means rare, represents an extreme of cultural alienation. Our normal, everyday life presents us with more discreet and concealed but in intention and effect no less dreadful examples of oscillation of behaviour between that guided by the secondary and that guided by the primary processes. The psycho-analyst is continually able to observe long and ingenious chains of secondary processes which turn out to be aimed ultimately at the satisfaction of an instinctual trend at the level of the primary processes; and, as both libidinal and destructive elements are able to gain the upper hand, that may be one of the reasons that led Freud to postulate a death wish.

# VI

# Ego and Ego Ideal

*Good examples and bad effects*

'Do you wish to become a universal right-seeing eye? Then you must do so as one who has passed through many individuals, the last of whom uses all the previous ones as functions.'

FRIEDRICH NIETZSCHE[1]

*Doubtful ancestor cults*

Our brief survey of the instincts enables us now to go a little more deeply into the processes of identification. We do not live in a stagnant, predominantly tradition-directed society, and that is bound to influence these processes. Nor do we live in a society which can be seen comprehensively, whose social processes work regulatively and permanently in a fixed area. On the contrary, the influence of sub-cultures continually overflows their original boundaries – one has only to recall the spread of jazz, for instance. This, together with continual technical and economic developments, brings about a permanent relativization of group-specific traditions. Orientation on the pattern of earlier generations, which took place as a matter of course in a tradition-directed society, is hardly possible. In a stable society one reason for clinging to tradition was the practical aid it provided in daily living, but in present-day conditions traditional methods often break down and hamper understanding of the requirements of the day. The various nationalisms, for instance, are a serious obstacle to trends that seek to go beyond them. Adherence to traditions that are losing their relationship to the rhythm of life and are increasingly assuming the character of fixed obsessional ritual tends to be increasingly motivated by fear of a profoundly changed environment. An outlook based on the past, on history, has been made vastly more difficult by the upheavals which have brought about radical changes in every field, not in the political field alone, for instance. Moreover, the peculiarity of all the abounding 'novelties' of our civilization is that they recall either not at all or only very remotely the once familiar working tools of the past. A power station means something totally different in human experience from the mill by the stream, though both use water power, and a car wheel is quite different from that of a donkey cart. Turbines, refrigerators, radio sets, have no history, but they absorb the attention of mankind, which has a history, a history of production and use. In drawing attention to the gap that divides the social furniture characteristic of the permanent technical revolution with that which preceded it, we are not to be taken as advocating shallow traditionlessness. Such a state of affairs indeed arose in the pioneering age in North America, for instance, where the 'unlimited' possibilities could be exploited because few traditions and institutions stood in the way. But this 'activity without history' (and the partially instinctual and ego-remote satisfactions associated with it) has long since invaded the older cultural areas and everywhere else where industrial and technical concentration has developed and set its stamp on town, landscape, and people. We are witnessing a slow change of this 'factory and management culture' by processes the yardstick of which is the aesthetic production of goods, which no longer takes place in reliance on the familiar. The lamentations about the loss of tradition that came from the old country, the 'olden days', at first reached neither the captains of industry whose smoke-stacks darkened the sky nor the workers who lived and worked in their shadow. The disastrous distinction between civilization (for the uneducated masses) and culture (for the educated few) dates from that time; and the retreat into romantic aestheticism – as symbolized by the museum – is essentially nothing but a confession of the loss of tradition in real, everyday life. The same probably applies to Sunday church attendance; a religious museum is attended for reasons of status. Goethe's injunction, *Was du ererbt von deinen Vätern hast, erwirb es, um es zu besitzen* ('If you are to possess what you inherited from your forefathers, you must first earn it'), nowadays requires the exercise of discretion, for first it is necessary to establish how many of the tangible and intangible possessions of the past are indeed inheritable and worth inheriting, what part of them has real value and is capable of yielding a good return, and what is likely to be a millstone round one's neck. We shall answer the question briefly. The traditional possessions, both material and mental, which we previously described as 'signal' possessions, are continually changing, being redistributed and – destroyed. This process is taking place very vigorously before our eyes, so there is little stability in such inheritance. Guidance from history must therefore be sought in a different direction; it is obtainable only by examination of previous experience in the resolution of historically constant conflicts. The storehouse of experience is what we have described as affective and social education. Where success has manifestly and unmistakably been achieved in subordinating man's instinctual nature to his ego nature, history has present guidance for us. The past is of course capable of imposing itself in many other ways through traditional institutions, but these are hardly likely to lead to adequate solutions.

St Paul may be recalled here: 'Though I speak with the tongues of men and of angels, and have not charity, I am become as sounding brass, or a tinkling cymbal.'[2]

There is a Jewish proverb with a similar implication: 'If someone says slay or I shall slay you, let yourself be slain.' Both quotations are timeless statements of the responsibility of the ego.

Appealing to such tradition is not retrospective romanticism – a critic might call it mere Utopianism – but it does not contain the whole truth either. The whole truth is that – our education being what it is at present – pressures to conform tend so to determine the structure of the individual character that the ego's power of resistance to collective states of mind and collective actions is no more effective than it is against his own instinctual trends. We have already discussed the individual as a creature of role in Chapter III,[3] and we shall now carry the subject further. We shall maintain our concern with the typical. Discerning the pathological element in the typical is the social psychologist's privilege, and he will defend his position with the anthropological theory that he believes to be correct.

*Conflicts of motivation*

We now turn our attention to conflicts of motivation arising from the coexistence of ancient traditional practices with ways of life that are entirely new, and also from the extension of knowledge about the ways of life of neighbouring or distant social groups. In this respect the idea of distance has also been relativized, for the strange and the familiar are drawing closer to each other, and the challenge to compare them, however unpractised in the matter we may be, is no longer so easy to evade. Where we see a community in which we could live differently without falling short of the accepted standards, our interest is first attracted by the things that are permitted in the alien group and are forbidden in our own. The title of the film *An American in Paris* neatly sums up this situation, but the passion for Italy that dominated the bourgeois century falls in the same category. The collapse of morals (continually lamented by the purists) that tends to follow cultural syncretism is the result of the disappearance of traditional conditions and society's consequent loss of ability to impose 'renunciations' on its members to which they had obviously not been deeply reconciled. This relativity of morals demonstrates the 'openness' of the human constitution, which can go all the way to a chaotic loss of orientation; that is to say, new mental equilibriums are sought and formed which may be freer or may be rigidly formal or wildly inconsistent, or for longer or shorter periods in the life of individuals or groups or society as a whole equilibrium can be totally lost. In Germany such a 'post-collapse' phase has occurred twice in a lifetime.

What light do these considerations throw on our theme, which is still the importance of the influence of inner objects on character development and hence on action? The child's first identifications are with persons in its immediate environment; later, of course, it identifies with heroes of all kinds (from Werther to pin-up girls), but these later identifications never attain the overriding significance of the first flesh-and-blood models. But these too are characterized by imperfect taming of the instinctual trends; were such taming complete, it would mean that 'every instinct is brought completely into the harmony of the ego and becomes accessible to all the influences of the other trends in the ego and no longer seeks to go its independent way'.[4] But such perfection is not attained by mankind. Even our greatest heroes, unless we idealize them, are able to achieve it only in part. Their character, in fact, includes defence mechanisms against instinctual trends entered on at an early age, that is, automatisms of action and judgement deficient in thorough knowledge of reality, whether of their own inner instinctual trends or of the outside world. Nietzsche's remark that every man is most distant from himself is worth remembering in this context. To a greater or lesser extent all our behaviour contains an element of double standards. We fulfil our own instinctual wishes with objects in a manner that is not moral, but disapprove of the same thing in others (our children, for instance) of whom total morality is demanded.

*How to evade the code*

The variations of these double standards are inexhaustible. The elimination of doubtfully moral or undoubtedly immoral behaviour from our conscious self-valuation has one especially disagreeable consequence. In the processes of introjection and identification which determine the growing child's behaviour, it internalizes, not only the super-ego and ego components of a model – that is, the model of ourselves that we want the child to see – but the model's whole pattern of behaviour as the child experiences it. Thus, if the model's double standards are very pronounced – if the part of the personality that ignores its professed standards and seeks direct instinctual satisfaction remains evident even though the ego refuses to accept this or tries to gloss it over – this aspect of the model, though kept out of his conscious, is introjected no less than is the 'official' aspect. In fact, something very disagreeable occurs: this aspect is seized on with special avidity. This is readily intelligible, for in it the young individual finds a powerful ally for his own pre-cultural trends. These, restricted by morality as they are, find a key to the circumvention of the latter in the way in which the model himself does forbidden things. The father who preaches good manners and self-restraint to his children but keeps the best bits at table for himself teaches them two things, both the code and how to evade it. This explains the persistence of identifications with what (from the point of view of the social code) are the model's negative traits. Careful scrutiny of one's own behaviour will often reveal the inclusion of traits taken over from one's father which the latter found particularly objectionable; for in its impotence the child hates this double standard without being able to avoid it in himself. But he also hates the prohibiting side of his inner objects and is alarmed by his own instinctual trends, which threaten to bring him into conflict with the official code. The untamed instinctual aspect of the model involuntarily comes to his aid in coping with this anxiety, for the model's actions proclaim that, if you go about things the right way, you will be able to get a bit of pleasure too. That, in a nutshell, is why good models sometimes have bad consequences. The idea that one is a good model may derive from an interpretation of the self in which the truth is very well concealed; it may be confirmed by neighbours, colleagues, seniors, and the parish priest, because social contact with them is restricted to the 'official' level. But members of a man's family and his close friends often have a picture of him quite different from that which he himself and the world at large have of him.

This double chain of motivation of our behaviour, the conscious and the unconscious, increases the burden of knowledge it is incumbent on us to acquire. To the conscious, with its desire to confirm that all is well, it is painful to realize that the conflict between pre-social, egoistical trends and moral, conformist behaviour is not capable of permanent resolution. It costs not a little effort and courage to have continually to recall this even when – and particularly when – the rightness of our behaviour strikes us as being especially self-evident. Only this exceedingly uncomfortable practice in relation to oneself can put us in a position of relative freedom of choice. Those who believe that freedom is not a potentiality of man's late development, but an innate and sovereign human characteristic, will of course be offended at our doubts about the inevitability of his maturation to freedom. But for those who refuse to sacrifice an unprejudiced view of reality for the sake of preserving an article of faith it is impossible to doubt how hard it is for all of us to bring about some degree of harmony between the demands of external authority and those of the internal authority of the super-ego. Habit, including the habit of self-deception, covers up a great deal; the truth is that the harmony is always partial. Distaste for such realism has contributed to the innumerable misrepresentations of psycho-analysis because of its refusal to underrate the instinctual component in human nature.[5]

There remains the question of what psychical capacities there are on which the individual can take his stand, that is, exert authority in the shaping of his thoughts, decisions, and actions. There must be some detached, Archimedean fulcrum through which leverage can be applied. We attribute this function to the ego, to which we concede the right and the ability to intervene. We shall now complete our survey of instinctual theory by considering some aspects of ego psychology without which our sketch of human behaviour would be very incomplete.

*The ego as energy transformer*

The id is certainly a more fundamental phenomenon in life than the super-ego or the still younger ego with its faculty of conscious decision. The achievements of civilization are associated with the functions of the ego and the super-ego, but both these 'organized'[6] components of the psyche are linked with the id, which supplies the energy for all the work of the psyche. In a description of the functions of the ego Freud states the situation as follows: 'The ego controls the approaches to motility under the id's orders but between a need and an action it has interposed a postponement in the form of the activity of thought, during which it makes use of the mnemic residues of experience. In that way it has dethroned the pleasure principle which dominates the course of events in the id without any restriction and it has replaced it by the reality principle, which promises more certainty and greater success . . . But what distinguishes the ego from the id quite especially is a tendency to synthesis in its contents. . . . The ego develops from perceiving the instincts to controlling them; but this last is only achieved by the [psychical] representative of the instinct being allotted its proper place in a considerable assemblage, by its being taken up into a coherent context.'[7]

However the energy processes of the psyche are conceived of, they are components of the living organism and thus of its total store of energy. As the task of organization devolves on the ego, it must have its own sources of energy, relatively independent of the processes of the id, if it is to fulfil this function. In other words, it must be able to deploy its own forces against the id. To erect a defence mechanism energy is needed, just as it is to integrate and organize. The many observations of this function of the ego have only recently been systematized into a theory. H. Hartmann[8] postulates that neutralized libidinal and aggressive energy is available to the ego for its work of mediation between the instinctual trends of the id, the demands of the super-ego, and the demands of the self to develop itself. The word 'neutralization' indicates a freer availability of the energy. It is released from the task of securing the quickest possible satisfaction for libidinal and aggressive trends; instead, the ego uses it for testing reality, detaching itself from external and internal stimuli. It is this detachment that results in a broader vision that makes possible a better, freer understanding of others, whom I am able to regard as other selves and no longer naïvely connect merely with my own narcissistic wishes. Thus the energies tied up in the ego obtain satisfactory discharge in spite of the renunciation of older forms of satisfaction. It is this that we previously referred to as renunciation that satisfies.[9]

As in the case of other human capacities, we must assume innate constitutional variations in the capacity for ego development. Whether the ego finds it easier or more difficult to appropriate and neutralize energy for itself in its own 'field' will depend on this innate potential. 'The ego is not the product of experience alone, but of experience acting on a prepared organism.'[10] The social psychologist, however, is concerned with the 'heredity' of psychical ability only to the extent that it co-operates with social influences. He is interested in pinpointing the social conditions that aid or hamper maturation of the ego. Though we are very well aware that we do not know nearly enough about this, we can nevertheless make some significant assumptions about conditions that work one way or the other.

We cannot see the ego; we merely assume its existence from what it does. Its central characteristic is the capacity for seeing cause and effect and for productive organization. The latter means that conflicts are experienced consciously and not disposed of without regard for the consequences. If a scientist, committed to the principle of causal logic, believes in a revealed religion such as Christianity without any sense of conflict, it means that his ego is not capable of coping with it. An unconscious component of his ego wards off the conflict, which is a permanent source of anxiety, denies it, and satisfies itself with the unprovable assumption that a reality beyond his empirical experience requires belief in the existence of a paradise. The outcome is an Orwellian double-think that keeps the two areas of experience in separate compartments having no contact with each other. Awareness of the presence of a conflict and ability to live with it even though unable to find a solution would be the sign of mature ego development.

## The necessity of empathy

Psycho-analytic observations have established that an essential condition for maturation to genital sexuality is a not too seriously disturbed progress through its pregenital phases. We also know that certain experiences are essential for the maturation of the ego capacities, and that pregenital satisfactions are among them. As for the ego functions that influence individual behaviour in the social conflicts that are always possible, we can say of them that their development is influenced by the nature of the inter-human relationships in which everyone is involved during the infantile period when we are most subject to imprinting. Let us try to identify three important phases:

(i) In the first place we must ask ourselves whether the child's closest relationships with people and things in its environment, its libidinal object cathexes, are encouraged by the emotional attitude of those with whom it is in contact, and whether these are at the same time able to tolerate its aggressive trends. What love really means to a child can be stated in psychological terms to be empathy, intuitive understanding of its needs. This enables the adult to compensate for the inevitable demands and prohibitions imposed on the child and at the same time to keep his own affective excitation under control. An essential condition for the proper development of the ego functions is the co-operation of education and self-education.

(ii) Only this tolerance, undisturbed by any excessive admixture of unrecognized, unsatisfied aggressive trends on the adult's part, makes possible introjections that do not demonize the child's natural sense of impotence. In other words, the super-ego must not impose itself terroristically; it must leave the ego elbow room for ambivalence and not enforce upon it traumatic fixations on definite defence mechanisms. The result will then be that excessive energy will not be absorbed in counter-cathexes against the threat of its inner trends. Instead, the organization of the ego will remain plastic, accessible to new experiences.

(iii) If this condition is fulfilled, the differentiation between the ego and the id will not widen into an unbridgeable gulf. Instead, the demands of the super-ego and the trends of the id will remain related, or at any rate not totally irreconcilable.

In these circumstances perception, thought, and the memory – the reality-testing functions – will not be excessively disturbed by the instinctual trends that may at any time be uppermost or by the injunctions of the super-ego. The ego will be able to bind energy for its specific tasks, and it will be able to use its capacity for libidinal object cathexis for integrative purposes. In other words, an individual who tackles difficult tasks with 'passion' or lasting interest and at the same time is properly adjusted to reality can gain pleasure, and specifically ego pleasure, from these activities and, when postponement of satisfaction is necessary, will be able better to accept the temporary unpleasure of the id. A good example of the opposite sort of situation is provided by the learning difficulties experienced by many children. They do not succeed in producing 'interest', that is, in organizing their curiosity into their ego and guiding it past the rocks of the unpleasure of the effort of learning. An insufficient libidinal cathexis of the ego capacities comes about; the gap between the wishes of the id that demand immediate satisfaction and the demands of the super-ego that call for renunciation and the unpleasure involved in learning is too wide. The ego is unable to mediate between the two functions; it has obviously failed to neutralize and appropriate sufficient psychical energy, but has submitted to the demands of the representatives of the primary trends. The distaste for 'work' in children can be very directly observed in their day-dreaming, dawdling, and aimless distraction. The explanation may be a dictatorial super-ego that has not been internalized but is embodied in a person in authority and is effective only so long as that person is actually exercising supervision. Alternatively, it may be due to neglect; the child may never have experienced enough libidinal attention to have enabled it to learn to assume unpleasure for itself for another's sake, which is the essential condition for the development of a tolerant or reliable super-ego structure. Often the two harmful factors co-operate. The inevitable identification with the negative component in the child's model then weakens the early stages of ego development in advance and prevents the development of a productive internal organization of the ego and the id and the ego and the super-ego.

*The passengers*

Thus our attention is concentrated on the dialectical relationship between instinctual and ego forces. Each is helpless without the other, though in a different way. Very primitive ego capacities can be sufficient to enable an individual to 'function' socially in an unobtrusive manner; he is able to satisfy his instinctual needs quite well. It was this that led to the bitter observation by that great psychologist Nietzsche that 'most men obviously do not regard themselves as individuals; that is demonstrated by their lives'.[11] In Nietzsche's vocabulary an individual is a man capable of thinking for himself and making independent decisions – in other words, a man who has achieved successful ego development. But if most men are not individuals, what are they? The answer can only be mass men functioning with varying degrees of efficiency, but totally at a loss when cut off from their frames of reference. The world in general, their environment, and the various kinds of pressure to which they are inwardly subject and the resultant anxiety and guilt feelings keep them so under their thumb that they shrink back from any independent thought about their situation. Being only passively adapted to the group, if its code falters or is faced with crises they are incapable of contributing to the search for rational solutions. They are passengers and, as is demonstrated by the history of all the ages, remain passengers, even to the point of a paroxysm of unreason.[12]

What is unreason? It is the predominance of the primary processes without the blessing of reality control. Cultures, in spite of obvious signs of rational achievement, are at many moments in history unable to provide the guidance in bringing instinctual wishes into tolerable harmony with real conditions which individual upbringing is capable of providing for the child. When disintegration of weak ego capacities takes place in the group in which political decisions are made, the same process takes place among the masses.

The most jeopardized area of the psyche remains the ego. At such times the temptation to be or to become a passenger is if possible even more irresistible than any individual temptation to infringe the common code – to steal, for instance. There is perceptible in this a compulsive behaviour trait common to all living creatures that live in groups, whether human or animal. The threat of loss of contact with the group is frightening; it leads to panic fear and a frantic effort to re-establish contact at all costs. What it does not lead to is cool and detached consideration of the situation. Such consideration would only intensify the conflict of the individual who does not approve of the behaviour of his fellows. Voluntary self-isolation from the group – in the spirit of the inscription on the tomb of Friedrich Adolf von der Marwitz, who 'chose disfavour when obedience would have brought no honour' – or at any rate withdrawal from the affective excitation of others, is obviously one of the ego's hardest control functions.[13] The medieval punishment of outlawry shows that to the individual loss of group membership is equivalent to death, as is well understood by those skilled in manipulation of the masses.

## A product of paternalism

The withering of ego capacities under the pressure of strong excitation, particularly when it is collectively communicated, has long been observed and deplored. Le Bon's *The Crowd* is based on this indisputable fact, but only since Freud's *Group Psychology and the Analysis of the Ego*[14] have we begun to gain a better understanding of the dynamic laws behind the phenomenon. If, as a result of intimidation and deficient empathy with childish needs, the ego has developed only weakly, any strengthening of outside authority, or equally well any promise of pleasure gain by repudiation of authority, can cripple its integration. The degree of vulnerability of the individual and of the community to such regressions to a primitive level of organization indicates the degree of cultural adaptation attained. Now, the traditional paternalist societies, that is, the existing cultural patterns, seem to favour early introjects that lead to primitive reactions such as aggression, flight, obedience, or asocial egoism when moderate excitations are aroused.

The average level of ego maturity reached in the process of socialization is low, and so is the ego's threshold of resistance to being overwhelmed by inner instinctual trends and dictation from outside. The explanation should be sought, not in nature, man's natural 'ego weakness', but in the conditions created for the development of the ego by the socially prevalent relationship between rulers and ruled all the way from the typical family to huge disciplined organizations administered on the largest scale. The 'irresponsible' character of mass man, the leading strings on which he is kept, are not, however, the result of a one-sided relationship of cause and effect; he is given orders because his powers of decision and criticism are weak. Also he is kept weak so that he can be given orders. Even the idea of any other kind of communal life meets with resistance, for it implies laying impious fingers on man's most sacred possessions, for example, the belief that the strong have the right to exploit and impose their will on the weak. That can easily be shown to be the guiding principle of typical reactions in the individual's character. These alone, however, are not enough to permit conclusions about his essential nature; first one must know something about the mental image he has of himself, and how he arrived at it.

In ordinary, non-scientific usage the word 'character' is often associated with ideas of heredity and of innate strength or weakness. Freud, however, points out that 'what is known as "character", a thing so hard to define, is to be ascribed entirely to the province of the ego'.[15] Character is not something that just grows, like the thickness of the hair or the colour of the eyes; at most it is 'potential destiny'.

*Ego ideal in the open social field*

Everyone, besides being what he is, also has a picture of himself, relatively blurred or relatively distinct, of what he would like to be, his ideal self. This again makes it possible to discern the nature of his adaptation. In one case the salient feature may be the self-indulgence the individual feels ought to be the reward of his passive submission – the ideal is to harvest the fruits of his conformism; in another the ideal may be to secure the approbation of his fellow-men by unusual achievement, enterprise, or energy. The ideal may be realistic, or it may be fed by infantile fantasies of omnipotence. In his ego ideal man lives in fantasy a future in which his unfulfilled wishes come true and his deprivations and strivings are rewarded. This process of forming ideals begins in early childhood, when the son wants to be like his father and the daughter like her mother. Ideals are later adapted to a large extent to those of the social class to which the individual belongs. Individuals belonging to a vital, lower social class which is on the way up will, however, include in their ego ideal many features taken from the image of the upper classes as they perceive it.

The importance of the ideal that the individual has of himself is to be judged by whether or not it has a noticeable influence – and if so what sort of influence – on the constant pattern of behaviour that we call his character. Or, to state the question in terms of the dynamics of behaviour: is the ideal closely related to the specifically organizing capacities of the ego and does it result in aims appropriate both to reality and to the ego, or do these fantasies cover representations of primary processes very remote from the ego, and are they thus an indication of the weakness of the organizing ego? The ideal of a member of a small community may be to be efficient at his job, enjoy a satisfactory sex life, and be the father of healthy children and a respected member of the community. His ideal follows the beaten track. Conflicts of development in his childhood have not led to a retreat from the reality offered him and a non-attainable fantasy substitute. But if he follows the drift to the big city, imagining he must seek his fortune in distant parts, in a vague fantasy of wealth that will secure him continual satisfaction of all his wishes, this betrays the formation and persistence of an infantile ego ideal that is a blueprint for failure unless his ego is capable of reality adaptation to the new environment.

There are, of course, any number of possible variations. Let us suppose that the member of our small community is a Greek fisherman. No amount of skill at his trade will help him if the fishing grounds are exhausted. If he decides to emigrate, the decision may be in perfect harmony with a high valuation of courage in his ego ideal. An ideal specific to a group that an individual makes his ego ideal can be acquired in very primitive and simple social circumstances. It can continue to have meaning and significance to an individual who moves from a fishing village to Coventry or Detroit, and the stronger the structure of his reality-testing ego functions is, the freer his ego is to learn and adapt itself actively and passively in the process of learning, the more significance it will have. If all this fails, however, in situations of temptation and adversity the ego will disintegrate; the super-ego will emerge as a rigid authority which in situations of conflict will not be able to indicate to the ego a decision in harmony either with traditional moral standards on the one hand or with the new group standards on the other. In these circumstances the ego ideal will be relegated to the role of a dispenser of fantasy consolations and unreal wishful dreams. This example is not intended to do more than make it plain that ego ideal and super-ego are not identical. The latter is formed out of the demands of society and calls for these to be followed as closely as possible. The ego ideal can anticipate this state of affairs. Its chief role is satisfying the individual's self-respect in a role he has himself chosen within the horizon of his experience. In a society which has crystallized into a relatively small number of traditional roles, the formation of the ego ideal presents few difficulties. In societies with a wide range of occupational and social roles and big differences of status the situation is different.

Role differentiation in our society is associated with differences of natural endowment. Liberation from economic want and group-centred and group-imposed habits of mind has given impetus and social prestige to a wide variety of aptitudes. A static social structure that had to be fatalistically accepted encountered a dynamic counter-trend that has opened up a relatively wide choice of roles. But this has made formation of the ego ideal no easier. True, everyone has a field-marshal's baton in his knapsack, which in contemporary terms means he has a chance of aspiring to any level of the 'establishment'; but the chances of failure are also greater than they used to be. Failure to attain the envisaged ideal strengthens the regressive trend present in every ego ideal, the trend to turn away from reality. The counter-part of a fantasy ideal remote from reality is invariably resentment, which is yet another factor that prevents the attainment of the attainable.

As this vicious circle − resulting from an ideal yoked to passive fantasies of surrogate satisfactions instead of being a blueprint for active, reality-adapted 'self-realization' able to face all the disappoint-ments on the way − is an important ingredient in neurotic character formation, let us illustrate it by two examples. They throw light on (i) social conditions that lead to failures of adaptation, and (ii) some of the factors that so often result in good models having bad conse-quences.

*The need for good counsel*

The following examples are not intended to throw light on individual cases, with which this book is not concerned. They are intended to show how social antagonisms can be reflected in psychical structure.

A forty-year-old hairdresser with a prosperous business, in the eyes of his neighbours a good father and husband, felt a compulsion to injure his customers with his razor or scissors. Fear of these unintelligible impulses made it almost impossible for him to carry on his trade, and he increasingly took refuge from his distress in drink. The first thing he told the physician after describing his trouble sounded odd; he ascribed his whole illness to the circumstance that, being a hairdresser's oldest son, by unanimous decision of the family he had had to carry on the family business, though he had wanted to be an engine driver. This last was of course no unusual aspiration for a boy; others want to be foresters, pastry-cooks, sea captains, or space-ship pilots. But a man still brooding over this ambition at the age of forty was a rather different matter, particularly as it turned out that he could quite well have achieved it 'if only he had seriously set his mind to it'. But what did that phrase mean? It assumed a 'will-power' that the patient had failed to show. He was by no means lacking in energy in the occupation that had been imposed upon him, so he was not really lacking in 'will-power'. But those words, that come so trippingly to the tongue to condemn people, tell us very little. What had happened in reality when one traced back this man's story? He recalled his parents in an almost impersonal manner, using words like 'strict', 'tidy', 'religious'; they were perpetually working, and had had little time for their children; he seemed to have had no experience of the fact that parents and children are capable of deriving pleasure from each other's company. The strangeness and inaccessibility of his parents to him was repeated in the structure of his super-ego. The inner authority that dictated his decisions was as alien and as dictatorial to him as his parents had been during his childhood. He could not remove himself from its sway, and it had trampled on his 'life's ambition' to become an engine driver, just as they had trampled on it. The harmony between their demands and those of his super-ego was far greater than that between his super-ego and himself as represented by the beginnings of an independent organization of the ego reflected in the engine-driver ideal. At the same time there was nothing eccentric about this ideal; engine driving was a respectable calling, at the same social level as his father's. But in spite of that he had been unable to assert himself against what he felt to be the united front of adult interests. The wish to be an engine driver went as far back in his childhood as he could remember; this made plain the 'hallucinatory' component of his tie to that role – in his fantasy being an engine driver was equivalent to being himself. The role expressed his identification in fantasy with a big, powerful figure in secure control of powerful forces; in fact, a more powerful figure than his father. So it could be concluded that the child had transformed his real experience of impotence and total subjection to his father's orders into a fantasy experience of tremendous power. To put it pictorially, the engine-driver image was the outcome of a whole stream of forgotten and repressed fantasies, expressing the very essence of the child's resistance. It was the result of his working up these fantasies to enable them to stand up in his self-esteem.

The symptom of his illness, the impulse to wound, perhaps kill, his customers, represented the return of the repressed content. It was yet another confirmation of the assumption that an impulse rejected by the ego does not for that reason lose its energy as long as it has not attained its goal. It also threw light on two other things: on why the patient had not forgotten and had been unable to give up his childish ambition, and why he had not been able to accomplish it. The working up of all his rebellious (Oedipal) wishes into the engine-driver ego ideal had been a notable achievement, an attempt to make himself acceptable in a social role. There was reason to believe that, had the patient's family shown understanding, had they supported his ambition, he would have been more successful in taming his instinctual trends and would have been able to live without the agonizing experience of being overwhelmed from within by impulses totally alien to his ego. But the rigid demands made on him by his group, its lack of empathy, had frustrated this. The ego ideal survived, because it was the form of organization in which the hostile, aggressive, socially still untamed id wishes remained alive under the burden of unforgiven and unforgivable frustrations, but transformed into a socially productive role; they were driven to conceal themselves behind the shield of that rational and reasonable ideal.

But the patient had been unable to attain his ideal, and thus integrate his id wishes, because the blank wall of refusal that he met had increased his unconscious guilt feelings. To state it in a very oversimplified form, what the refusal to allow him to become an engine driver meant to him was that he was not loved because of his aggressivity; for even the attempt to tame this in his engine-driver ideal had been rejected. The ambition was the symbol of liberation from the domination of primary impulses and guilt-rousing introjects, and it was here that the patient failed. To minimize his unconscious guilt feelings he yielded to his parents' wishes and followed the career they chose for him. His submissiveness further strengthened his super-ego as an alien power reigning supreme over his ego. Instead of helping him to strengthen his ego by the organization of his id impulses, the behaviour of his group, in the fashion of these impersonal contacts, caused him to set up and obey inexorable commands from his super-ego in order to preserve his qualifications for membership of the group.

Thus the result was the apparent paradox that it was his own guilt feelings brought about by his super-ego that forbade him to become an engine driver. When we say his own guilt feelings, we are of course making plain the weakness of the ego in his total personality. What Freud calls the 'incorporation of the early parental authority as super-ego' proved to be the irresistibly powerful agent of an inner alienation. His parents were long since dead, their authority had long since vanished, but the patient could still not free himself from their domination, which had become a structural component of his character.

This is certainly not an unusual example of the unintended effect of 'well-intentioned' models. But it also makes plain the genetic principle of character formation as such. For it is in this way and no other that the stabilization of affective relations takes place between human beings. In the disastrous combination of his personal ego characteristics with the all too harsh pressure of his family group our patient was a borderline case, but his character structure provides a model of the educational process in an authoritarian social group.

In Chapter I we mentioned pairs of siblings who grew up in different social environments. It is conceivable that in an environment in which there was a lesser predominance of impersonal, collective standards our patient would not have been reduced to such a state of helpless suffering. There is a Jewish proverb which says that the best horse needs a whip, the cleverest man good counsel.[16] It was good counsel that the patient lacked; or more specifically an upbringing that provided good counsel and guidance for his ego instead of merely reinforcing his super-ego.

## The enlightened official

That is why we quoted this case history. It is intended as an example of how socialization of behaviour can be imposed in a fashion entirely inadequate to the demands of our society. When we consider that authoritarianism in upbringing is repeated with variations in innumerable families, it is clear that the fact that it has this effect is far from insignificant. Such authoritarianism belongs to a thoroughly paternalist tradition associated with a relatively high degree of independence based on land ownership. In modern social conditions it is obsolete, that is, it is no preparation for dealing with the sources of conflict that arise in a mobile social order characterized by a relatively high degree of interdependence. Power is in the hands of officials, trade union leaders, party leaders, etc. Even if this new type of leader often still confuses functional power with feudal power in his personal manner, this is an anachronism. In their self-regard the key figures in our technical mass civilization must be guided, not by a modified form of more or less enlightened absolutism, but by a historically totally new imago, that of the enlightened official.

Two trends are discernible in the followable course of history: increase of population (in geometrical progression), and the much slower growth of the share of the ego in the psychical sphere. We may describe the ego as the faculty that enables us to find our way in strange situations – which applies increasingly to life lived among strangers at the present time. Development of the ego forces has always been a greater necessity for the ruling group than for the masses; it took place at the expense of the masses. Today mass man needs a capacity for self-orientation instead of blind or fatalistic loyalty to the imagos of paternal figures who in the present structure of society can no longer possess the overriding authority attributed to them by conservative fantasy.

The ego is not only indispensable for taming instinctual forces that have outgrown the behaviour patterns of pre-industrial times; it must also mediate with the inhibiting force of reason between the sources of energy that have become available and their exploitation by the primary trends. Fear of the atomic extinction of mankind is only one side of the coin; the other, hidden side is the pleasure, the intoxicating power, of being able to bring it about. Tremendous goals beckon to the aggressive tendencies. Those who have seen whole countries reduced to rubble while men fought to the last round abjure the hope that intelligence, resourcefulness, and ingenuity have made the id sensibly friendlier to reality. The oldest and deepest foundation of the psyche is still the force of the instinctual trends that try to reach their aims by short circuit – circumventing the ego. Moreover, the hope that ego and id had drawn closer to each other was based on false premises. For our culture acts as before with deficient understanding of the instinctual trends; it alternates between provoking infantile defence mechanisms against them and approving their primitive satisfaction. No earlier form of society possessed power comparable with our own, and none had such urgent need of reason, that is, developed ego capacities, in all its members. It is this difference between us and the past that makes orientation by traditional forms of organization seem to be of very limited utility.

Thus we are led to the conclusion that a style of education must be developed that will accept the ego needs of the individual in the very early stages of his development. The psycho-analytic contribution to knowledge in the social sciences is the formulation of the necessity of taking into account the strength of the instinctual trends and the way in which they seek to attain their aims, and hence the necessity of social compulsions in order to make social group life possible. The question is what kind of social compulsions must be opposed to the instinctual compulsions. The vital factor is not so much the nature and the quantity of these compulsions as the amount of insight that is associated with them and can develop in spite of them. Are they to remain external, of the carrot and the stick type, with their counterpart of inner compulsions reflecting and continuing the same pattern, or is the aim to be the compulsion of insight, that is, acquisition of the power of meaningful, rational decision based on the ego capacities? We believe the historical challenge involved in the evolution towards consciousness is to achieve this development. Many of our traditional patterns of behaviour have become anachronistic from this point of view. Social reality differs from the ideologically coloured pictures of it we are offered. They stem from a past that is so dead that appealing to it no longer serves to throw light on the present, but is equivalent rather to an anxious erection of defence mechanisms against reality. The rapid advances of technology in unforeseeable directions, the political and social upheavals of our time, are alarming, but the withering away of unambiguous role models and the chaotic effect of irreconcilable introjects are just as alarming. The seat of anxiety, according to Freud, is the ego, which will have to be very strong indeed to deal with these sources of anxiety. But that remains the only hope in our unsettled time.

## Fathers who can learn from their sons

If the needs and capacities of the ego are to be promoted, the dynamics of the group, its methods of social education, the way in which it establishes its equilibrium, integrates the primary, egoistical, asocial interests of its members, will certainly differ from those that may have been adequate hitherto, even though they failed to prevent dreadful break-throughs of the death wish. That is the conclusion we may draw from another, happier case history that contrasts with the one we described above.

A motor mechanic had a son whose passion was books and study; manual dexterity did not come nearly so easily to him as to his father. If the son's inclinations and the ego ideal associated with them were to be taken seriously, a process of active adaptation was required of both. The father had to see and to recognize the different nature of his son's interests, no easy task if he had his own plans for the boy. His own ego ideal knew nothing of the satisfactions drawn by his son from poring over his books. For his part the son was faced with a no less difficult task. He had to learn to accept the fact that in many respects he could not compete with his father's strengths, as he would naturally have liked to do, and also he had to learn how to fulfil his own ideal in practice. Did his aspiration to autonomy involve breaking the tie with his group? On the contrary, the mutual respect of father and son for each other strengthened the libidinal tie, and with it the family equilibrium. The father's good will in respecting his son's initiative and autonomy promoted the ego maturation of both; both solved their own problems in accordance with their respective degrees of maturity, the son by finding his own ego ideal as an outcome of his previous character formation, the father by learning not to regard his child as a function of his own narcissistic desires but as a human being with his own individuality. By doing so he strengthened both his own and his son's sense of responsibility more than he could have done by any amount of lecturing and injunctions based on his own experience, which in his son's actual situation would have been of no use to him. The father's authority, to mention one feature only, was better manifested in the reliability and equilibrium he showed in his work than by trying to bully his son into following in his footsteps. Identification with the trait of dependability is better assured when the choice of object on which to demonstrate his own dependability is left to the child. Thus upbringing aided a process of maturation that prevented the super-ego from developing a preponderance that left the young person no freedom of manœuvre, as occurred in the history of our frustrated engine driver.

This educational process calls for an inner detachment from one's own aspirations. In less mobile cultures, with less occupational and status differentiation than ours, this task of resisting one's own impulses in order to leave the way open to others to lead the life of their choice does not arise with such acuteness. In these the taking over by the son of the external marks of his father's role takes place much more unquestioningly. But our culture has still to fashion a pattern of social behaviour based on a new insight: the necessity of perceiving and recognizing the autonomy of the individual from the outset. Preparedness to do this must be consolidated into a socially established parental role. Mere permissiveness, leaving the child alone – that is, completely passive socially integrative behaviour on the part of the parents – should not be confused with the task of aiding and promoting its ego development. The great variety of potential aptitudes present in people before they are developed in the innumerable fields of cultural activity in most cases makes the old form of parental model obsolete. Men can no longer learn their trade from their father; instead, they can learn from him the basis and essentials of dependable behaviour in whatever field it may happen to be. The happy relationship between father and son in the instance we have quoted was based on the father's ability to be a model independently of the content of any particular role. The experience of feeling that his ego needs were understood, in spite of the difference between the things in which he and his father were interested, gave the son a foundation of security which would stand him in good stead in dealing with any occupational or social situation and, last but not least, would one day preserve him from using all sorts of rational-sounding but in reality rationalizing arguments in an effort to deny his children what he did not have himself.

## Ego-strengthening education

There can be no doubt that the sum-total of the traditional and presently effective stereotypes of our society perform the task of education in strengthening the ego very feebly indeed. That is not contradicted by the cult of popular idols who are taken to represent the maximum achievable human happiness. These idols have too many marks of autocracy, eccentricity, or sheer rebelliousness to be regarded as successful examples of ego maturity achieved in co-operation with the instinctual trends. Too much unresolved infantilism attaches to them to justify the continued evocation of their names in tones of heartfelt cultural responsibility. 'There are problem characters,' Goethe wrote, 'who are not adequate to any situation in which they find themselves and are not satisfied by any. That is the origin of the tremendous strife that causes life to be used up without pleasure.'[17] Many of these 'problem characters' have laid claim to the highest distinction as personalities, and their claim has been accepted. Yet many have turned out to be monsters, in the family, at work, in school, and in the state. That ought to provide food for thought.

Under the educational conditions that prevail in our country it may be true that in innumerable cases neurotic illnesses such as those of our hairdresser represent 'the mildest possible outcome of the situation'.[18] If he had had grandiose ideas to which a whole nation paid homage, and these had resulted in his being put in a position in which he need have no scruples about the impulses he felt in relation to his customers, the outcome would have been less mild. For where did the organizers and executors of Hitler's terror come from, whether they were commercial travellers or professors, if not the army of neurotically sick who were enabled by circumstances to shake off their painfully maintained cultural hypocrisy? The terrifying number of such evil consequences of 'good' models casts doubt on their utility. Such doubt is no sacrilege when one contemplates the cemeteries of Europe.

It is obvious that the technical miracles that we produce do not suffice to consolidate our love ties with each other. It would be reckless optimism to believe that the development of inhuman reactions, some of the breeding grounds of which we have tried to throw light on in this chapter, will not again grow on the soil of the customs and habits that we take for granted; and they will continue to do so so long as we have not explored them with our ego capacities. Social psychology can make no small contribution to this task. It tells us that a start must be made, not on a mass scale, not from above, but by ourselves, in the way in which we so love and so tolerate our children that they will love us in a better way and tolerate us in a less embittered and uneasy way than we have hitherto enabled them to do. That is a not insignificant field of action in which we can correct destiny.

# VII

# The Invisible Father

*Creating the behaviour repertoire*

In the course of our reflections we have continually been brought face to face with the overriding importance of the primary family group to the process of individual socialization and hence to society as a whole. If in addition we learn to understand how people attune to one another, and why this happens in the way it does and not otherwise, depending on the nature of their relationships, we shall have obtained a basic model of the possibilities open to a culture in its affective contacts and in dealing with inter-human conflicts. In this connection an important feature is the question of which emotional impulses can be expressed only from above to below (and vice versa) and which can be disclosed reciprocally.

Our method, which will show the genetic links of psychical development on the one hand and the interdependence of successive social roles on the other, will enable us to trace back the multiplicity of the patterns of behaviour that we meet with in life to the original, more easily intelligible emotional relationships from which they sprang. The ways in which an individual behaves in situations which his sensibility feels to be similar we call typical of his character. These will depend on the course that his instinctual development has taken in relation to his environment and the degree of ego maturity he has in the circumstances been able to acquire. How far is he capable of seeing the external world realistically, that is, correctly assessing the motives of his fellow-men and appreciating real connections? To what extent is he able to tolerate the conflicts of his own instinctual impulses – his ambivalence? To what extent is he able to risk conflicts with his environment, and to what extent are these conflicts reasonable? To what extent does he hold fast to what seems right to him under the influence of the prejudices of his society when these come into conflict with his own super-ego? In other words, to what extent is his protest guided by insight into reality, and to what extent is he guided by a distorted view of reality, deficient insight into his own unconscious motivations? These are the questions we are confronted with when we try to find out why an individual makes no social contacts at his place of work, why he joins this party or that, why he has friends or not, why he wanders restlessly from one sexual relationship to another or is unable to find his way to the other sex at all, why he quickly joins a mob or remains cool and detached when collective excitation tries to draw him in. Why is one individual covetous and full of envy when another knows his limitations and more or less satisfactorily adapts himself to them? All these questions, which are related to the behaviour of the individual in the group, his harmony with group tendencies, the demarcation between his own way of life and the group style, are real socio-psychological questions.

The psycho-analyst must impose modesty on himself. Interesting though it may be to try to probe the psychology of political party formation, or of national consciousness, or of a class or occupational group, the first subject of investigation must be the behaviour imprinting with which people grow up until they show themselves to be satisfied or dissatisfied with their religion, their working conditions, their possibilities of advancement, the policy of their government, and develop into sociable or solitary human beings. The psycho-analytic method is a genetic one. Like other sciences, it assumes that later events are determined by earlier ones. In the mental sphere, however, connections between cause and effect are not easy to track down, because only a small part of the life of the mind crosses the threshold of consciousness. That part of it which Freud called the unconscious system is permanently inaccessible; another part is prevented from crossing the threshold by active exclusion from consciousness.

Lasting cultural habituation is unalterably associated with the question whether, apart from the repression involved, some instinctual trends are allowed direct satisfaction. Naturally, it makes a great deal of difference whether the concessions made to instinct are palpably related to the instinctual renunciations, or whether the repressive side embodies the 'official' code while the concessions are in some way 'unofficial' and not respectable; in short, which areas of instinctual life are in good repute and which in bad. Finally, behind all human cultural unrest – that is, in every single human individual – a struggle goes on about whether the suppression and renunciation of pleasure imposed by society are right and necessary, or arbitrary, the result of the privileged position of the few.

The repertoire of behaviour that an individual is able to acquire through a sequence of identifications depends on the nature of his earliest emotional ties, and so does the extent to which he is able to gain awareness of the world of internal impulses that arise in him and the way in which he learns to cope with them. The 'offers of identification' made to each individual are his destiny – his social and therefore changeable destiny; the strength of his innate instinctual drives and ego qualities, which can cover a wide range, are his inherited destiny.

In the multiplicity of human life and experience the social psychologist also follows the flourishing growth and development as well as the inhibition of hereditary dispositions. We should not forget that the pursuit of this knowledge in a demonstrable form, namely, as a science, is of relatively recent origin: and it is interesting to note that the investigation both of the laws of heredity and of those that govern human behaviour are very recent sciences too. So strong was the belief in man's exceptional position in the universe, his being made in God's image, that both Darwin and Freud were put in the rogues' gallery as enemies of Christianity. But it was easier for Darwin's theory of evolution to overcome affective resistance than it was for Freud's theory of psychical determinism. The theory of the inheritance of characteristics, quite independently of its validity, turned out to be usable as a sedative, to comfort the ego for its weakness in relation to the id. Because the psycho-analytic theory of development restricts the compulsion of destiny to a traditional form of behaviour in which we are actively and responsibly involved, it was and remains disturbing.

What does one really inherit from one's father, apart from his physique, perhaps, and what does one acquire from him? What happens in emotional communication with him, and what social task is associated with this relationship? One can admire one's father, one can feel sheltered and protected by him, or one can fear him; and finally one can despise him. At different times one can do all these things. Besides these so varying emotional attitudes, however, there is something else. One can learn from one's father, one can be initiated by him into ways of dealing with things, or one can do without him in the process.

It should be noted that in this chapter we are dealing with only one social relationship, that between father and son. It must stand as an example for the other relationships in the family group: those between father and daughter, mother and son, mother and daughter, brothers and sisters, brothers, and last but not least, those between the parents themselves. If we have singled out the father-son relationship, there is a reason for it – its special position in a paternalist society. The changes in that relationship brought about by social processes enable one clearly to see that the paternalist social order has manœuvred itself into a critical position, from which it will not emerge with the same secure sense of permanent stability that it possessed in the age that lies behind us.

*Affective and object-related alienation*

As a civilization develops and grows more complicated, the more situations arise in which the father's teaching role is taken over by others – until teaching finally emerges as an independent profession. Teachers then assume very definite aspects of the absent father. Investigation of learning failures (at school and in the process of adaptation to life in general) has shown that the learning process is closely associated with the tone of the emotional relationships between the child and the adult world. There are two areas in which the father-child relationship can be weakened or eliminated altogether: that of affective contacts and that of object-related contacts, both of which always affect each other, positively and negatively. At the outset, of course, the supremely important relationship is that with the mother, on which the establishment of 'basic trust' (E. H. Erikson)[1] depends; whether this is successfully achieved or not depends entirely on the sense of security, the harmony of conscious and unconscious emotional trends, that the infant feels. But as soon as trends to autonomy and initiative appear (between the third and fifth year), that is, when the ego begins to form, the decisive factor in the development of character, that is, the basic pattern of behaviour, is the process of instruction and its affective guidance.

The first form of inter-human relationships is the unconscious process of introjection. Behaviour patterns of the primary figures of mother and father are taken over and internalized. With progressive development and integration of psychical experience these primitive introjects coalesce and are identified with the behaviour pattern of the child's model – or in unfavourable cases they survive as isolated, compulsive reactions. Psycho-analytic observations show that these reactions originating in identifying imitation are marked by a strong tendency to repetition; they take place far from the conscious level and are hardly accessible to conscious control. We must again recall that the characteristics of his educators that are consciously most rejected are also taken over into the nucleus of the individual's personality.

The phrase 'invisible father' may suggest to the reader the notion of an omnipotent, omnipresent, invisible God, but that is not what we are referring to in the present context. It may also suggest a father who has been really lost, as the result of a divorce, or a marriage that never took place, or because he was killed in the war. But that is not what we have in mind here. We are thinking rather of the disappearance of the father imago so closely associated with the roots of our civilization, and of the paternal instructive function. The imago of the working father is disappearing and becoming unknown. This is the result of historical processes and is accompanied by a revolution in values. Exaltation of the paternal principle as exemplified in *Land of Our Fathers* and national anthems in praise of *la patrie*, the fatherland, etc., has been broadly followed by 'socialized hatred of the father',[2] 'rejection of the father',[3] alienation and its psychical concomitants anxiety and aggressivity.[4]

The assumption that paternalism is the basic and unshakeable structural principle of society can easily lead one into minimizing the importance of this process of alienation between fathers and sons. The striking inaccessibility of many young people, their provocative manners, their indifference to the values of their elders, the loneliness that they try to stifle by a hectic pursuit of experience – in short, the severity and the protraction of the crisis of adolescence – are dismissed as psychopathological phenomena laid at the door of youth, who are blamed for everything. By way of explanation hereditary mythologies (for instance, the ne'er-do-well in the family tree) are drawn on, as well as unspecific circumstances (discrepancies in maturation, acceleration of physical growth accompanied by retardation of mental development, etc.). The more delicate question whether the family itself might be responsible for the surprising fact that good models can have such deplorable results remains unmentioned, as well as the question that logically follows, namely, that of the extent to which social processes contribute to shaping family life. Affective fixation on the traditional model of a society in which the father-figure predominates makes it difficult to see a reality in which very little of the old attitude survives.

The effects of a father imago that has faded into invisibility are strikingly illustrated in Luis Buñuel's Mexican film *Los Olvidados* (called in English *The Young and the Damned*), which tells the story, reconstructed from court documents, of two abandoned youths. One is a brutally antisocial teenage gang leader, an individual who has never experienced love or understanding and ends by being shot down like a wild beast. The other is an Indian boy of nine or ten, who is taken by his father to the big city. His father leaves him at a street corner, telling him to wait until he comes back, but he never comes back. The boy, who is thoroughly imprinted with cultural values, manages to survive and to establish friendly contacts in the strange, big city until he too meets a tragic end at the hand of forces he does not understand.

The gang leader in the film is at the mercy of irresistible instinctual forces; he possesses no reliable non-instinctual base that would enable him to know himself or guide his conduct. He had never known his father, his mother threw him out, and he makes a living by violent parasitism. To state it more exactly, his ego listens only to his basic urges; he does not possess a culturally useful ego. His whole perception of his environment and himself is in the ruthless service of his instinctual drives. We have described the 'cultural ego' as a psychical development that advances from the first primitive introjects (the earliest imprintings) to conscious appreciation of one's fellow-men. Only the experience of having been loved and understood makes it possible to have consideration for others later. The early introjects are the primary patterns of instinctual experience before ego development can have an integrative influence on them. At this stage there is not yet any clear demarcation between the self and the environment; moods prevail that depend on physical stimuli, and these succeed each other in a vegetative rhythm. The gang leader's behaviour is characterized by these unformed, presocial reactions to vegetative urges accompanied by 'either-or' reactions such as aggression or flight. No doubt this description unduly simplifies the picture even in such an extreme case as this; some higher achievements in coming to terms with reality – for instance, communication by means of speech – stand to his credit, but the archaic introjects continually reimpose their sway. He never developed the socializing identifications the foundation of which is the love and understanding of dependable figures in the environment; in his environment no such human figures were available. So he found his model (for without models human development is inconceivable) among the strong and fearless 'heroes' of legend. Such a model, being the creation of fantasy, differs in one essential respect from models who have been really experienced; it never prohibits, never calls for moderation or self-control. Instead, without any protest being made either from without or from within, it combines with the hallucinatory trends of the primary instinctual wishes, the primary psychical processes. All the aptitudes which this young person might have developed in more favourable conditions are thus yoked to the service of these fantasy formations. They are reflected in a self-awareness that imagines itself to be omnipotent and indestructible. This failure of social development is discernible in every detail in Hitler. The nucleus of his following was provided by like-minded individuals, his impact and the fascination that he exercised were due to regressive association with these fantasies of indestructibility, and the means of communication was the preverbal cry of excitement.

The other boy in the film, having been brought up in a traditional peasant family, has received a unified imprint. He has a conscience, and also – and this is what concerns us here – he is able to work. He has observed and learnt a whole series of skills that were his father's or belonged to his father's world, and, after a short period of agonizing distress and bewilderment, these enable him courageously to find his way through the thickest of human jungles.

Thus his contact with his father had marked the child in two ways. It had left him with the development plan for orderly behaviour that we call the conscience (super-ego), and also the rudiments of practical life had been passed on to him. In social conditions characterized by regular, seasonal tasks handed on unchanged from generation to generation, this formative side of education seems hardly worthy of notice; it is a social phenomenon of a self-evident kind. No problem arises until this way of doing things becomes subject to permanent revolution. If the revolutionary process takes the form of a fragmentation of labour and an increase of social activities with 'non-visible' results – such as all administrative and office work, for instance – the result for the young is a loss of direct contact, which means deficiency in social education. The point that we are making is that this deficiency is not without a retroactive effect on the whole formation and imprinting of the present generation of sons by their fathers.

At this point let us recall the contribution of psycho-analysis to anthropological theory. In the course of his analytic work Freud came across traces of a cultural inactivation or deformation of originally instinctual human characteristics. He interpreted character development, hitherto generally regarded as a process that had to be fatalistically accepted, as the outcome of cultural methods of dealing with or subduing the vital instinctual base. He regarded this base as the more powerful, because the more conservative. In spite of cultural efforts to impose order on it, from behind the scenes and by circuitous routes it plays a decisive part in human life. A great deal that strikes us as being completely rational turns out on closer examination to be mere rationalization of the satisfaction of presocial, selfish, instinctual trends. In this the function of the ego is that of an advocate who has to establish an alibi that explains a great deal but conceals the truth.

## Magical thought and conservatism

Freud's cultural analysis began with a systematic survey of man's instinctual nature of a kind that had not been previously attempted. Ludwig Binswanger says that by systematic instead of haphazard observation Freud expanded and organized the basis of our understanding in an unprecedented manner.[5] The process that he set in train led to the later psychology of the ego. His work makes it plain that the ability to make free decisions in new circumstances is a complex psychical achievement, in which unconscious instinctual trends and fantasies of satisfaction combine with insight into reality in guiding the available object libido towards appropriate purposive action. The ego sees to the realization, the exercise, finally the institutionalization of its achievements. In modern times these processes of discovery and institutionalization have taken increasing precedence over the older, ritualized patterns of behaviour which professed to derive from higher inspiration and originated in a magical order of thought. The only social task of the ego in relation to them is that of their respectful preservation.

The conservatism inherent in societies, which they do not lose even under the impact of revolutions, is rooted in the stubborn persistence of the earliest identifications, that is to say, the survival of the magical pattern of experience associated with the earliest stages of life side by side with later patterns of experience in which there is a larger element of conscious critical control. Societies consist of individuals all of whom have passed through these phases of development, and a substantial amount of magical thought, anchored in the super-ego, survives as a regulative factor in the attitude to the world and to the self. In particular, the patriarchal structural components of our society are closely associated with magical thought. It assumes the omnipotence-impotence relationship between father and son, God and man, ruler and ruled, to be the natural principle of social organization. Historical development, however, has been marked by a strengthening of the conscious critical capacities, which have relativized the omnipotence-impotence relationship. This makes filial dependence and paternal authority no longer seem to be necessary and permanent, but concessions subject to revision. Paternal authority can be outgrown, need not continue through all the stages of life on the pattern of earliest childhood. A period of life in which one had to adjust oneself to those who were bigger and stronger and remained strong even when one grew bigger oneself could be followed by one of association between equals, all of whom enjoyed the same privileges and respected each other on the same level. That was the content of the Enlightenment. But trends inspired by it, such as the development of science and a scientific technocracy, and the recognition of equal rights for women in the eyes of the law, do not simply displace older social patterns of behaviour; they become tied to them, just as rational thought in the individual does not completely supersede magical thought, but at best outweighs it. It would be an ideological oversimplification to regard the slow advance of conscious criticism at the expense of the magical habits of thought of the paternalist age as a guarantee of a better form of human coexistence. All we can say is that social processes have made a paternalist culture more and more functionless, and that many of the challenges that face the individual cannot be met by following or repeating the pattern of internalized models. The individual at work is involved in a structure of extreme complexity, and the fact that its functioning is accompanied by so much inner loss is connected with the fact that the institutionalized authorities in our society still tend by their imprintings to extend the obedience natural to the infant to men's whole lifetime instead of seeking to advance to a state of equal, fraternal responsibility.

There are at least three influences from which cultural development is fed (leaving aside for the moment those of the natural environment and of technological developments in the broadest sense, though without forgetting their impact on human behaviour). At work in what we call civilization, then, are constitutional factors and their individual variations, the inter-human affective relationships which create the destiny of the instinctual constitution, that is, in forming the individual's character, and finally the group's specific way of dealing with the stock of cultural achievements. This includes not only usages (and consumption habits) but also presupposes a capacity for handling these things, and this involves the learning process. Ability to learn and the direction taken by it clearly depend both on constitutional factors and on the environment, but the problem that requires systematic study is a different one. What comes out of the learning process? A kind of circus act produced by conditioned reflexes? Knowledge acquired without libidinal satisfaction, merely to keep out of trouble or achieve some practical aim? When gained in this way it can indirectly satisfy aggressivity in the battle for prestige; that is the commonest outcome. Or do learning and knowledge represent an enrichment of the ego, a widening of the area of affective contact? All these levels of learning and the use of knowledge are in practice mingled, of course, but we are concerned with a mounting line of cultivation, and in considering an individual in history or one with whom one has dealings one would like to know where it breaks off.

It must be borne in mind that most cultural and practical knowledge throughout the history of civilization has been transmitted through fathers or father-figures. This buttressed the esteem in which they were held, and they transmitted their knowledge in person. Skills were acquired by watching one's father, working with him, seeing the way he handled things, observing the degree of knowledge and skill he had attained as well as his limitations – in short, the point he had reached on the rising line of cultivation.

## Authority loses its substance

The progressive fragmentation of labour, combined with mass production and complicated administration, the separation of home from place of work, the transition from independent producer to paid employee who uses consumer goods, has led to a progressive loss of substance of the father's authority and a diminution of his power in the family and over the family. It is interesting to note that an examination of American culture as acute as that of the Englishman Geoffrey Gorer[6] begins with an analysis of the American rejection of the father. A country in which sons have taken their fathers' place seems to provide exemplary confirmation of Freud's theory of the origins of civilization as stated in *Totem and Taboo*. But in the interests of historical accuracy a not unimportant qualification is required. The situation in America today is not that the sons still need a symbolical patricide and a ritual reminder of it in the form of a totem meal to keep alive the memory of their crime and to prevent any of them from stepping into the slain father's shoes. That spirit may have survived as long as there was still a western frontier. The cultural behaviour pattern of North America has meanwhile developed into mere contempt for the father. Present-day American culture is no longer motivated by rivalry with the father arising from ambivalence between respect and hatred of him. What is taking place is centred elsewhere, and incidentally includes a non-respect for the father which is associated with very little affect indeed. American cultural development was undoubtedly set in train by the revolt against the British autocracy, but the Declaration of Independence was followed by an involvement of the self in new ways of tackling life that ended by allowing the efficacy of a vital ingredient of traditional culture, the father's authority, to wither away unpunished – at any rate by the fathers themselves.

'The making of an American,' says Gorer, 'demanded that the father should be rejected both as a model and as a source of authority. Father never knew best. And once the mutation was established, it was maintained; no matter how many generations separate an American from his immigrant ancestors, he rejected his father as an authority and example, and expects his sons to reject him.'[7] Gorer's subtle analysis is naturally a generalization, and there are exceptions. There are long-settled agricultural communities in America, in Pennsylvania, for instance, in which social standards anchored in religion have to a large extent survived. As John Gunther's description of them makes clear,[8] a Europe of the pre-revolutionary period, which in its birthplace has long since been obscured by later social realities, persists relatively unchanged. Many of the Pennsylvania Dutch are still as subject to paternal authority as were European peasants in the century before the incursion of the technical revolution. Thus it was not the shaking off of the leading strings of European authority that brought about the shocking collapse of paternal authority in America but, after the interesting beginnings of a style of development of their own, the process of uninhibited expansion of industrial organization and the consequent continuous changes in living techniques. Technical development resulted and continues to result in the elimination of centuries-old traditional forms of craftsmanship and styles of life, and the conservatism in ways of living associated with them is unable to survive. When one entrusts oneself to the accelerated pace and progress of technical civilization, the hierarchy of the old social orders breaks down, and this extends even into the structural elements of the family. Actually it is obvious that where the social pattern of work changes all other social patterns must be affected.

*Classless mass man*

From the conventional point of view, and from that of the old forms of social organization which are disappearing over the historical horizon, a process is taking place which certainly exhibits what Ernst Michel calls signs of the defective social structure of industrial society.[9] But from the historical point of view 'defective' is always a relative term. Vanished or vanishing characteristics and values must be seen in relation to new ones which have taken their place. We must therefore train ourselves not to look at things from the point of view of the museum of our history. In this connection it should be noted that the exhibits in this museum represent the 'best' and the 'most beautiful', without necessarily indicating what part they played in the social reality of their time as a whole. Insufficiently considered retrospection can easily lead to myth.

In the absence of direct and immediate instruction in practical life under the paternal eye, and the consequent lack of dependable tradition in this respect, contemporaries orient themselves by each other. The peer group – that is to say, one's contemporaries at school and place of residence and work – becomes the guiding line of behaviour. That applies to adults as well as children, and the logical consequence is that parents reprove the latter not so much for failure to comply with inner standards as for insufficient success with their fellows and not being 'popular' with them.[10]

David Riesman has based a new 'cultural typology' on these observations. He distinguishes the 'tradition-directed' type, the predominantly 'inner-directed' type, and finally the 'other-directed' type guided by conformity with the group. This last is the average citizen of the new middle class created by technical mass civilization.

This new cultural environment, like its predecessors through the ages, is naturally marked by a trend to conformity. In contrast to the tradition-directed group man and group style, however, the conformity of the inner-directed individual – of the bourgeois period in Europe, for instance – rested 'less on continuously encouraged obedience to customs and more to obedience to internalized controls instilled in childhood by the individual's parents and other adult authorities'.[11] The other-directed type, on the other hand, 'is prepared to cope with fairly rapid social change, and to exploit it in pursuance of individualistic ends'. Of this new human type, which has spread until it has become typical of modern man, Riesman says very pertinently that 'in the place of life-long goals towards which he is steered as by a gyroscope, the other-directed person obeys a fluctuating series of short-run goals picked up by a radar'. The result is a lasting change of trend, for a characteristic of the 'other-directed' man is the appeal of short-term goals, which he quickly takes up and as quickly drops again. This susceptibility is also learnt in childhood. It results among other things in the appearance of the father-despising technical progressive type, who feels in himself no aspiration for inner development, but for whom to a large extent only two standards of value exist – being socially with the trend, or popular, and being forgotten, out-of-date, worthless. The idea of maturity as a collectively acknowledged aim is beginning to fade.

Riesman sees the dangers of this style of life very plainly. 'The character structure of many people today makes them tense and anxious lest their radar not bring them the latest bulletins. Consequently, psychic strains which one would regard as neurotic, if they occurred in a lone individual, pervade groups whose adaptation in terms of social and career success seems good.'[12] This indicates a deep change in social structure, that is, in the functional ties between men.

But let us again return to our point of departure, the question of what determines man's behaviour among his fellows. On the one hand, as we have seen, there are basic instinctual trends that produce inner tensions, in part rise to consciousness, and seek discharge of tension by way of action. On the other hand there are inter-human experiences. The learning of behaviour patterns in which the vital drives are bound, stylized into group-specific outlets, combined with each other, or suppressed, originates in these. If one follows psychological literature, one finds again and again that it is the affective climate that is analysed and adduced to explain character development. Let us, however, recall the peasant boy in the film. He was a member of the tradition-directed form of society of which peasants have always been the most striking representatives. But was it only 'affective contact' that enabled him so surely and unerringly to find his way about in a totally alien environment in spite of all his childish anguish?

## The father as bogy man

'We are instructed by words but educated by our eyes,' says Carl J. Burckhardt.[13] One of the characteristics of the peasant tradition is that, no matter what the affective climate in the home may be, the life of the parents takes place before the child's eyes. No important aspects of the life of the adults surrounding him take place out of his sight or beyond the range of his experience. Thus he grows up quite naturally into a way of life consolidated by tradition, articulated with the seasons and the course of nature itself. All its aspects are lived out before his eyes, and he can fit in with them. When we compare our own way of living with his, we can distinguish two phases in the process of alienation that has taken place. The first was the separation of the world of work from that of family life. This is reflected in the fiction of the first half of the nineteenth century. That highly important thing, the way in which his father gained his livelihood, ceased to be visible to the child. He may still, perhaps, have been able to talk about it and demonstrate some of his acquired skills in the home. But those whose careers were determined by the next step in technical progress and worked in offices could no longer do this, for the work they did had no tangible, visible results, and they could not 'take it home'; all they could take home was their irritations and frustrations, and office gossip.

In these circumstances, the father often makes his appearance in the child's world only in the form of a terror-striking figure, a bogy man. That at any rate is the case in our own cultural environment, which is still impregnated with the spirit of paternal authoritarianism, while in America, where bigger advances have been made in toppling father from his throne, he tends to be regarded rather as a figure of fun.

A typical case history is the following. A student aged thirty-five had twice failed in his examinations. He was severely inhibited and unable to concentrate either on his work or on any other aim in life. His father was an official who had suffered throughout his life from the fact that he had not taken his matriculation examination; he spent his working life among colleagues and seniors who enjoyed that distinction. In spite of their bad performance at school, the patient and his brother were forced by their father to sit for their matriculation. Their mother's horizon was narrowed by obsessional neurosis, and she had grown depressive under her husband's resentment-laden tyranny. When he came home in the evening she filled his ears with tales of the boys' misdeeds during the day, and the result would be a paternal punitive expedition to their room. And so it went on. The boys lived in perpetual terror of their mother's denunciations and their father's severity. Characteristically enough, the patient's few happy memories of his father were connected with the few hours they spent together engaged in practical hobbies at home. But even this activity was not emotionally constructive, created no bond between the two, for the whole of these children's lives was overshadowed by the spirit of disciplinary didacticism. School was a torment, a never-ending sequence of conflicts with the teachers (who, as so often occurs, had to taste to the full the suppressed attitude of ambivalence to the father). The stronger the paternal pressure, the more insuperable was the inhibition on learning. The only element of positive relationship between father and son was their common interest in technical matters, which finally decided his choice of occupation. Though skilful enough in practical matters, he was a failure as a student because of his complete inability to apply himself. In spite of his natural ability, he put up a total resistance, based on his unconscious introjects and his defence against them, to all systematic and logically coherent knowledge. His inability to work was his only way of simultaneously avenging himself on his father and punishing himself for doing so, for to his conscious the idea of the former was horrifying. As for his father, he narcissistically identified himself completely with his sons; to him they were mere tools with which to attain his ideal, and their failure was a severe narcissistic blow.

The young man's chaotic psychical state, which provided yet another example of the bad consequences of a model's 'good intentions', is hard to describe briefly. A primitive-sadistical super-ego devalued all the achievements of which the ego might have been capable. The super-ego preserved the unconscious projection of the father on the son. His fanatical wish that his sons should be more successful in life than he had been was in part a defence against destructive wishes directed at them, for no one must be so strong, so perfect, as he was in his fantasies of omnipotence. This super-ego, imposed on his son in the 'magical' phase of early infancy, carried out this unconscious wish, which turned out to be stronger than the conscious one. Thus a libidinal tie unhampered by primitive aggressive impulses could hardly appear. To the son the lack of loving paternal and maternal support, combined with their great demands on him, meant the growth of an intolerable sense of inadequacy, a reinforcement of guilt feelings reaching deeply into the unconscious. To the child his father's severity meant retribution for his aggressive wishes directed against him. Such wishes are inevitable even with the most loving upbringing, but when parental severity so far exceeds parental empathy they become uncontrollable. Such a child never experiences 'basic trust', and later has no secure foundation on which to build his autonomy. He can never shake off the scene of his terror-filled childhood; feelings of rivalry and guilt remain its only affective content. Of the disturbance that prevented him from learning mathematics, for instance, the patient remarked, very much to the point, that 'mathematics is the intellectual emanation of masculine authority'. He had experienced masculine strength only in a perverse, masochistic, terrifying way, and that put him in no position to make identifications from which he could learn to love. The counterpart to his inhibitions in relation to work was that his sexual impulses were also disturbed and guilt-laden.

This is certainly no unusual instance of the sad consequences of educational efforts that have not been associated with any thought of self-education by the educator. It also, however, represents a typical conflict between generations in our administered mass society. So long as the son could see and join in with his father's work, there was always at least a chance that even the most unbridled paternal aggressivity might be compensated for. For in the 'pre-work' that the child does there is included something of the happier side of the model's personality: that part of it in which there has been a successful fusion of aggressive trends with pleasure in work and the exercise of skill. If the paternal efforts are not skilled, this can be experienced without guilt and can be worked up to become a stimulus. But our patient did not have this experience; all he had was an *emotional* father imago. His contact with his father extended only to that aspect of him in which unsatisfied destructive wishes dominated. This was the image on which he had to build up his own guiding image, and it was such a disturbing one that he never succeeded in adapting himself to reality.

*Conflicts of ambivalence*

Comparable disturbances, more or less pronounced, are to be found among so many young people that they can be regarded as a typical contemporary phenomenon (of the relatively affluent society); the predominant features may be a 'don't care' attitude, indifference, irresponsibility, or reluctance to accept responsibility. These attitudes are inadequately explained by attributing them to the conflicts of puberty. It must at least be admitted that the puberty of these young people is very protracted, often extending far into the twenties, and that it points to unusually acute disturbance. The 'crisis of identity' natural to the transition from childhood to adulthood seems to involve a much more violent shaking up of the personality than in tradition-directed or inner-directed (that is, super-ego-directed) societies. If we regard the course taken by this crisis of development as characteristic of our age, we have to show what special conditions there are that account for it. That is a difficult task, however, for we cannot be satisfied with stereotyped judgements of the kind made by popular cultural critics – and not by them only. Undoubtedly a combination of factors lie behind this typical or at any rate frequent phenomenon, and many of them are not susceptible to precise demonstration. Let us attempt, however, to indicate some of the psychodynamic forces at work.

The crisis of puberty arises from a resurgence of ambivalent emotional attitudes. The young person is torn this way and that between opposite feelings to one and the same person. He expresses the sharpest and most contradictory opinions about others, but it can also be noted that his opinion of himself is liable to swing rapidly from the heights of over-confidence and self-esteem to the depths of a terrifying sense of inadequacy until, with the growth of his ego capacities, he returns to a more balanced attitude to himself and to the persons in his environment who are important to him. The way out of his difficulties that he previously sought was to concentrate the negative side of his ambivalent feelings on his parents and transfer the positive side to newly idealized models.

This pubertal crisis of ambivalence was preceded by a similar crisis at the age of four or five associated with the Oedipal conflict, when the child was painfully torn between love and jealousy, admiration and envious hatred, of both his parents. Different cultures deal with various degrees of skill and tolerance with both these great crises of identity in the developing individual, and it can hardly be doubted that their patterns of reaction have a decisive influence on the prevalent affective tone.

But people do not live only in immediate affective relationships with each other. They live in an environment, and in an affectively very definitely coloured and distinct environment. That means that as they mature physically a part of their affectivity is transferred to the things about them. In a society in which there is relatively little division of labour, relations with things and relations with people take place in the same area. Association with men and with tools is emotionally linked; the boy sees the men working with them, and eventually joins in himself. The reciprocal relationship between man's interest in man and his interest in things is a matter of direct experience. There is obviously no sentimentality in seeing in these basic experiences – which include the actual shaping of the landscape itself by man's labour – the origin of the sense of belonging symbolized by the word 'home'. The fact that the word has been sentimentally exploited, both politically and industrially, serves only to illustrate the devotion to a past that has been lost but is associated in the mind with happiness. The townsman's sense of home is of course based on a similar experience of gradually gaining familiarity with a strange environment, but the houses, streets, and districts of a town contain far more strange and unfamiliar things than the village whose life extends into the neighbouring landscape.

It would, of course, be foolish to idealize the peasant world, with its narrowness and inbreeding, its rigid conformity and conservatism, its back-breaking labour, insensitivity, and superstition. Nevertheless, the further it recedes into the past, the more completely agriculture is transformed into yet another specialist branch of the economy; it offered a chance of productively solving the conflict of ambivalence in spite of the permanent poverty that characterized it. It was able to do this because of the unity of its field of action. Rivalry with the father could be worked out in non-verbal but directly visible competition with him, working with tools. The son could plough his father's field in the latter's presence and show what he was capable of. This direct competition contributed to the resolution of affective tension; it did not have to be directly expressed, it did not have to come out in quarrels; it could take place indirectly, by way of doing a job equally familiar to both of them.

The separation of the father's world from the child's in our civilization does not permit such direct and immediate experience on both sides. The child does not know what his father does, and the father does not see the child daily developing its skills. A refrigerator or a car is not a possession in the same sense as a barn which you have built with your own hands.

In our highly specialized working world the paths by which identification takes place are certainly very different from those of the world of the peasant or craftsman. It is difficult for the child to find his identity because, instead of seeing and getting to know his father in his working world, too much is left to his fantasy. The same situation is repeated during the pubertal crisis of identity. He cannot easily find his identity in roles performed by his father or forefathers before him, but has somehow to pick his way and make up his mind between a vast number of possible occupations of which he can have no real knowledge, and no first-hand knowledge based on childhood experiences. All this must give him a sense of isolation, and may suggest to him that his father is weak, incompetent, and not to be depended on; and the father for his part may find in his son a non-understanding reserve that makes it difficult for him to say the right thing at the right time.

Thus we have arrived at a partial understanding of the specific difficulties that stand in the way of mutual comprehension between the generations in our contemporary culture. We have not yet discovered how to improve the situation. Moreover, critics, in order to make us see our own helplessness in the proper light of human imperfection, might remind us of the appalling hostilities between father and son that occur in the peasant world, of unfeeling exploitation of children by their parents, of lovelessness of the young towards the old when the time comes for the latter to retire, of the many instances of life-long distrust and pettifogging envy. Unfortunately, such reminders of the blind alleys of human development that appear wherever we look in history serve no purpose except to warn us to keep our hopes modest. They only illustrate by contrast the problem of the paternal role and the child's specific deprivations in present-day society.

*Roots of the social-climbing mania*

It is not, however, sufficient to mention only what the child misses because of his father's invisibility (incidentally, there are many trends that indicate that his mother too may soon vanish into a similar shadowy realm). It must also be borne in mind that the father, too, suffers from doing work that does not enable him to develop his own aptitudes and thus express himself. He works for pay, by time or on piece rates, but the final product shows no trace of his individuality. This keeps alive in him a permanent sense of frustration. He is involved in a process that provides no outlet for his need to 'make' things or express himself, whether he is conscious of this or not; this is bound to reinforce his aggressive tension. In a world in which the division of labour prevails, the resentment that accumulates cannot be worked off in work, for the work is itself inherently frustrating. Opportunities of 'creative' work bearing the mark of individuality exist only for a minority. Consequently even high rates of pay fail to compensate for the dissatisfaction involved in the working conditions of an advanced technological society. To a large extent the tensions are transferred to affective relations with others at the same place of work; hence the great attention that is paid to the 'working environment'. Or tensions may be caught up in affect-releasing entertainments, sporting events, etc. Both the sympathy and antipathy groups that tend to form in factories and offices and intrigue and gossip at each other's expense, as well as the urge to be entertained in some way (preferably in the way associated with the greatest possible prestige), must be considered substitutes for the frustrations felt at work.

It must again be emphasized that this situation is specific to the conditions existing in our civilization; in other conditions different disappointments and limitations had to be faced. When we look at the past we tend to see only the advantages it offered that have become inaccessible; we overlook the disadvantages, contemplation of which suggests the depressing idea that a permanent, satisfactory social order is to be found nowhere.

The loss of prestige suffered by craftsmanship is illustrated by the life story of a young drunkard and poriomaniac, the son of a locksmith and a mother who was an insatiable social climber.

She had no peace until her husband got himself an office job, whereupon his tools were stowed away in the attic. As the boy became old enough to gain pleasure from using them she cleared them out of the house, in spite of the distress that this caused him; she explained that she had lived long enough with one man with dirty hands; he, the son, must do better than that for himself in the world. This was another instance of a personal neurosis fitting in with a collective prejudice that regards the white-collar worker as inherently superior to the 'primitive' man who works with his hands.

Such valuations must of course be considered against their historical background. The machine age promises liberation from bondage to back-breaking physical labour; the latter is its prehistory. The optimism with which mechanization is pursued is the measure of men's suffering under the old yoke. The broken life of the young man we have just mentioned illustrates the new problems that have arisen, which are social as well as individual.

What interests the sociologist in such cases is their general implications and the extent to which the relationship between hope and reality is changed by developments. The field anthropologist – which is what the practising psycho-analyst feels himself to be – is struck by the same processes of alienation that recur with innumerable variations in individual cases. A girl office worker aged twenty-one, illegitimate by birth and leading a life not far removed from prostitution, was troubled by nightly attacks of anxiety in which she felt that someone was in her room who might kill her. She said she felt as if some part of her that she did not know, but which belonged to her, was wandering about somewhere in the world. This turned out to be a fantasy about her unknown father. Her lack of a father caused her to engage in a continual affective search for a father-figure, whom she simultaneously felt to be very dangerous (because unknown). At the same time she was unable to find a real partner, which again seemed to be connected with the fact that her object libido had never had a firm footing, either in people or in things, that would have made love of them valuable, and she felt that life had no meaning.

At all events, this loss of relationship to things greatly encourages the highly paradoxical reaction to be observed in the mother we mentioned above who regarded manual work with such contempt; that is to say, the tendency of increasing numbers of people to seek out the 'abstract' work – abstract in the sense that it does not produce visible, tangible results – which is also what the economic and administrative apparatus of society, with its extreme division of labour, has to offer. 'Brain workers', however, have long ceased to be encyclopedists surveying a broad intellectual landscape, and become white-collar workers, specialists in a narrow field just like workers on an assembly line. In a study of guiding patterns in present-day German family life Gerhard Wurzbacher speaks of the strong parental pressure exercised on the child 'to achieve all the unfulfilled parental desires for education, their ambition to rise in the world and their desire for prestige'.[14] In its culture-specific way this attitude of German parents is of course comparable to that of the parents of the 'other-directed' American child. In both cases the parents desire the child to live a life different from their own, and exert pressure on it to do things that will enable it to advance in the world, attain a higher standard of living, fulfil a larger number of aspirations. These excessive demands made on the child are a consequence of their own lack of relationship to their way of earning a living. The mobility of the radar-guided conformist (a fantasy that also occurs in Orwell's *1984*) enables him to seem adapted to the requirements of a technological mass civilization that is organizing itself round new centres of gravity, but at the same time it demonstrates his homelessness, his deficient libidinal object attachment in his social situation.

### *Unassuaged thirst for identification and prolonged adolescence*

The Oedipus complex, as we have seen, involves a basic conflict in the affective relations between child and adult. The way it is dealt with lays the foundations of the child's cultural adaptation and – looked at from the point of view of the final result – enables one to see whether and to what extent the adult has advanced along that path or has been left behind on it.

There are many indications that our social order has added new difficulties for the child in the conflict of generations inherent in the Oedipus complex. The adult working world has become inaccessible to it. There is no room for children in factories or offices, and they are excluded from identifying watching and learning. As we have seen, however, there is a close connection between affective mood and learning ability; they form a functional unity which in the previous history of humanity was never seriously imperilled, for our society was the first to bring about a far-reaching separation between the two. Stated symbolically, the unity of father as temperament and father as teacher has been destroyed. Father as temperament remains, but not as a factor of continuous experience. Instead, it makes a sudden irruption after being absent all day long, and the affectively charged instruction to be derived from it (with all its risks of violence) that gave things the stamp of 'home' is missing. The connection between affective contacts and the direct experience of things is reflected in negative form in the following dream of an eighteen-year-old who was a failure at school. He was the illegitimate son of an artist and a factory worker. His mother never told him the truth about his birth, and he knew his father only as an 'uncle' who appeared at intervals and then disappeared again; his departure was always a relief to the boy. Punishments and spoiling had bound him completely to his mother and kept him away from reality wherever this presented itself, whether challengingly or alluringly. He grew up to be a day-dreamer, unpopular with his comrades, envious of children who had a father. The extent to which his plight extended beyond Oedipal fears and consisted of a sense of being exposed helpless in an alien world, his helplessness unmitigated by the presence of any good father-figure, is shown by the picture of himself that emerges from this dream.

'I was at a crossroads in the midst of heavy traffic,' he said. 'In a black car I saw an old man dressed in black and with a skull instead of a head. He was driving straight at me, I dodged, and he drove straight on towards another car. I wanted to see the accident, but nothing was left in the road but a heap of sand. I walked on a long way, went into a park, and saw some goldfish in a fountain. At the bottom of the fountain I saw a town and heard bells ringing. I put my hand in the water, but was terribly frightened, for when I withdrew my arm my hand was missing. I ran away, and saw that the old man was following me, pointing a pistol at me. I saw a flash and lost consciousness.'

The dream shows the violence with which the Oedipus conflict survived. It may well be that this is a consequence to be generally expected when the 'temperament father' is not also the 'teacher father' against whom one learns to measure oneself, thus causing him to lose the demoniacal characteristics with which one equipped him in childhood.

In the unconscious even a 'dead' father remains dangerous, but without his guidance the world is totally inaccessible and incalculable, continually changing shape and producing sinister surprises. Whatever the personal interpretation might have been at various levels of meaning (the castrating power of the father, for instance), what concerns us here is the hallucinatory picture of the world that had been worked up by the patient, the total unreliability, alienness, and dangerous nature of men and things. This attitude to life, the sense of being utterly at its mercy, the lack of any basic experience of love and comfort, might well be described as the Kaspar Hauser complex.[15]

Kaspar Hauser, whatever his prehistory may have been, is the prototype of the individual who has suffered from birth from impoverished relations with his cultural environment. His apathy and helplessness contrast strikingly with the violence of the young bandit in *Los Olvidados*, but both alike are the victims of abandonment, the difference being that the bandit is active, excited. Kaspar Hauser represents passive lingering in an inarticulate fantasy world – that of the primary psychical processes. The outside world is experienced only in the form of direct stimuli to instinctual wishes searching for satisfaction, but no contact with the complicated signalling system of cultural symbols has been established; or, to state it at its most extreme, the world is enjoyable either at the level of the primary processes or not at all. Anxiety hardly exists, but only unpleasure. Many of the 'artificial paradises' of our time are adjusted with technological perfection to this primary process level. The opposite, ruthlessly aggressive type, to whom the outside world is just as much of an alien jungle, searches for such paradises. Both types of abandoned individual are parasitical and unproductive. Their development has never advanced to the stage of the Oedipal conflict, which presupposes constancy of relationships in the pre-Oedipal period of childhood. Only by working through this conflict, with its fully developed ambivalence of emotional relationships to one and the same person, does it become possible for the individual to develop the secondary processes through which we grow into civilized human beings. The stormy, unbridled loving and hating of the first stages of life must be shaped and consolidated in human relationships if they are to develop into activity and interest in the things of the world. 'Hypertrophy of instinct' as exemplified by our bandit is, as Konrad Lorenz says, a 'behaviour change resulting from domestication'. Looking at the apathetic Kaspar Hauser, we might similarly speak of a hypertrophy of fantasy. Both forms of degeneracy are out of contact with reality, and there is no doubt that they are the result of 'domestication'. They arise at the point where cultural ties break down and admit the individual, not to a state of nature of the kind imagined by Rousseau, but to a state of instinctual chaos.

There is also no doubt that these contemporary 'defects' have a specific colouring and correspond to deprivation of very definite experiences (for instance, that of co-operating in work that leaves a definite trace). The patients we mentioned failed in the environment in which they found themselves, but many others before them had failed as a result of other abandonments, cruelties, failures of understanding. To anticipate a commonplace criticism, let us make it clear that human civilization has always been in danger, and particularly so when it was believed that everything was in order. Also one consequence of suffering is always that efforts are made to put an end to it;

it stimulates initiative in those who have remained capable of feeling sympathy for it. It would be one-sided not also to look for signs of the ways in which a society that is becoming fatherless is trying to reorganize the world it has created and is seeking to familiarize itself with new object relations. It cannot do so by looking to past forms of organization, for more of the old and familiar is disappearing daily. Many characteristics of contemporary art are significant in this respect. Art is always interpretation, and interpretation implies a search for order. Artistic production also combines fantasy with technique, which is precisely what so many people are deprived of in their work.

*Fatherlessness in an over-organized society*

The long, impersonal chains of production of the technological age increasingly exclude man from the experience of producing, and in his capacity as consumer he is also quite differently related or unrelated to the end-product in comparison with earlier times, when at any rate to some extent it bore a personal stamp. The 'subjects' of contemporary art reflect this situation. Finished objects have become inherently uninteresting. What the artist is trying to express lies behind them; they mean something only to the extent that they rouse the artist's curiosity. The great interest in technical experimentation combined with the creation of new effects shows there is no liking for or reliance on the ready-made, but that the artist is seeking a way of combining craftsmanship with fantasy. The shaking off of traditional forms of expression is thus a symptom of fatherlessness. What is taking place in this field is a fascinating combination of inarticulacy and aesthetic subtlety, and is challenging and completely new, as new as the departure from the old forms of emotionally laden relationship with one's fellow-men and things. The self-feeling that makes it possible to objectivize this subjectively acquired outlook in the form of art makes man's new plight manifest and communicable – and thereby relieves it of some of its anxiety. Kaspar Hauser's pregenital, almost preverbal, anxiety is of a type different from that of Robinson Crusoe or Columbus or the men of the age of imperialist discovery, who took their catechism – both religious and practical – with them in their baggage. Kaspar Hauser's beginnings were quite different. He did not set out; he was put out when he was a child.

The conclusion to which all this leads is that this process of alienation, of dropping libidinal object ties to the environment that sometimes looks like a schizophrenic total loss of reality, is slowly proving
to be an 'alienation from old fatherlands' in every sense of the word.
New tensions between the individual and society obviously arise as a
result. We know from Karl Bednarik's study[16] about 'young workers'
cool relationship to the state'. The young worker, he says, has 'turned
into a son who is perpetually only demanding and taking. The only
reason why he is not totally indifferent to his father, who has receded
very far into the distance, is that he has to listen to his injunctions
and decrees in order to be able to evade them.' This gives us access to
understanding another distorted form taken by the modern slave of
the machine, that is, the completely asocial type, the 'forgotten man'
whom we mentioned above. Inhibition, loss of concentration, loss of
contact with the physical things that he should make 'his own', are
obviously only one aspect of the reaction; the other is unbridled
aggressivity, destructiveness, making demands, and indifference to
others. These things are not the signs of innate bad character, but the
consequences of an environment by which broad sections of the
population are being affected. As Riesman has pointed out, if one met
them in an individual one would be forced to say one was confronted
with a neurotic behaviour pattern. What we said earlier about the
historical relativity of all social behaviour referred to its content, its
style of expression, the direction of its interests, but not to processes
of pure and simple loss of relationship and, above all, not to any
process of regression from activity to aggressivity. Aggressivity in
this context is man's neurotically distorted capacity for work. The
best way of producing neurotic sons is to give them neurotic fathers.
Thwarted of 'productive' work, banished for the greater part of their
lives to a shadowy realm in which the work they do is psychologically
lopsided and deprives them of the sense of 'making' or 'doing' something, the fathers fulfil neither their 'human', conciliatory, emotional
role nor their second role of setting a visible example of how to deal
with things, how to live in their civilization. The consequence is the
great army of neurotic climbers and the host of 'forgotten' men who
search in hordes for surrogate satisfactions. The examples of Kaspar
Hauser and the young Mexican bandit should not blind us to the fact
that growing up in the state of 'forgotten men' is not associated with

any class, but is becoming more and more frequent at all social levels and is thus a trend in social relations. Bednarik's 'indirect protest against the over-organized paternal world' may take the form of anxiety or may be a 'disease', and in many cases it may merely take the form of apathy, but dealing with it is a task with which civilization is now faced.

In Ionesco's *Victims of Duty* there is a scene in which a son in dream-like fashion digs back into his memory and meets his father. His mother, whom his father had abandoned, had said to him: 'You will have to forgive, my child, and that is the hardest thing of all. If you are not good, if you do not forgive, you will suffer.' He says to his father: 'Father, we never understood each other. You were hard, perhaps you did not mean badly. Perhaps it was not your fault. It was not you, your violence and selfishness, that I hated; it was your weaknesses with which I had no sympathy. You used to strike me, but I was tougher than you. My contempt hit you much harder; it killed you. The avenger always suffers. We might have been good friends. I was wrong to despise you. I am worth no more than you. Look at me. I am very like you. If you were willing to look at me, you would see how like you I am. I have all your faults.' His father's complaint begins with the words: 'My child, I was a travelling sales-man. My job sent me roving all over the world. From October to March I was in the northern hemisphere and from April until September in the southern. So there was nothing but winter in my life.' These monologues of father and son who cannot see or understand each other, between whom there is only an exhaustion of hatred and hence a grudging forgiveness, sum up the seriousness of the situation some of the factors of which we have been trying to analyse in this chapter.

# VIII

# Obedience, Autonomy, Anarchy

'I should rather have a dead son than a disobedient one.'

MARTIN LUTHER[1]

Obedience is as necessary as it is obviously not natural. It is one of the greatest and most insuperable sources of suffering. A tremendous amount of thought, writing, and laying down of the law has been devoted to the question of its necessity and how far it should extend, and it has seldom been imposed with a gentle hand. The surest ally of the commandment to obey is destructivity. Of these two heavenly twins, the former lives in the full daylight of legality while the latter, often mercifully concealed in deep obscurity though sometimes only by moderate shadow, serves a totally different purpose, the pleasure of securing submission.

Laws are the reduction to writing of what is held to be right according to the religious, bourgeois, proletarian, or Fascist code, as the case may be. The man in the street combines the pleasure of obeying them with that of finding fault with them. Customs, respectability, prestige, are the direct aids of average conformist behaviour, even though some of the values involved are acknowledged by the rest only in inverted commas. A voice raised in favour of disobedience rouses resentment.

The right to disobedience? That could arise only in a situation so incredibly remote that it is unworthy of serious consideration. When is 'authority' so bad that it ought to be disobeyed? No harm is of course done by mentioning the theoretical possibility in legislation, but in practical life it requires colder blood than most people have to recall the clauses dealing with human rights, the rights of the weaker. So people go about things in a more circuitous way.

Nevertheless a model is required to make plain where the demarcation line runs between the duty of obedience and that of refusing obedience. It is obviously right to refuse to obey an order to do something that the law condemns. But supposing what is generally recognized as legal and right turns out to be manifestly wrong? Who would not hesitate in such circumstances, and submit his rebelliousness to very careful scrutiny before proclaiming it? Querulousness, craziness, Utopianism, blindness, intervene in unforeseeable and convincing rational disguises when the intelligence exerts itself.

Disobedience, the intelligence says, may represent the higher right. But how is that right to be established in the eyes of society, how is it to impose itself against an established authority that refuses to listen to reason? By bloodshed and violence? When is reason entitled to use violence to impose obedience? And does its unseen, twin, dark brother not immediately raise its head? Is there a natural justice that must be obeyed, and where does it end? Animals – in particular the social animals – have no choice but to obey their nature, and some such principle must also apply to human beings. But where is it positively and indisputably to be found? And how do our typically human laws, which are always conventions, come about? They do not depend solely on a natural order of the kind to be found in animals, but on a social order that claims to be natural, divinely ordained, self-evident, and therefore right and just, but is nevertheless, as history shows, subject to incomparably more rapid collapse than the natural orders developed by other living creatures. Birds live and raise their families in the ruins of the past exactly as they do in the cities in which we still live.

Are we too obedient, too ready to fall into line with behaviour as it is laid down? Are we lacking in civil courage? Or are we too disobedient and, if so, in what respect? What are the historical reasons for the breakdown of social orders based on obedience? What are the social circumstances, the roles, in which we are capable of being too ruthless and destructive, too contemptuous of legality and obedience, and those in which we can be too submissive, too loyal, and too obsessed with obedience? What is socially liberating and what is socially enslaving?

Before we can answer such questions in the situations in life in which they force themselves on our attention, we must examine obedience and disobedience in the conditions and on the scale of the very beginning of life. Bearing in mind the impotent situation of the child, we must look at situations in which a similar obedience is demanded and expected – when it is regarded as an equally obvious necessity, so to speak. Who is entitled to call for such obedience? The physically or economically superior, the senior, the more experienced, the representative of numinous powers? In the individual case the question of his understanding of the relationship of interdependence between him and the authority that expects obedience will always arise. The more complicated a society is, the longer is the process of learning required of the individual if he is to find his way from the relatively simple situation of childhood to the intricate and many-layered pattern of authority to which he has to adapt himself in adult life. Contradictory orders often come from different agencies both in the outside world and in one's own head and breast. We need insight into the structure and dynamics of obedience if we are to gain a better understanding of the psychical processes that lead to discipline or indiscipline; that is, we must investigate the levels of conflict that are resolved or avoided in obedient behaviour. Perhaps it will turn out that, though they assume innumerable forms, only a few fundamental conflicts are involved.

Obedience is obviously the corner-stone of every social order, whether human or animal, though in the human sense it does not arise in the instinct-directed behaviour of animals, who are free of conflict in the matter. They are totally subject to their innate behaviour patterns, while man is practically totally subject to conflict – though to a greater or lesser extent he forgets the fact.

Structurally obedience can be very easily defined; it indicates an unequal power relationship. Primarily it is imposed by fear of the much greater strength of the party that imposes it. Anticipation of a threat that has been really experienced leads to the habit of obedience. But continuous reiteration of the sense of impotence and fear of punishment is required if obedience is to develop into an 'attitude'. The economic purpose served by obedience is that of sparing oneself unpleasure; it helps the weak to get by relatively unmolested. Though it may be associated with unpleasure, this is generally less than that associated with the anxiety of again trying to find out how far it is safe to go with one's own wishes and impulses in the existing power relationship.

The picture we associate with the word 'obedience' stems from our own infancy, when we learnt it. On the one side is an individual who orders or forbids, and on the other one who obeys. The inner experience of the weaker party in this situation is easily overlooked; he seeks to obtain what another withholds, and he does this under the pressure of his own imperious impulses. Thus there is a clash of two demands for obedience: an inner wish that demands fulfilment and an outside order that stands in its way.

This simple conflict situation applies of course only to the infantile phase of human life. In the course of our development the situation becomes more complicated. We distinguish three levels of real obedience, namely, obedience to instinct, learnt obedience, and obedience to conscience, as well as a fourth in which the use of inverted commas is required, namely ego 'obedience'. The differences between these will become plain if we describe the conflicts they impose upon us and try to spare us.

*Obedience to instinct*

The most primitive level is that of obedience to instinct. An instinctual need announces itself by unpleasure and demands immediate satisfaction. At first there is no inner authority able to 'work' on it and bring about acceptance of postponement of satisfaction. The instinctual wish uses all the channels open to it to signal itself to the outside world. As soon as the child begins to have some control over its movements, it makes for the object that will remove its unpleasure; an example is the suckling's search for the breast, an innate movement directed towards the instinctual object. An instinct can be described as the innate factor that causes an object to be sought; hunger, for instance, causes unpleasure in an animal that releases instinct-guided behaviour. Only when the state of instinctual excitation is high does the behaviour associated with it take place 'in the void', in the absence of an external stimulus or object. It is meaningful in this context to talk of absolute, 'blind' obedience, for the animal has no alternative to this compulsive behaviour. The individual's instinctual patterns of behaviour are in many ways geared into social behaviour. The arrangement of the head feathers of one kind of heron, for instance, strikingly displayed when it approaches the nest, causes the young ones to open their beaks for food. Most of the objects that promise satisfaction to man are, as we have seen, not so unalterable and unexchangeable. Many objects are capable of offering his instinctual wishes relief from tension. But he needs long training before being capable of exercising choice in the matter. Nevertheless instinctual wishes find their way to primary objects, that is, objects that offer immediate satisfaction, much more frequently than appears. The complicated situational clothing they are given in order to justify them is entirely superficial, a kind of camouflage for the selfish instinctual trend.

Thus basically the instinctual demands have remained rigid; the superstructure erected on top of them consists of: (i) the ability to find satisfaction in objects that sometimes may be very remote from the original goal; and (ii) the ability to tolerate postponement of satisfaction of many instinctual needs that is associated with this. An equilibrium is established between primary instinctual needs and secondary cultural forms of satisfaction, but it is never a stable equilibrium.

The ability to postpone action is a very obvious distinction between the human and the animal personality. The more modern level of organization of the ego succeeds in binding instinctual energy to itself, 'neutralizing' it (Heinz Hartmann) and using it for its own ends. Nevertheless a substantial proportion of our instinctual trends remain tied to their primary objects, and we are not capable of removing ourselves altogether from their influence. Men have continually rebelled against the categorical character of the instinctual trends; the Spartan way of life and asceticism are instances of such rebellion. Such refusal to accept the domination of the instincts generally elicits almost automatic respect. On the other hand, hedonistic and epicurean refinement of the pleasures of the senses, which is of course perfectly compatible with moderation and moderate means and is impossible without guidance by the ego, is not so highly regarded, at any rate in our culture.

This is a striking phenomenon, the explanation of which is to be sought in the unsatisfied instinctual surplus. The many instinctual renunciations, the long postponements of satisfaction imposed by a highly specialized culture in order to achieve its ends, are in many respects frustrating. Frustration means involuntary deprivation, which both rouses anxiety and sets free aggression aimed at getting rid of that state. Thus aggression here fulfils as it were a regulatory function, though at a primitive level. For in this form it has lost its connection with libidinal impulses and manifests itself as envy and resentment; dissatisfied tension of this kind can end by completely overshadowing the capacity for enjoyment. Simple pleasures no longer suffice; one cannot enjoy just sitting in the sun, for instance; one has to read an illustrated paper and have a transistor set playing away at the same time. Excessive demand for pleasure originates in deprivation that has long since been covered up and concealed, and that is why no satisfying relief of tension is attainable; the element of aggressive want clashes permanently with the element of regressive soothing and lulling that is present in all libidinal satisfaction. The frustrating aspects of our total social situation powerfully stimulate the individual's instinctual demands but, because anxiety and anxiety-soothing behaviour dominate, obedience to them results less in pleasure than in the mere passing of time. The lavish provision of means of entertainment that is so characteristic of our age serves two functions of a very different type, one open and the other masked. The propaganda of the pleasure providers is based with apparent *naïveté* on the promise that they will relieve our burden of unpleasure, but the concealed dynamics that makes them so successful is of quite different origin. It arises from the anxiety produced by the frustrations of mass living. The individual must be very ill armed against them, or the violence with which the anxiety has to be warded off would be inexplicable. The morbid plunge into surrogate pleasures can be explained only as a reaction-formation against an anxiety with which the ego cannot cope. Obedience to instinct and anxiety reactions fuse in patterns of behaviour the only common factor in the multiplicity of which is that they are to a large extent inaccessible to the critical ego. They are produced by social processes and promote conformity, but they also bring about a state of pathological obedience to the instincts and a chronic pathogenous state of anxiety.

*Learnt obedience*

We have just described the form of obedience which is closest to the biological sphere. The next level is that of learnt obedience. This enables the individual to adapt himself to the conditions that hold out the prospect of instinctual satisfaction within the society. He habituates himself to the prevalent restrictions and power relationships. The first stages of ego development consist in the erection of a structure of usable memories. With these an emotionally toned external world makes its appearance – emotionally toned by the child's predominant trends and the responses provoked in others by his behaviour (depending on their emotional tone).

A hitherto autonomous command-and-obey system meets with restraints that provoke unpleasure as great as that of unfulfilled instinctual demand. The conflict of duty begins, the conflict between rival obediences that creates the 'reality' peculiar to the individual. So long as the expression of instinctual wishes brings about rapid satisfaction in infancy the world is a single unit, which may be charged with emotions but is not objectively detached from reality.

The child's behaviour begins to be guided by what he learns. Slowly he succeeds in obeying this guidance, to avoid the pitfalls into which his desires might lead him. Memories of situations in which other persons were involved and in which he would have gladly followed his instinctual wishes are activated and begin to work inside him, as if the person who did the forbidding were actually present. A boy of three alone in the kitchen sees a basketful of bananas. He strokes them longingly, and ends by saying aloud: 'Tommy must not take.' He says this to himself, but it is as if his mother spoke the words. The unpleasure of the threat of punishment or his mother's disapproval gets the better of obedience to the desire stimulated by the forbidden fruit. In contrast to 'blind' obedience to his instinctual nature, this second stage of 'learnt' obedience is tied to backward-looking memory. The behaviour even of simple forms of animal life is capable of being guided by experience in this way. But in the case of man this learnt obedience opens the way to further possibilities. The child first learns to control its instinctual trends, to break their compulsive sway. It may go on so to adopt and make its own the outside order that it has learnt that it will also learn how to reflect on it and guide it, with the result that its psychical development in this respect will go beyond the acquisition of conditioned reflexes. But that depends on the style of its upbringing; that is, on whether the outside authority that gives it orders does or does not behave as dictatorially as the inner authority of its instinctual wishes has done since it was born. If the outside authority does so behave, if that is the predominant experience, the individual will remain the plaything of blind obedience, submitting now to instinctual trends, now to learnt patterns of behaviour, depending on which command-post is the stronger at any particular moment. But there will be little elbow room for free decision by the ego. In learnt obedience we begin by adapting ourselves to others, unconsciously imitating them. That is the first form taken by our contact with reality over and above the affects and fantasies stimulated by the instincts. If the imitation develops into empathy, the result is a greater knowledge of the individual who is imitated. But this last cannot be a one-way process; it cannot take place in the absence of response. The individual's further development will be vitally influenced by its reciprocity and the disturbances its reciprocity may suffer. As long as the child is completely helpless and dependent on the mother, the latter feels and responds to its instinctual needs and knows when she must impose obedience. She senses the child's instinctual needs, and that enables her to satisfy them. But she can lose this closeness to the child if her capacity for empathy is restricted, whether by personal disturbance or by obedience to cultural patterns of behaviour. When the child's physical development enables it to establish the beginnings of autonomous behaviour, empathy of quite a different kind is required, not of the mother alone, but also of the father and everyone else in its environment. All those with whom the child lives must learn to respect, recognize, support, and at the same time restrict its trends to independence, because the conflict between obedience to its instincts and learnt obedience while identifying with demanding and prohibiting adults is extremely painful to the child. It is not for nothing that memory of this phase is subsequently almost totally obliterated; this is an example of relief secured by repression. In the course of development the repressed content may gradually lose the force that it unconsciously continues to exert (its cathecting energy); but in less happy instances it may remain practically undiminished for a lifetime. The outcome – that is, whether or not there is a fixation on what has been repressed – is decided solely by the extent to which renunciation of obedience to instinct is balanced by instinctual fulfilments which have remained directly attainable. How often suffering imposed on the child could be diminished if adults were more capable of empathy – if their own development permitted them undistorted perception of the child's world. But the instinctual trends that they themselves wanted to obey in their own childhood may have been so spoilt for them that they phobically avoid all memory of them that may later be recalled by the behaviour of their own children. This prevents the intuitive understanding of the child's experiences and difficulties that might be so helpful to it.

## Ambivalence

Here the great problem of ambivalence arises again. To the extent that human beings are the objects of our instinctual aspirations, they can never fulfil these as completely as the insatiability and ruthlessness of our instincts would like them to. The individual who is the object of these aspirations has his or her own life to live and his or her own instinctual needs to obey. Sometimes the adult has a perfectly justified need for rest and quiet while the child has a need for motor discharge. The child is then, with greater or lesser mildness, made to keep quiet. Thus situations continually arise in which an instinctual object fails to be a source of satisfaction. There are occasions when even the best and most loving of mothers necessarily becomes a bad mother, a witch, to the child because the reality principle allows her no alternative but to deny it something. She can, however, also become an evil object by projection of the child itself. The child is at first unable to feel its way into the object's own world, that is, its subjectivity. It is completely cathected by its own instinctual trends, and when the object does not completely satisfy these the frustration is ascribed, not to the excessive demands on it made by the child, but to the nature of the object itself.

It is this archaic ambivalence towards the object, however, that shapes once and for all our relationship with the people and things whom we cathect with interest, love, or passion and who consequently play a vital part in our lives. Our learnt obedience forces us to suppress many of our ambivalent impulses, whether libidinal or aggressive. Thus the social roles offered us by society allow no elbow room for fully living out the ambivalence. Our ability to deal with ambivalent feelings in ourselves depends on how much understanding or lack of it we encounter in the earliest phases of our lives. The more role-tied our parents are, the more harshly and at the same time the more anonymously the model of them introjected into us in the form of our conscience condemns all our impermissible aggressive or libidinal ambivalent impulses. But if the parents are able to be more tolerant towards the child's ambivalent feelings, the latter will be able to feel that it can love and hate one and the same person and will thus discover that it is not just others who have two faces but that it too can have divided feelings.

Plenty of good intentions in regard to drawing the teeth of this conflict of ambivalence were contained in the education of the last generation. These had many social roots, all of them more or less directly connected with the rebellion against the crumbling paternalism of the bourgeois age. One of the most direct signs of the weakening of paternalism was the emancipation of women; and the trend to feminine independence was again connected with economic developments, for the modern economy cannot do without women as workers and consumers. The emancipated woman's diversion of interest from the home at the age when children need active and constant attention results in a conflict of interests that is often smoothed over by a passive permissiveness towards the children on the mother's part and spoiling them with presents. Emancipation, however, brings her not only freedom from household ties (which are felt to be tedious), but may also involve her in new forms of slavery as a result of changes of political régime. Under a dictatorship, for instance, she may be conscripted to take the place of men of military age in factories or offices. The children are then cared for by institutions. This attempted compensation is a doubtful benefit, however, for neither alienation nor genuine emotional rapprochement is any answer to the intervention or encroachment of the state.

In societies in which the tradition of feudal and bourgeois paternalism has survived, the weakening of paternal authority is reflected in the fact that the state, which in earlier times exercised its influence through the family, which sometimes (as, among religious minorities) was able to offer resistance to society, now sets out to exercise a much more direct influence on the child over the head of its father, who to a greater or lesser extent has become invisible (and also over the head of its mother in her pursuit of emancipation). The school plays an incomparably wider role, as do the means of mass communication, such as television. There is often no countervailing agency within the family that subjects these influences to criticism or gives rise to fruitful discussions that might interest all its members.

This weakening of care for the next generation also derives from a vague but increasing sense of discomfort and guilt at being unable to communicate meaningful guidance to the child (or to the self) in a world in which all the traditionally familiar elements are slipping away. Many respond to this by regressing to selfish satisfaction of instinctual trends. Because permissiveness, which is a combination of helplessness with a narcissistic lack of interest in others, appears to be a good thing, and is unexpectedly associated with continuing educational advances, it is worth emphasizing two fundamental facts that no society can ignore. It must be able to impose prohibitions on its members and to teach them to work up these prohibitions without alienating themselves from themselves, thus neither passively adapting themselves nor asocially ignoring them; it must teach them how groups cope with the ambivalence of feelings caused by these prohibitions and are able to reach productive ways out by sublimation. Not the least factor in this task is that obedience must not be taken for granted and must not be enforced by unilateral communication from above to below; instead, *conscious* consideration must be given to the weaker party. The party that is the weaker now will one day be the stronger, and it is essential that its demands should not then be excessive.

## After-effects of punishment

When the child encounters brutal and tyrannical adult behaviour, not all remembrance of it is repressed. On the contrary, its memory remains full of such scenes, and they determine its expectations of the social environment. As we have seen, the child often rouses unsatisfied revenge wishes in its parents. The natural inhibition of aggression towards the weaker – an innate behaviour pattern – is overlaid by another automatism, the tendency to unload upon the weaker un-expended aggression stored up in relation to the stronger. This is yet another way in which aggressive tension can find relief in automatic discharge. The pecking order is an adequate social regulator in the chicken run, but it is a sub-human, disturbing factor in human society, illustrating yet again that the residues of innate instinctual behaviour do not necessarily have good effects when they make their appearance among mankind. The inhibition of aggression by empathy and insight, which is the civilized method, runs counter to the ideology of authoritarian superiority and its right to impose punishment, and this is consequently a by no means finished chapter in the story of humanization. Only in a social environment in which the possession and exercise of power are reflected in critical consciousness can aggression be so tied to libido that a broad field of interests lies open. The release of primary instinctual energy then loses primacy and consciously guided activity increases accordingly. This applies not only to the acquisition of skills but also and even more to emotional contacts with others.

In the absence of the moderating libidinal component which the ego has learnt to control brutality will be carried on from generation to generation in the form of a truly morbid disturbance, a traditional symptom. When ruthless instinctual behaviour unmodified by any learning process acquires pathological significance in our human society we are justified in calling it a morbid disturbance. Luther said he would rather have a dead son than a disobedient one, but in another passage later he said:

'Children should not be too severely flogged; for my father once flogged me so severely that I fled and became averse to him, until he accustomed me to him again.'[2] He also wrote: 'My parents treated me so harshly that I grew quite dispirited. My mother once flogged me till the blood flowed all because of a nut, and the hard and severe life they made me lead caused me later to enter a monastery and become a monk. Their intentions were genuinely for the best, *sed non poterant discernere ingenia, secundum quae erunt temperandae correctiones. Quia* punishment should be dealt out in such a manner that the apple lies next to the rod.'[3]

Luther here describes the disturbing effect of punishment that we can see in the case of the whipped dog that has slowly to be 'accustomed' to its master again. He also mentions how he tried to escape from this *ordo* by rebelliously handing himself over to another. Finally he mentions that his parents' intentions were 'for the best', a concession in which we can see the attempt to forgive described by Ionesco as well as the attempt to justify the parental introject inside himself represented in his statement that he would rather have had a dead son than a disobedient one. Though there is no conscious connection between the statements we have quoted, we can nevertheless see the unconscious one. The whole illustrates how fear and irreconcilable feelings hamper the acquisition of learnt obedience, so that relief can be obtained only by escape to an environment that seems less intimidating. Draconic punishments not only stunt the child's aspirations to autonomy but simultaneously greatly excite them.

There seems to be something in common between this running away and escaping and the psychology of travel, particularly the modern craze for it. At the age of eighty Freud in a letter to Romain Rolland mentioned the 'limitations and poverty of our conditions of life in my youth'. He said that the passion for travel certainly reflected the wish to escape from this pressure, and was related to the urge that made so many adolescents run away from home; and that it had long been clear to him that a large part of the pleasure in travel lay in the fulfilment of this early wish, that is, in dissatisfaction with home and family.[4]

Non-understanding and brutality experienced in childhood leave permanent traces in our character. We are again reminded of Pascal's remark that evil is never so thorough and complete as when done with a good conscience. Now we can see the whole difficulty of orientation by the ego that comes to light in the relation of parents and children. To Luther's parents the 'evil' that they did was morally justified and good. The childish ego was faced with the tremendously difficult task of obeying two unalterably opposed introjects, one of which called for obedience, because his parents' intentions were 'for the best', while the other, the remorselessly punishing, humiliating, intimidating, irreconcilable element, was destructive to his self-esteem. Such a situation was bound to make his life incomparably more difficult, and that is what happens when the conscience is distorted and the imperative of obedience is guided not by insight but by an inaccessible absolute.

One should try to realize the enormousness of the demand that is made on the child when it is called on to see the hand raised to strike it, to prevent it from obeying its instincts, as a kind and loving one. The kindness and lovingness of the owner of the hand have vanished into violence; in psychological terms, his aggressivity is libidinized, but no tie of instinctual outlet is established on both sides in which – as in a chemical process – their qualities change from the level of the primary to that of the secondary processes. Here lies one of the most important differences to which the destinies of instincts are subject. Aggression which has associated itself with libido but remains unchanged differs from unfeeling cruelty; it is closer to sadism. Sadism as a fully developed perversion may be rare, but a half-conscious or unconscious way of obtaining satisfaction by behaviour reminiscent of it is very common.

Also education by the carrot and the whip, the apple as well as the rod, does not derive from empathy with the child. It exploits the child's learning ability by imposing conditioned reflexes, as in an animal training act; it teaches it to avoid pleasures that bring punishment in their wake, but it leaves it with an automatism of experience that is not associated with understanding. Henceforward the child necessarily identifies the good and the right with reward and punishment. Its behaviour differs in no way from that of cattle which refrain from enjoying the greener grass in the next field for fear of the shock they will get from the electrified wire fence.

It is interesting to note that when Luther approaches critical reflection on his parents' educational principles he drops into the 'language of reason', Latin. *Non poterant discernere ingenia*, he says, they did not possess the intellectual capacity to discriminate, but remained subject to the automatism of their behaviour stereotype.

### Rigidity or openness to development?

We travel the road to insight, to self-control in social contacts, wrapped in affect taken over from others. The closeness of the relationship between the acquisition of knowledge and the affective reactions of the environment is acknowledged by all modern theories of education. The contribution that psycho-analysis would like to make is indicated by the concept of introjection, that is, the ability in very early stages of human experience to turn into an 'inner voice' a demand we encounter in the environment in the course of following our instinctual impulses. This becomes so very much our own that we find it difficult to feel it as something distinct from us, an outside order or prohibition, and to deal with it dialectically. The introjects become parts of the self, of the whole character, and embrace the ego so closely that it is practically or totally impossible for it to gain critical detachment from them. We often sense this in others when we notice characteristics of theirs to which we cannot draw their attention because they would be unable to respond on the reality plane. These are the blind spots in self-awareness; if their concealed content is forcibly imposed upon the conscious, we react with panic, depression, or immediately form projections: we transfer to others what is intolerable in ourselves, and thus justify the self-hatred it rouses in us as being hatred of another.

Many close friendships have been shipwrecked by infringement of the frontiers of this blindness.

The suddenness and unexpectedness of the automatic reaction of his previously familiar friend strikes the observer who is alienated by it as totally unintelligible; it stems from the strength of archaic introjects that survive within the self though at the same time they are total 'strangers' to it. At a stage of development when critical detachment was still impossible we adopted the attitudes of others towards us and began judging ourselves by their pattern. An individual who was continually scolded and ridiculed for his inadequacies during his childhood, or was continually beaten or morally condemned for breaking the rules, will adopt this trend as self-criticism and build up reaction-formations against it – and vigorously carry on the practice himself at the expense of other victims. He may be lacking in self-confidence, he may be timid and perpetually carry about 'a bad conscience'; or he may take the opposite course, become arrogant and ruthless, that is, take panic flight in the other direction. In either case his ego will never succeed in philosophically accepting his strengths and weaknesses, for it will be lacking in intuitive understanding enabling him to find 'bridges' and solutions appropriate to his capacities and thus open the way to a conscience tolerable to himself.

By the term 'good conscience' we mean to indicate an operational factor in the psychical apparatus, the ability to be active in interdependence; to receive 'information' both from the id and from the outside world through the mediation of the ego and to absorb it. Such a conscience will affect the total behaviour of the individual and in a manner close to reality. A conscience built up of dictatorial early introjects lacks this capacity for communication, it is tied to rigid earlier judgements and is always completely cut off from learning processes subsequent to the first imprints. Its influence is strong, but in actual situations is sometimes totally non-understanding. It is capable of lovelessly humiliating the world as such as well as the self-respect of the individual.

Thus with the advance to learnt obedience from obedience to pure instinct an alternative is opened up. A short phase of learning ending with definitive imprints of crude behaviour stereotypes for all situations that arouse affect can end in the establishment of an intolerant inner agency that makes absolute demands – a terroristic and dictatorial conscience. Alternatively a long learning process can be set in train involving the formation of a conscience inherently capable of development. In this case the super-ego will be an agency of self-awareness, a yardstick for measuring oneself in relation to models and standards of value. This will be a consistent process, and a tolerant one. The conscience will be able to recall its own history and its own questionable past behaviour, and thus acquire the confidence and the ability to forgive both self and others. Only on these foundations can a morality be built up with which the individual will be able to live without a hypocritical denial of double standards.

To understand the development into one or other of these kinds of conscience, the rigid, anonymous kind or the kind open to development, we must again recall the processes we dealt with in the last chapter which take place simultaneously with the formation of the conscience. Learning is associated with a model, a human being who does something that can be imitated. But in its origins in infancy it is a unified process of learning contact with things and contact with people, or rather people's affects. In the initial stages the emphasis is certainly on affective relations; the way in which these are stabilized depends on how pleasurable or unpleasurable is the appropriation of the skills and knowledge required. Not only does the conscience we build up in ourselves by means of introjection and identification depend on our models, but the ideal we are able to build up for ourselves to follow depends on those models too. If our instinctual impulses, or our demand for love, or our aggressivity encounter harsh rejection by the person closest to us and are thus shown no way forward by which they can develop, no alternative is open to the weak and unconsolidated ego except the strength-draining task of repressing them as far as possible. Only when it has succeeded in doing this will the child have adapted itself sufficiently to be acceptable in its parents' or guardians' eyes and thus be able to establish tolerable relations with them.

But this process of adaptation is many sided. In spite of superficial adaptation to adult demands, the child may cling to its 'ideals', that is, the representatives of its unfulfilled instinctual trends, and develop them in the sphere of magical thought. Our hairdresser's fantasies of power survived, not only in his ideal of becoming an engine driver, but also in his terrifying desire to wound his customers. The fantasy of being lord over life and death, of being able to act entirely according to one's desires, is a direct repetition of the infantile feeling of adult omnipotence. In his fantasy the later adult is still the same child; he still sees the world in terms of the satisfaction or disappointment of his primary wishes. The fear and anxiety produced by these fantasies and impulses reveal the impotence of his ego to pass beyond this infantile level of experience. Adults introjected at a level far above that of any law or human kindness impose themselves as 'compulsions' inaccessible to subsequent rational correction. The discovery that such primitive ideals are at work in himself is no light task for the individual.

The development of the childish ego ideal will also depend on the extent to which he succeeds in suppressing his spontaneous instinctual trends, and in particular his ambivalent impulses. Because of his condemnation he will condemn these as evil; at the next stage the condemnation will be dictated by his conscience. The more successful the repression, the closer he will be to his ideal of himself. The caricature of this is the successful, over-adapted 'yes-man'.

'Repression', says Freud, 'proceeds from the ego; we might say with greater precision that it proceeds from the self-respect of the ego.'[5] This self-respect is the reflection of the respect one has oneself experienced in the environment. We have already pointed out that an early established ego ideal can often remain unalterable throughout a lifetime, and this is not difficult to understand when we consider that it develops in close association with defence mechanisms such as the conversion into their opposite of repressed impulses. The courageous, enterprising individual who accepts many risks may perhaps be over-reacting to desires to be sheltered and protected that were interpreted as weakness in his childhood and threatened him with loss of the love he refused to do without. Only the touch of arrogance about such an individual, his compulsion to be prominent always and everywhere, betrays the presence of a feeling of non-worth that has been warded off.

All the defence mechanisms – such as conversion into the opposite and repression – made use of by the weak ego belong to an infantile stage of development of the psychical organization. They imprint themselves deeply and at the same time automatize the psychical equilibrium, which at this stage still largely aspires to obeying instinctual trends. How high the price is that has to be paid for such equilibrium, which no further development can disturb, is shown by the frequent outcome in neurosis by no means necessarily involving illness. On the contrary, the clinical neuroses, such as agoraphobia, counting compulsion, etc., may show the severity of the milder course chosen, namely, character neurosis, in which psychical energy is largely diverted to defence. In cases of the latter kind the individual may regard his morbid limitations with semi-naïve pride as character traits, not character distortions.

## Sublimation and ego development

The alternative – if for the moment we are to look at things in terms of sheer contrast – would be guiding the individual towards sublimating his instinctual trends instead of repressing them. Above all, more tolerant, intuitive, imaginative guidance of the child from obedience to instinct to learnt obedience and knowledge would lead to the formation of an ego ideal that was not so demonized, did not imagine itself to be as omnipotent as its model. A model that does not exploit its sheer physical and intellectual superiority by violently imposing itself will not be idealized in a fashion so remote from reality. It will be appreciated that we are not questioning ideals as such; what we are concerned with is the extent to which a model is 'human', close, attainable, 'loved and revered', to use an old-fashioned phrase, or is the product of magical thought, unreal, one-sided, transfigured, un-attainable, and excessively demanding. A 'high' ideal (there is always a correspondingly 'low' ambivalent counter-ideal formation, in a word, a demonization) would seem to be a worse outcome of upbringing than a pragmatic ideal with which one can cope and grow up in greater freedom and respect for one's fellows.

The parting of the ways in education, at all events in so far as the social world is concerned, comes with the choice between sublimation and instinctual repression. Do educators understand the human constitution sufficiently, are they able to understand the individual's trends, mitigate the harshness of the necessary prohibitions, and thereby help the necessary repressions across the bridges to a satisfactory sublimation, thus promoting the development of the ego, or not? Sublimation and development of the ego are closely linked. In the absence of the capacity to sublimate, the possibility of acquiring more conscious freedom of choice is not within the ego's reach.

In the sublimation of instinctual wishes and their affects learnt obedience plays a part, but it is a modified kind of learnt obedience, being accompanied by some satisfaction of primary trends which do not have to be immediately cathected with guilt and anxiety. A child, for instance, who is trying hard not to help itself to forbidden sweets should be shown that its efforts are appreciated and occasionally be given a sweet. When it grows up it will not be perpetually preoccupied with the 'struggle for life', for security and possessions, without inner permission ever to relax and enjoy itself. How hard the psychological mechanism of this is to describe can be concluded from the fact that such incapacity for primary instinctual pleasure may arise either from a puritanical fear of sensual enjoyment or from a morbid surrender to surrogate satisfactions (consumption habits of all kinds).

Not only do extremes meet here, they also have the same function in the psychical economy; the only difference is that the incapacity for enjoyment is at a different distance from the conscious. The experience of relaxation of tension belongs to the phase of development following that of 'social womb', the shelter of the mother-child unit, and precedes the work of the ego. It is the continuation of that work that first creates a more subtle relationship with reality, in the course of which we acquire a better knowledge of men and things. It must sound very heretical to the 'cultural consciousness' of many men to say that it is our 'ideals' of all things that betray very little of this ego work. When a magical interpretation of reality imposes itself in spite of contradictory facts, it is the sign of a process working in the opposite, regressive direction. Wishful thinking devises an interpretation – a picture of the self, or of a leader – of the national virtues, and so on and so forth; these are devised in the service of id processes, which by such idealization create the prerequisites for their satisfaction. The ego, which has to produce evidence to show that the wishful thinking is justified by reality, thus becomes the agent of more primitive psychical organizations. Whole historical libraries bear witness to this subservience of the ego, just as historical research in general, when it devotes itself to interpretation, so clearly demonstrates the impotence of the ego to establish itself in the 'struggles of power of motivation'.[6] Investigation of motive that cannot distinguish between aspects of a phenomenon originating in infantile ideals formed in the service of powerful unconscious instinctual trends and ideals based on the critical capacities of the ego certainly contributes little to the understanding of history-making mankind, even when it is based on a huge apparatus of scientific historiography.

What applies to history writing on the grand scale applies equally to the way in which we compose our own private 'biographies'. Even when our conduct has been selfish, and even more when it has been guided by fear or ruthlessness, we like to see it idealized, and we like to regard our experiences of failure as 'tragic'. Even the cynicism that ridicules all idealism as self-deception has its own ideal of deeper insight and fearless freedom from prejudice. True, the great ideals demand a great deal from us, but they do not reveal – without lying – how they are arrived at. The most lamentable lies are those of which we do not become aware perhaps for a whole lifetime, because we use them stubbornly to defend the infantile ideal to which we remain in bondage. As Freud says, 'formation of an ideal . . . heightens the demands of the ego and is the most powerful factor favouring repression; sublimation is a way out, a way by which those demands can be met *without* involving repression'.[7]

Men's thoughts and aspirations remain 'open' and plastic so long as the ego is able to ask questions without knowing the answers in advance. Learnt obedience restricted to the dogmatic level, a previously experienced pattern from which it is impossible to escape, prematurely cuts the thread of development towards a critical ego capable of independent decision. Rigid repression of all impulses that might shake this system of ideals – and their counterpart, the standards of non-value – cements characterological infantilism. Even the steps towards biological maturity often fail to disturb this finality and make things fluid again. We are bound to conclude that these ideals must be associated with a tremendous amount of anxiety if the individual is unable to question them; as the answer comes from the world of magical experience, merely questioning it is equivalent to sacrilege. Much of the mimicry that is practised in connection with the collective ideals that are so often assumed to be self-evident must be regarded as superstitious magic. This leaves little elbow room for sublimation in the affective sphere.

*Repetition compulsion*

In spite of the use of what, from the point of view of a later stage of maturation, are outdated aids in social orientation, our capacity for adaptation enables us to fit into the most varied cultural environments. Common to all of them is that they call on us to restrict obedience to our instinctual trends and adopt the prevailing rules of behaviour. This shows that the average man is able to tolerate a great deal of repression of undesired ambivalence without necessarily advancing from infantile obedience to reality-adapted behaviour. A favourable social constellation, a stimulus, is of course required if the individual is to feel called on to make a fresh effort to understand himself and his environment; and there must not be an *a priori* disproportion between the social demands made on him and his vital energy, whether in the form of excessive strictness or excessive indulgence. In these latter cases the possibility of development towards a critical attitude to reality is either very restricted or absent altogether.

In general, the demands for obedience that come from the social environment must be adapted to the individual's stage of development, in order to allow him time to deal with the ambivalence In the first year of life, for instance, the mother's attitude must be predominantly protective. Even then the child suffers enough frustrations of its instinctual trends, which it feels to be utterly strange and overpowering. If the mother multiplies these by ill-timed social demands, premature toilet training, or excessive restriction of the child's movements, its feelings of ambivalence towards her are increased; she is then felt more violently than is necessary in this period of inevitable conflict to be an evil, prohibiting object. It can be assumed that such a mother shows little intuitive understanding of the child and is uncritical of the intolerant practices recommended to her. A mother who is a trainer rather than a guide will be unable to cope with her child's rejection of her. The child's ambivalence of feeling unconsciously rouses in her the memory of her own suffering that was the consequence of similar 'naughtiness' on her own part. Because she was then forced to resort to violent repression, she cannot remember now but instead can only 'act', that is, adhere to the line of infantile defence, guided by an ideal standard of what a child ought to be like. Real experiences bewilder her, and the 'stereotype' of imposing obedience is the simpler and less ambivalent course. Thus earlier experiences, perhaps defects in her own development, are reflected in her behaviour to her child.

*Regressive idealization*

Freud pointed out that the 'child's super-ego is in fact constructed on the model, not of its parents, but of its parents' super-ego'; the super-ego thus becomes 'the vehicle of tradition and of all the time-resisting judgements of value which have propagated themselves in this manner from generation to generation'.[8] In discussing the father's recession into invisibility, we tried to describe the changes brought about in that centre of integration, the super-ego, by the separation between the child's experience of the model in practical action and its purely emotional experience of him, and the increasing impoverishment of the former. This results in a weakening of object relations and a fickleness of identification that is reflected on the social scale. The individual's psychical constitution is of course the result of interaction between collective and individual processes. The separation of home from place of work brings about alienation in the family group, and the loosening up of identifications makes the individual more adaptable but less fit for criticism and responsibility. This again is reflected on the social scale in political practices that assume an individual psychical constitution in which the contents of the super-ego are easily changeable. If the number of oaths of loyalty are recalled that Germans now in the sixties have been required to swear in the course of their lifetime – and in most cases they complied without objection – it becomes evident that the super-ego has assumed the quality almost of a dummy. This easy exchangeability of ideals reveals a regressive trait to which mass man succumbs. There is no longer any clear distinction between the internal authority of the super-ego and external authorities, ruling figures, ideologies, etc. The situation has reverted to that which prevailed between the ages of four and six.

That is the real characteristic of 'cultural hypocrisy'. The requirements of civilization are not assimilated and firmly associated with the attainments of the ego, but are complied with provisionally. The other-directed man, to use Riesman's terminology, does not have a super-ego with permanent contents; or, to state it more precisely, his principles do not evolve, but merely follow one another in catastrophic succession as the ideologies born of catastrophe require. It may be that this has occurred in all ages; the only peculiarity of ours may be the accumulation of collapses and upheavals into a short time. But the frequency of the necessity for reorientation must nevertheless have qualitative effects on the character structure of those involved. To say nothing of the real question: Which takes precedence or is dominant, the rapid and often incoherent socio-economic and socio-political development or the regressive (or retarded or at any rate weakened) capacity to hold fast to objects, that is, keep them libidinally cathected, and be able to remember them? A multiplicity of interactions is of course at work here, but for that very reason we must be on our guard against ideologically primitive oversimplifications.

There are certainly plenty of extra-psychological reasons for unrest in the field of social values. The contrast, at any rate in the Western world, between experimental curiosity in technical matters and the tendency to idealize 'grand old men' and choose them as leaders is another illustration of the regressive trends of the ego ideal. Obviously we are confronted here with something approaching a realm of magical fantasies of greatness which has not lost its influence on behaviour. Also the ego ideal of many of our contemporaries was formed on the model of adults who in principle knew everything better and had little understanding for human weaknesses, for the groping, fallible child. That at all events is the basis on which the characteristic form of communication between adults and children in our society takes place. This authoritarian form of initiation into the social field has, however, had an unexpected consequence, namely, a reinforcement of the tendency to dependence and an acceptance of non-responsibility. The counterpart of our characteristic mass heroes are the unenterprising 'young pensioners' who have no desire to stand on their own feet in their welfare states.

This, let us repeat, is unfair criticism of existing conditions to the extent that it omits consideration of such material factors as urbanization, concentration in big industrial units, and increased fragmentation of labour and responsibility, all of which produce reaction-formations in those affected. All the same, it would be underrating the autonomy of psychical life if the contribution of psychological factors to the actual situation were ignored. Hence, instead of always blaming social processes directly, we should try to gain a better understanding of the motivation of this regressive, passive attitude, with its background of irresponsible fantasies and impersonal pleasures (mass pleasures almost indiscriminately enjoyed), and its roots in infantile experiences at the imprinting stage. In the first place, the so-called social superstructure (its system of values, its theory about itself, its legal relations, and so on) is not directly dependent on the 'infrastructure', the conditions of production; the relationship of each to the other is dialectical. Then it should be recalled how much in the social field is communicated to the child by parental attitudes, educational practices, affective situations, etc. This communication at the infantile imprinting stage requires investigation; if the family's communicative function is declining, we must find out who is taking over this role. Above all, we must find out how and in what conditions 'society' in the form of its individual behaviour patterns turns into psychical structure and what are the psychical conditions (early experiences) that cause these influences to be effective. Quick and unconsidered recourse to society or other material factors (as 'scapegoats') can amount to seeking an alibi. If human subjectivity is left so completely out of account, the way can be insidiously opened to a passivity that could lead to permanent postponement of change in these conditions. If we do this, if we surrender the dialectical relationship between the world and the self, we surrender the self as well; and the functioning individual is reduced to a mere plaything of his economic system, a point of intersection of political, moral, and other lines of force. All these things affect the individual's life, of course. But we must also look at the psychical impulses at work in them, as well as the psychological impact that they themselves make. We must note, for instance, the enormous increase that has taken place in the attitude of curiosity, which has led to the development of modern science, or the increased sense of rivalry and responsiveness to challenge; and it must not be forgotten that these conditions and circumstances have been brought about by man's open possibilities of self-realization. They both reveal the marks of new forms of sublimation and are also reaction-formations, both individual and collective, to the surviving, still unsuperseded past. Marxist social criticism sees this very plainly. But, because the anthropology that it assumes lacks the dimension of a psychical determinism of its own, it is undialectical in this respect; it works with a concept of man in which man is the product of his material and social conditions. That concept is adequate in many respects, but it will not do as a description of the nature of man. Above all, we are not entitled to assume an eschatological state towards which humanity by reason of its nature is striving. The characteristic of human nature is its open-endedness. This is reflected in the inadequacy of all social orders, but such inadequacy cannot be held solely responsible for the 'immaturity' of those who live in them. That is no excuse for social injustice; on the contrary, it is an invitation to correct this, though with the awareness of the inevitability of new imperfections. Human nature has become 'historical' in a specific sense; it fulfils natural history in a human historical context. This is something we sense in broad outline rather than know for certain.

The psychological set-up in mass societies, independently of the political trend that prevails in them, is characterized by regressive idealization and an increased readiness to obey, accompanied by a loosening of permanent ties to men and things and values and ways of behaviour. This is obviously a result of the growth of population and the changes in working and living conditions that made the population explosion possible. In an organized, specialist society subject to rapid technological changes obedience plays no smaller, indeed probably a bigger, role than in societies based on established status and covering smaller areas. The danger of an over-organized social structure producing 'mass units' totally trained in learnt obedience and totally manipulated has been thought of often enough, and attempts have actually been made to produce it in practice. Though this wishful thinking would not produce all the results expected of it and the individual's fears of completely losing his identity in the mass may be exaggerated, the dangers of development in this direction are the specific dangers with which our social order is faced.

The counter-forces available to the individual lie in the expansion of consciousness in relation to calls for obedience made with the claim that their justice is self-evident. A primitive way of defying restriction of freedom of action by the administrative machine and the pressure of the masses among whom our lives are spent is the anarchy that springs up in many places (and quite naturally in the behaviour of many young people). But only an increase of consciousness in relation to this mass life which we cannot escape but might treat with greater sympathy will enable us to understand the regressive trends and at least avoid them ourselves.

If it were possible, with the aid of a more subtle understanding of the different types of obedience, to make observations in the most varied fields – if it were possible, for instance, to study the relationship between the progress made by children at school and the behaviour pattern of their families, or similarly to study how much elbow room is really available in reaching judicial decisions, or how much freedom of judgement the character structure (as distinct from *esprit de corps* and group affect) of members of a cabinet allows them in arriving at government decisions – we should reach a new dimension of understanding of the social reality of which history is made. The way in which the three types of obedience we have described intertwine with each other and with the social institutions which are cut to their measure and call for obedience of such different types would then be plain. We possess, however, only the most rudimentary beginnings of field studies of the type that would enable us to answer these questions. They will, however, enable us to answer the question why at this moment in history tendencies to regressive ideal formation, passive submission, and dependence on social institutions, as well as anarchical trends, appear on a mass scale.

## The seat of anxiety

The social behaviour of animals is regulated on a single level, that of obedience to innate behaviour patterns specific to each species. Man's behaviour on the social level is regulated by the trinity of obedience to instinct, learnt obedience, and obedience to conscience; and he is also capable of disobedience at all levels. Obeying his conscience gives stability to his decisions in relation to his inner, instinctual demands and the outside demands of society. Thus it has the effect of reducing conflict. Freud, as Waelder has pointed out,[9] describes the ego as a 'problem-solving agency', and thus uses a 'teleological concept'. 'Just as the ego controls the path to action in regard to the external world, so it controls access to consciousness.'[10] It can do this effectively only when it is able to anticipate dangerous situations, and for this it depends on memory. The foresight of which it is capable depends on the resemblance of the present and the anticipated to remembered experience. If the concomitant affective phenomena of the latter were very frightening, the ego will choose the narrow path it previously took with relative immunity. It will adapt its decisions to previous decisions, the patterns laid down by models, taboos, custom, etc. It must again be recalled that this work by the ego takes place unconsciously (as also does a large part of the activity of the super-ego); the integrating, guiding activity of the ego is not identical with the conscious.

Thus the more strongly learnt obedience and obedience to the conscience are associated with experiences of fear, the more will the functioning of the ego be taken up with unconscious defence measures. For the ego is the 'seat of anxiety'.[11] Anxiety results in a retreat, not only from the outside world, but also from the experiences of the inner world. If for a moment we follow the practice of applying the word 'instinct' to all spontaneous elements in behaviour (the 'play instinct', the 'dressing-up instinct', and so on and so forth), we shall agree with Erich von Holst that 'fear is an instinct that even in small doses keeps all other instincts in check', and 'that long persisting suppression can end in the apathy of natural social tendencies in behaviour'.[12] All we have to add to this observation, which is based on the study of animal behaviour, is that in human beings fear is a more complicated phenomenon than it is in the animal kingdom; in man's case fear is not just a matter of hostile patterns that automatically put an end to other activities; elements of danger can be seen in an incomparably larger number of social experiences in the secondary learning processes. Fear may spread by association to quite incidental concomitant circumstances, which thus similarly come to symbolize danger. With the maturation of the ego such sources of fear can be dismantled again, activity can be resumed, and an anxiously tabooed situation can be mastered. But the conditioned reflexes that arose in early experiences of fear can so weaken the later development of the ego capacities that they remain stunted.

### Instillation of fear as a method of control

We believe that the educational methods used by our civilization, which requires life-long adaptation, that is, learning capacity, on the part of an ever increasing number of people, on the whole rouse far too much totally unnecessary anxiety in early childhood and create an obstacle to learning thereby. The lack of intuitive understanding of the infant and the young person in the crises of puberty represents the most underdeveloped social relationship in our society. The excessive demands made on the child by imposing on him learnt obedience to social stereotypes on the one hand and the heedlessness with which the needs and difficulties peculiar to his age are overlooked on the other are direct products of the surviving unchanged values of the status society of the pre-technical age. The belief still prevails that in the nursery everything is quite simple, straightforward, and self-evident. Adults, parents, teachers, and other well-intentioned individuals fail to appreciate that what they take for granted to be 'good', natural, right, and so on is merely the outcome of their own obedience to learnt social standards. Neither these standards nor the question of obedience itself, so far as they are concerned, come within the field of critical examination. But the amount of juvenile neurosis, the innumerable symptoms of neglect (which appear most violently in puberty, or during the period of adolescence as a whole), the appearance of which is quite independent of poor living conditions and does not spare the 'best families', should make them less complacent. However politics may be bedevilled by trite phrases idealizing the child and mother-love and problem-free family life, we cannot blind our eyes to the burdens imposed by our society on the psychical development of the child. The building of new roads, and of course defence, and even the encouragement of school and university education, all take precedence over the vital question of the treatment of children before the age of school entry or the final adoption of adult roles. It is here that taboos are the most tenacious. Everyone is willing to submit to a medical examination to obtain life insurance, but hardly anyone thinks it necessary to seek the aid of others with a view to ensuring success for his children in the ordinary business of living. We must ask ourselves how our society, which has moved so far from the stabilizing security of social values and standards of behaviour that survived for generations, will be able to afford this blind clinging to patterns of behaviour which have become void of content with the disappearance of the conditions on which they were based. Wolfgang Hochheimer complains that it is 'the habitual limitation of our anthropological field of vision' that continually causes us to shake our heads in astonishment at 'how war came about, how people could possibly be like that, how we could be so grossly deceived, how basically evil our enemies are', etc., etc. Instead of this *naïveté* resulting from inhibition of thought it would be better 'to take all this material rejected as "unintelligible" into the real anthropological balance sheet'.[13]

But at this point we have closed the circle. Learnt obedience requires the acquisition of techniques and the pragmatic style of society and the rejection of disturbing primary trends. This is broadly speaking imposed by education, which achieves only a partial socialization, however. The degree of adaptation enforced by repression is the whole point. Too much repression combined with too little initial fundamental satisfaction of the primary trends creates a very wide area of repression and requires a great deal of energy to ward off the repressed. The individual and the community are consequently forced to create outlets for the repressed trends. The most important of these are projections upon others of what is intolerable in the self and reaction-formations, for instance, morbidly sought surrogate satisfactions. As no one succeeds in complete sublimation or leads a life totally satisfactory to his instinctual trends – because nobody lives in an ideal society – transitions from 'normal' to morbidly intensified search for outlets for the primary trends are continuous. Features that suggest the pathological are for long periods regarded as 'normal' in societies. Liability to bias of this kind makes 'the real anthropological balance sheet' difficult to draw up, even very roughly. But working towards it must be the real objective of all anthropological theory; it is the real challenge to psychology.

Let us therefore surrender neither to an ideology that explains man by his social circumstances nor to that other ideology that derives in the truest sense of the word from the image of a dominant individual (the ideal self of a ruling or would-be ruling group) and consequently condemns the non-conformist either to exploitation or to extermination. The so strongly regressive processes now taking place in super-ego formation will then become somewhat more intelligible to us. Among the masses the tendency to passive social conformity is spreading; or perhaps it has always been the only form of socialization available to the 'small man'. If the latter is true, its inadequacy has only become more obvious now that critical independence combined with frictionless 'functioning' in the social field has become indispensable, and critical consciousness is the only corrective against the dangerous preponderance of technology and bureaucracy. If we had better methods of investigation and a broader foundation of experience for drawing up a 'real anthropological balance sheet' of the social forces which are 'producing' the kind of men now living in our society, we should be better able to understand why they are no longer guided from within by a super-ego but from without by the political conditions of the time, with their fashionable and ideological trends. The circumstance that a change of régime involves a mass 'loss of face' would then be less unintelligible. We could spare ourselves a great deal of negative cultural criticism (which in any case is generally based on a reactionary overvaluation of a self well protected against the prevailing ideology), if we took into account that, as we have pointed out, society nowadays has a much more direct influence on the individual than in earlier times, when withdrawal into the family or the clan or emigration were more easily possible. We can assume from our rudimentary psychological anthropological knowledge that the regressive assimilation that is observable arises from 'conditions' to the extent that these are making previously habitual ways of dealing with people impossible. But that does not mean that the effects of this process are unalterable. On the contrary, we need only point to the fact that the inertia of behaviour patterns leads us into living in a world of 'as if', the clearest consequences of which are to be seen in the autonomy of subjective feelings, tastes, and valuations. But psychological analysis shows that what appears to the individual to be autonomy is often anarchy, an anarchy originating in weak object ties that quickly takes up people and aims and as quickly drops them again. The roots of the capacity to establish lasting object cathexes reach back to the learning experiences of early childhood, the period when the forces that oppose object ties, the instinctual trends that are aware of an object only as a means to an end, still try ruthlessly to attain their aims. The attitude of the model, not his mere words, enables the child to discover how an object can slowly change from the role of being merely a means to an end (that is, the satisfaction of primitive trends) into a known and familiar component of the world. The model thus enriches us, not just by being present for the duration of our vital needs, after the satisfaction of which all interest in it ceases, but by assuming the features of another self distinct from our own whose identity engages us and involves our feelings.

Compensation for real object loss is provided by idealized exaltation (and cathexis) of objects with which we have no direct contact, which are in actual fact 'unknown' to us. We idealize the family in its tradi-tional historical form, for instance. We do so as if the peasant, artisan, or bourgeois family were an ideal form of human association in which the object was never a mere means to an end, exploited as if it were not a human being at all. We act as if such a family could still be an un-changed oasis in urbanized industrial society, as if it were still a reality, though in this idealized form it can hardly have been a reality at all, or at any rate a typical reality. Consequently we miss the chance of care-fully analysing the various aspects of family life – the relationship of the parents with each other and their relations with their children – in existing social conditions, and so bringing them into our balance sheet. From an altogether different aspect, this balance sheet would be useful for making more rational use of an abundance that earlier times never knew. But we are hampered at every step by the anxiety which every tradition keeps alive and simultaneously appeases by obedience to its commandments. Solid interests are always associated with conditions as they are, and they can be opposed only by overcoming the anxiety that rises to their defence. Ideologically manipulated anxiety is not a defence mechanism that works in the interest of preservation of the species, but a doubtful tactic that is best resisted with doubt.

*Obedience to the ego*

There remains to be discussed what is historically the most modern form of behaviour, which we have called obedience to the ego. Many of the conditions essential for its development have already been indicated. The phases of obedience to instinct and learnt obedience must have been passed through without excessive intimidation of the instinctual trends and without an excessively anxiety-cathected restric-tion of the area over which learning extends. In these conditions the attitude of curiosity is maintained and is not too easily put off with dogmatically final answers. In psychological terms, the dynamics of ego development must not be excessively burdened with defence against ambivalent inner representatives of instincts, that is, conflicting wishes, affects, and fantasies, if the psychical tendencies to maturation are to advance on a broad front to the establishment of a stable, conscious, critical ego. The constitutional factors involved in this development interest us only to the extent that we do not doubt the differences in innate human aptitude that exist in this field, as in others. Leaving aside the extremes of exceptionally high and exceptionally low aptitude, the differences among the great mass are not significant enough to cause evolution to a greater critical consciousness to fail. On the contrary, psycho-analytic experience shows that social imprinting processes are enormously important, and that they are responsible on a very wide scale indeed for the frustration and atrophy of the trend towards more consciously guided behaviour. As we have shown, the explanation is to be sought in the fact that the development of the conscious – as a possession of the *species* – represents a very recent and insecure biological variation in the process of evolution. The critically conscious ego makes a late appearance in the development of the individual, long after the beginnings of social education, and all too often the latter blocks its normal maturation.

We are continually told that it is useless to appeal to human 'reason', because it is too rare, so it is essential to have strict laws and patterns of behaviour and strict education, meaning the imposition of reliable conditioned reflexes. This is putting the cart before the horse. The opposite argument is closer to the truth. That is to say, since the socialization of members of our society takes a partly prohibitory, partly non-understanding, form and the necessary backing is not given to the child, because the child is filled with guilt feelings from the first without receiving the benefit of the good counsel and gentle hand that would show it how guilt can be avoided and how one can learn to discriminate between guilt and attempted outside intimidation; and because a social structure depending on the division of labour requires specialists who think critically only in a narrow field and are otherwise expected to conform; because, in short, these influences are interlinked with and superimposed on each other, most people are unable to realize the rational potentialities of which they are capable.

The tried and tested system of imposing early 'inhibitions of thought',[14] developed by ruling groups over the centuries as the guiding educational principle for the masses, is still successfully applied with the aid of the mass media and their way of presenting information and encouraging habits of consumption at all levels. It can indeed be stated without exaggeration that had one single political agency taken up the cause of applying psycho-analytic knowledge for the purposes of strengthening the critical ego with as much enthusiasm as the economy has taken up that of increasing consumption (while simultaneously frustrating criticism), our political landscape would look quite different. For instance, an important element in the fear of the Eastern world would be modified if the inner command-and-obey structure were less alien to the ego and therefore bore less resemblance to the autocratic system that prevails there – and prevailed in our own history. The capacity for criticism begins at home, with criticism of the self, which is the basis for reinforcing the ego against anxiety. Only those early subjected to the principle of inhibition of thought tend to attribute their own defects to others, thus almost certainly missing the chance of realizing their own potentialities.

Education confined to the transmission of learnt obedience and the imprinting of an absolutist conscience leads to men's partial infantilism, prevents the development of a personal conscience, the prerequisite of which is the experience of closeness and intimacy. In the process of identification with models, the model's own thirst for knowledge, awareness of its own fallibility, and honesty in the face of the doubts which no one is spared must be closely experienced so that they may be closely communicated.

*Empathy and detachment*

The experience of closeness presupposes the surmounting of obedience to instinct, in which the other party has only a functional role as a means to the end of securing satisfaction. Whenever that is the motive for seeking a person out, whatever the excuse we may make for it, that person remains a stranger and, in so far as we deceive ourselves about our real motivation, we remain in the dark about ourselves. The distinction between intuitive understanding (involving closeness) and autistic, instinctually motivated behaviour concealed behind a cloak of humanitarianism is described with great acuteness in a letter of Goethe's. 'And, so far as goodness of heart and excellence of character are concerned, I have only this to say: Our actions are really good only in so far as they are accompanied by self-knowledge; darkness about ourselves does not easily permit us really to do good, and so it amounts to the good not being really good at all.' In terms of the character, the self-assurance with which rationalization is clung to can be described as 'darkness'. Goethe continues: 'But darkness certainly leads us into wrong and actually, if it is unqualified, into evil, but without justifying us in saying that the man who acts evilly is evil.'[15] Both the structure and the influence of the model on the individual are always more subtle than is evident to either party. The individual identifies with the model with whom he is presented, and the process of taking over attitudes, reactions, habits, etc., includes unconsciously transmitted behaviour patterns as well as those that the model consciously desires to transmit. Thus one also takes over the 'darkness' and other forms of self-concealment that one is offered. Only if we are ourselves willing to learn about the blind spots in our self-awareness can we create the conditions necessary for education in obedience to the ego. Intuitive understanding of the child's intellectual and emotional immaturity will prevent the premature application of adult moral standards.

This empathy brings about an affective contact in which the child's own impulses are not suppressed. For this it is necessary that the adult's attitude of curiosity should not have congealed into one of unchallengeable certitudes. Curiosity is a sign of object interest, and aggressive and libidinal trends are tied to the object of the interest. Also, curiosity is the instinctually conditioned psychical prerequisite of all sublimation, and we have seen that the possibility of developing a conscious critical ego depends on the capacity for sublimated instinctual satisfaction. By this path energy flows to the ego, which is able to 'neutralize' and store it up, keeping it available for the constant exercise of its vital capacities of perception and thought.

Obedience to the ego must therefore be regarded as obedience only in a qualified sense. In situations of conflict the reflex-like response gives way to a synthesis of intellectual reality judgement and empathy with the object. One of man's psychical capacities is that of critical reflection before decision or action, and one of his affective capacities is that of feeling his way into the minds of others; mentally he can go a part of the way with another person, and he can also change his mind and withdraw. In the process he learns to know the other person better. Without the ability to change his mind he would be merely a conformist.

In sub-human societies, in swarms and herds, such conformity prevails. The mark of intelligent behaviour, however, is a capacity in affective situations for simultaneous empathy and reflective detachment; decisions made are not totally dependent on the other party's advantage in strength. Renunciation or acceptance of instinctual impulse, the taking over or rejection of a prescribed role or recourse to an original solution, are possibilities that can be taken into account before a decision is made; or at any rate the ground is clear for the ego to have its say, and not only in the minor decisions of everyday life which have little affective cathexis, but also when the ego is under the influence of great instinctual excitation or anxiety-arousing demands by the social environment.

What do all these reflections lead to? The demands for obedience have very different roots. There are hereditary biological necessities and traditional social requirements. Some of these are absorbed by the individual and become a regulatory mechanism in the form of his superego, his conscience, his social standards. The process is very accurately described by Nietzsche: 'The contents of our conscience are everything that was regularly demanded of us without reason in the years of our childhood by persons whom we revered or feared. Thus the conscience is the source of the "must" feeling ("I must do this, I must not do that"), but does not ask why I must. Whenever a thing is done for a reason, men act without their conscience, though not necessarily against it. The source of conscience is belief in authority; thus it is not the voice of God in man's breast, but the voice of other men in man.' When such a conscience functions well, it assures practical adaptation and more or less successfully wipes out all memory of scenes of collective lack of conscience. 'All so-called practical men,' Nietzsche says a little later, 'have an aptitude for service; it is that that makes them practical, useful both to others and to themselves. Robinson had an even better servant than Man Friday; his name was Crusoe.'[16]

*Education for insecurity, and some thoughts on ideas of political unity*

Social reality is uncomfortable, because conflict is inherent in it. It seeks to attain equilibrium, but the means by which it does so inevitably create conflict. At one end of the scale of human societies there is the totalitarian system, which tries to suppress all resistance by force. At the other there is the permissiveness of the *laissez-faire* system which, however, can never lead to liberty, because the stronger will always try to overpower the weaker without regard for his arguments, so that violent conflicts arise and the final outcome is their brutal suppression. The numerous compromise formations, apart from some relatively satisfactory ones, include a painfully obvious abundance of short-lived arrangements based on short-sighted decisions.

With our increasing knowledge of the large number of different societies that have arisen in the course of history and the large number that exist today, confidence that any world outlook based on one particular group can be correct is severely shaken. At the same time we are involved in another process for which there is no historical precedent, namely, an incursion of ideas from which no existing political unit is able to isolate itself, whether it is organized as a state or is based on community of race, language, or religion. The most effective of these ideas are those of national independence and of sharing in technical progress and the exploitation of new sources of prosperity. A contemporary phenomenon scattered all over the world is the setting up under the banner of national independence of states in which a poverty and want prevail in the face of which we seem to be as helpless as we once were in the face of hunger and disease. In many places the Western liberal idea of national self-determination meets autochthonous social and political traditions which, far from capitulating to them, use them on the international level primarily for the purpose of blackmail, thus reducing them to absurdity.

The idea that every nation has the right to determine its own way of life belongs to the superstructure of the social thinking of our time, but it has also taken on the character of a fetish, because it assumes a similar attitude to the problems of humanity on the part of everyone. Nevertheless we must bear in mind that, for whatever complex reasons, the idea of national autonomy has come to exercise such a fascination that we must count on its being a primary source of conflict for the foreseeable future. The force with which claims based on it are made rouses anxiety in the previously dominant political entities, the traces of which are reflected in the phenomenon of a collective inhibition of thought. So far few ideas have appeared which might help in effectively bringing the autonomy of national units into a system of social responsibility on the international plane. Even where they have been the beginnings of the development of such a broader outlook – as in establishing the rudiments of European integration, that is, among nations with a long experience of ambivalent contacts, and in the United Nations – a many-layered system of affective resistances has to ne overcome. Identity feelings and feelings of self-esteem are associated far beyond any rational level with concepts such as national dignity, nationality, and so on; included in these are not only self-centred fears about self-preservation, but also rationalized defences of one's own 'individuality', with all the presocial and partially socialized behaviour patterns associated with them.

The 'pride' with which one is here confronted turns out to be not only an expression of the self-realization that has been attained, but also a form of readiness to discharge aggression if it is infringed on. The indignity of having to live under alien rule or 'imperialism' is irreconcilable with this pride. Its violence is certainly not a sign of resolved conflict or successful social integration. It belongs to the category of collective rationalizations from which the great majority, who use it as a defence mechanism against their feelings of unpleasure about the existing order, are unable to escape. But when chronic anarchy affects whole continents (South America, for instance), or a system of archaic terror is superimposed on endemic poverty in Haiti or Albania, no amount of sympathy or rational understanding can do anything, because no form of organization yet exists that can interfere with national independence.

The idea of national individuality, associated with the most varied levels of development of group consciousness and the most varied forms of social conflict, has become an ideological entity that seems inaccessible to our powers of mediation by critical reflection. Each individuality puts up the same claim to responsibility and total freedom from interference by others, though a similar claim by a small group (family, school, productive unit) would be too absurd to sustain. The idea that they should subordinate themselves by integration into larger groupings in accordance with their productive contribution offends their self-esteem. There is no style of international intercourse – which, like all styles, should have teeth – that can give emphasis to the representations of the dominant groups. On the contrary, a relatively passive, tolerant attitude prevails, in the granting of development aid, for instance. The older nations, who used to have recourse to imperialist solutions, are now confronted with a large number of young states over which their authority is very weak; they are like many parents, unable to make intuitive contact with their adolescent children. The adolescent-like development of these communities would seem, however, to be more liable to crisis the less ambivalence was dealt with and organized into inner patterns of self-guidance during the period preceding the violent obtaining of independence. The paternal structure of imperial colonialism was obviously not a good preparation for independence, not the best possible initiation rite.

If there was ever a misleading slogan, it is that of the 'family of nations', for no nation would ever admit to 'childishness' or unfitness for responsibility. On the other hand, the weakness of paternalist imperialism has been evident since the end of the Austro-Hungarian and British Empires, though there is no uniformity of development in this respect either. Federalism, however, has shown its strength in the face of nationalist particularism. The Soviet Union succeeded in giving a new sense of cohesion to the multi-national empire of the Tsars, and only on its western perimeter, where Russian imperialism (old-style) advanced into areas where other imperialisms had prevailed and there was a long-standing political tradition aspiring to responsibility and self-determination, did a ring of satellites arise that had to be kept within it by the exercise of force. The first and oldest of the federations to arise from the conflict with the monarchist imperialist system, the United States, was also the luckiest, because it could begin its work of national construction and social organization in a new country in which there were no established traditions to be superseded.

The analogy between the history of societies that have created institutions and individual processes of maturation may be frail in many respects, but there is one in which it is real. Groups that possess a high degree of decentralized conscious control, that is to say, a high proportion of members capable of criticism, replace the older, pyramidal, hierarchical structure by another in which horizontal *rapprochement* is highly developed, both in material and affective relations. The phase of history we are entering on is leading to the end of the predominance of paternalist régimes, and many individual phenomena herald the advent of the age of the fatherless society, or rather the society that has outgrown paternal leading strings. What from the old viewpoint looks like unbridled anarchy may also be a state of groping for new solutions. Everywhere there is great sensitivity to instructions from above. However, the realization that if one is responsible for one's actions one can no longer project responsibility upwards hobbles along painfully in the wake of the aspiration for autonomy. This may be connected with the conflicting trends inherent in all social processes. The typical conflict – it may well be called the central conflict – of our time arises from the inconsistency between the aspiration to subjective autonomy in the meaningful decisions of life on the one hand and on the other the necessity of adapting oneself to bureaucratic super-organizations and accepting limitations of responsibility in specialist fields, while at the same time often developing disproportionate claims for social assistance. The trend to parasitism is discernible not only within societies but also on the international plane. Emergent nations which have little to contribute to the economy of the nations of the world unashamedly make blackmailing demands for international aid. The only possible moderator of this ambivalence of 'sibling envy' is the sense of partnership, an understanding of the law of reciprocity which can keep uncontrolled selfish aspirations in check.

The multiplicity of associations that have sprung up between groups that had never previously shared any historical experience makes tremendous demands on the patience of the critical conscious and on the ability to find intelligent solutions that will make coexistence possible. It seems obvious enough that this process of horizontal socialization of mankind will not be permitted the length of time required for true evolutionary processes. That sounds resigned, and is indeed a feeble consolation, particularly to those who have seen the possibility and necessity of a critical assessment of themselves and their society not based on an appeal to traditional certitudes.

We are faced with the unpredictable at two levels of experience. Technical developments promise discoveries and possibilities that are incalculable in advance. The efforts to land man on the moon seem absurd when compared with the foreseeable practical results, but that is exactly what his contemporaries thought of Columbus's project. The other field of unpredictability is that of the consequences of the population explosion and the use of the same technical equipment by all mankind. The consequence of the great differences in historical development and awareness among contemporaries all of whom use the same techniques must be the development of a very high degree of tension in vast areas of the world in individuals engaged simultaneously in rapid learning processes (learning to drive a car, for instance) and processes of maturation (such as shaking off magical modes of thought). The sudden dropping of familiar ways of life and the adoption of techniques in the absence of familiarity with the historical background against which they developed is bound to activate elementary anxiety. The less security the old patterns of behaviour are able to provide, the stronger are the regressive tendencies, in particular the break-through of primitive instinctual trends, especially aggressive ones. Many new states on being freed from ancient tyrannies have promptly undergone a massive structural social collapse and a regression to horde-like terror organizations. So-called military dictatorships have sprung up all over as a consequence of the acquisition of national freedom, and the rivalries and struggles for power and the fashion in which they succeed each other, the dynamics that these 'revolutions' follow, differ little from the struggles for the number one position in the herd. The modern weapons and the rest of the arsenal that assure the victor's position only remotely affect the motivation processes on the social level. These demonstrate the permanence of man's instinctual organization and the regression to primitive ways of assuring survival when traditional structures collapse. In these circumstances imposing 'order' on the political scene means keeping oneself and one's followers alive at all costs.

The turmoil the world is in must be painful to optimistic humanists who believed that the conquest of epidemics, improvement of the soil, the spread of literacy, and better living conditions would lead to a diminution of human stress; it must be painful for them to see old-established human equilibriums (and wants) profoundly unsettled by these achievements of human intelligence and resourcefulness. But if calculated expectations are followed by unexpected and paradoxical consequences, and if these conflicts are inevitable, what follows is the necessity of what Robert Merton calls education for insecurity. For not only the idealistic but also the pragmatical humanism of the Western tradition has turned out not to be immune to the lure of wishful-thinking Utopianism. Nor is there any immunization against the decline of even the oldest established parliamentary democracy – the highest level of conscious control of group conflict so far reached in history; and it is at a loss when faced with organized bands and regression to authoritarianism when it assumes the mantle of social responsibility.

When we say that world-wide social conflicts and the irresistible advance of technology call for an education that will enable the individual to find his way through these manifold uncertainties without lightly shedding his identity, we are again reverting to what we have already described as the possibility, which we deduced from the dynamics of individual maturation, of an obedience to the ego equipped to organize and co-ordinate the purposes of blind instinctual obedience and uncritical obedience to the super-ego. The most antagonistic forces are at work in the social field in which each one of us moves. On the one hand are the residues of a paternalism which is becoming increasingly void of content and is no longer able to provide guidance in the real decisions that have to be made, and on the other the rules of a society of the 'band of brothers' type that have hardly developed beyond the rudimentary stage and therefore do not yet provide binding and compelling patterns of behaviour. That is the state of transition in which the destiny of the mass society is being decided, and with it the destiny of each and every individual. The dice will fall not just for today, but for a present that will determine the future.

*Postscript: the disciplined body*

The individual may rough hew his ends, but society shapes them. It does so under the pressure of the conflicts at work in it. One element in the individual's destiny is the group into which he was born. Groups can, however, develop rich or poor dialectics for the aspirations of their members. The group style is always the outcome of the harmony or polyphony or disharmony of individual contributions, but the variables in the double process of behaviour formation are incredibly numerous.

At all events, the functions that fall to the individual in society make him liable to conflict in very varying degrees. The fate of a whole group may depend on the smooth carrying out of many tasks, and unquestioning obedience is therefore required in carrying them out; and the nature and permanence of a task may make it necessary to hand it over to a disciplined organization (such as the army). The existence of the religious orders of the Catholic Church show that religious tasks, for instance, can be carried out on the military pattern. As we have reiterated, no society can manage without compulsions. The question arises whether these disciplined bodies can be used as models for the carrying out of more or less all intra-social tasks.

Any limitation of the requirement of absolute obedience is always a thorn in the flesh of traditional institutions that exercise their authority on that principle. It is not disputed that this 'conservative' principle meets biological needs for an equilibrium of vital urges and reduces conflict. So long as the authority of their seniors is felt to be meaningful and binding, both those privileged under this system as well as the ordinary recipients of orders accept it as a plain and straightforward distribution of responsibility. Those who looked to revolutionary ideas alone for liberation from an inequitable burden of discipline will have been disillusioned by ample experiences in our lifetime. No sooner were régimes that promised such liberation in the saddle than they started tilting the balance in their favour by setting up new disciplined organizations. The alleged infallibility with which they set about out-trumping the old certitudes of their fathers was in reality a reaction-formation to the insecurity of their position. Another sign of this was their paranoid fear of persecution. To escape this, an externalized conscience was established in the form of an infallible party and an omniscient secret police. The ordinary citizen was put back into the infantile situation of being apparently continually exposed to adult observation and even having his thoughts read.

The educational system that ensued was to hand over the young to a succession of disciplined organizations, giving them the unhealthy feeling that by totally subordinating themselves to the omniscient ruling group they too attained omniscience. In these conditions the art of government consists in exploiting the libidinal tendency to idealize favourites and transfer aggressive impulses to scapegoats. Because of the severity of the discipline, aggressivity reaches a sadistic degree of intensity. The oppressed has imposed on him such a degree of identification with the oppressor – by way of idealistic exaltation of the latter – that he actually enjoys the humiliations he suffers when he becomes the system's victim. The confessions enforced in the Stalin era developed this process into a public ceremonial, as in the days of the Inquisition. When with the aid of this technique the authorities succeed in crushing intellectual doubt by the steam-roller of the dogmatic certitudes to which they appeal, they not only obtain dog-like obedience but also an intellectual servility which to outsiders is perhaps even more repellent than the brutal exercise of force.

The essence and the justification of a disciplined body is that it carries out subordinate tasks (however vitally important they may be) and does not claim to be an end in itself. Where this demarcation line is crossed, when obedience to orders becomes a virtue in its own right, the result is slavishness. Slavishness always includes a great deal of hate which, however, cannot be extended to its idealized (and simultaneously disappointing) object, so it has to be turned inwards against the individual's self; he is forced to gain satisfaction from his own self-humiliation.

The successes gained by this method of handling people are indisputable, and it still overshadows education in human self-respect. It would be unfair to the older tyrannical institutions not to admit that their defences against an education in ego strengthening are now being slowly taken over by new disciplined organizations. But even in these distorted methods of government, which would be unthinkable in the absence of psycho-pathological deformation on the part of the governors, a subterranean transformation of the conscious is taking place. George Orwell hit the nail on the head when he spoke, not of 'Big Father', but of 'Big Brother'. Even the father-repudiating society of the 'band of brothers' will have to remember this quotation from Bertolt Brecht: 'I need ... a great new custom which we must introduce immediately, that is, the custom of thinking afresh in every new situation.'[17]

# IX

# Taboo

'Taboo' is a Polynesian and thus a very foreign word. Since words cannot be imported like pepper or bananas, it was only to be expected that it should have undergone a change of meaning in everyday speech. It means holy, untouchable, an idea as familiar to us as it is to all other cultures. Infringing a taboo is an outrage, a sacrilegious act. Perhaps the reason why this fascinating-sounding word has been adopted by all the languages of the Western world is that it provides a strange sound to describe a strange and uncanny experience. Its opposite, the word '*noa*' – meaning the profane, the familiar, the everyday – failed to enter our vocabulary in spite of Gauguin, probably because everyday life in Oklahoma or West Kensington does not possess those specific qualities. But 'taboo' is 'taboo' everywhere, even though the things that are tabooed vary very greatly.

When the medical student for the first time enters the dissecting hall with its display of dismembered corpses, the feeling of nausea and faintness with which he has to struggle testifies to the fact that he is infringing a taboo, though he knows that it is expected of him. He is infringing the 'holy dread' of death, though from the highest motive – that of making it useful to the living. But it is by no means certain that his conscious intentions will get the better of his primitive emotional impulses. What is holy is obviously also dangerous, and what is dangerous is also tempting. Freud points out that 'touching is the first step towards obtaining any sort of control over, or attempting to make use of, a person or object'.[1] When the first human couple picked the apple, they broke a taboo. The marking off of a forbidden, sacred precinct is as ancient a feature of man's life as is the wish to penetrate into the holy of holies. 'Taboo is a primeval prohibition forcibly imposed (by some authority) from outside, and directed against the most powerful longings to which human beings are subject. The desire to violate it persists in the unconscious; those who obey the taboo have an ambivalent attitude to what the taboo prohibits.'[2] Freud here describes a process to which it is difficult to gain conscious access. When the medical student goes deathly pale at the sight of opened abdominal cavities, exposed nerves and organs, it is easier to dismiss him as a 'sensitive soul' than to recognize the racing feelings and fantasies with which his faintness or sensation of sickness is associated. He does not recognize them himself; all he is aware of is that something is happening that is too much for him. But he is not just a victim of weak nerves, for even those stronger and more experienced than he have to fight the same revulsion and fear; the difference is merely that they are better able to conceal them. No human being has ever approached the dead body of a man or woman with the intention of laying hands on it without a sensation of the uncanny, fear of the wrath of God or of the gods, of retribution for an impious act that will turn him into a corpse himself.

In due course the student becomes a doctor, perhaps a surgeon. In the latter event his primary act of impiety is itself subjected to taboo, for no one other than himself is allowed without penalty to infringe the taboo on 'inflicting bodily injury' (in this case, performing an operation). The rational argument that he had acquired the skill necessary to estimate the dangers correctly *(lege artis)* and is therefore worthy of the privilege is valid enough; it refers to the formal, technical contents of the process. But one has only to recall those who would have liked to become doctors and had the necessary intelligence and skill, but were unable to cross the threshold of anatomy because they were prevented by an inner resistance, to realize that here a different system of selection is at work. Because another factor besides ability and experience is required – courage and determination to defy the taboo to secure membership of a group which not only forgives the infringement but also unconsciously transfers to it a degree of pleasure in so doing. The same thing also applies to the 'discoverers sailing unknown seas' of the past and to the space travellers of the future. Those who first violate a taboo are always a socially by no means highly regarded group who drive away the demons from the taboo precinct and make it safe enough for the majority to dare to follow them. This involves an extremely interesting socio-psychological process. Those who remain in passive dread are able to go on infringing the taboo in their unconscious fantasy, while those who do so in fact have consciously to accept these instinctual impulses and successfully control them by standards of reality. It is only this reciprocal relationship between the passive observance of the taboo by some and the active violation of it by others that makes possible the step of defying an originally universal taboo and simultaneously establishing a socially demarcated new one. The instinctual forces that are simultaneously so alarming and so alluring to our conscious are, however, never satisfied. In many cases when a surgeon is faced with a difficult decision regarding whether to operate or not, the question is decided by what is called his temperament or, to state it more accurately, his ability or lack of it to make a reality-based decision in spite of his instinctual trends. How essential is the social control of historically attained liberties in relation to the infringement of ancient taboos is demonstrated by the crimes of the Nazi régime, when unpenalized violation of taboo led to a collective break-through of destructive fantasies. An individual like Dr Rascher, who at Dachau made pseudo-rational excuses for committing murders the course of which he described in full medical detail, was able to carry out such outrages in defiance of taboos only so long as the pleasure of so doing was made possible and shared in by a criminal community which, like all human communities, immediately created new taboos, the sacrosanct figure of the Führer or the blood barrier by which it tabooed its victims. For, like many primal words, of which it must surely be one, taboo also means its opposite; the unclean is taboo as well as the holy. The emperor on the throne of Byzantium or Peking was 'untouchable', like the Indian outcaste. It is also of the essence of primal words that they can never be fully defined, though one 'knows', or rather feels, their meaning. They always communicate something extra that cannot be paraphrased; they are witnesses to the survival of magic, animistic modes of thought.

Thus taboos never coincide exactly with laws and usages. All effective social ties contain some element of the mysterious, fear-provoking quality inherent in a taboo. 'Etiquette', a code of good manners, is not a taboo in the strict sense of the word, though it has a great deal in common with it; people are offended, for instance, even by an unwitting infringement of it due to ignorance. Purely administrative law, as every tax collector knows very well, is far from being closely associated with taboo, while so-called natural law is very close to it, as is shown by the efforts made to establish a Charter of Human Rights after the taboo-destroying horrors committed by the dictatorships of our time.

Apart from the incest taboo, which is universal, though even here there are wide differences in the degree and criminality of prohibited unions, very different things are covered by taboo in different cultures. The only possible explanation is that there is only one basic restriction on man's 'strongest appetites', but that his instincts are not tied to definite objects and are not cyclically regulated; he lives from one historical adaptation to the next, creating new living conditions in response to the challenge of adaptation. Looked at from the outside, taboos may seem repellent or comic, but if one impinges on them the fun stops immediately, and we note the appearance in every individual of the dangerously destructive trends contained in the rituals intended to cleanse them of the taboo object. These rituals may involve the strangest sacrifices and compromises and remain unintelligible to the outsider, but they nevertheless help to preserve the psychical equilibrium of those who observe them. The multitude of neurotic symptoms echoes on the individual scale the collective practices associated with taboo.

When we consider with detachment the 'racial madness' of the Nazis or the revolting arrogance of the *apartheid* policy, we are indifferent or hostile to the taboos involved, as in Hans Andersen's tale about the emperor's new clothes. We are able to look at this particular sector of reality unthreatened and free of its demons, but that does not mean we are able to look at the whole world with the same detachment. He who simply denies the existence of taboos is a fool who has not learnt the meaning of fear and does not understand the world; or probably it would be truer to say that he cannot allow himself to feel fear at any price, because it would sweep his weak ego away in panic. Criticism of reality based on cool consideration of the evidence inevitably finds itself quickly trespassing on taboos. Even thinking about forbidden things causes a shock of anxiety; imagining the infringement of a taboo in advance often calls for more courage than the act itself.

Utopians are great dreamers, often childish ones, who charge headlong into enclosed areas and act as if that justified them in behaving as if they owned them. Thus Henry Miller, writing as if dreams were not a cunning device by which our instinctual nature both presents and conceals itself from consciousness but were straightforward revelations of ultimate truth, says: 'In dream it is the Adamic man, one with the earth, one with the stars, who comes to life, who roams through past, present and future with equal freedom. For him there are no taboos, no laws, no conventions. Pursuing his way, he is unimpeded by time, space, physical obstacles or moral considerations. He sleeps with his mother as naturally as with another. If it be with an animal of the field he satisfies his desire, he feels no revolt. He can take his own daughter with equal enjoyment and satisfaction.'[3] The most interesting thing about such visions is their stereotyped nature. They reappear in masked form in all eschatologies. Both the Anabaptists and the Russian revolutionaries believed themselves to be on the threshold of Adamic man. Utopians dream of the stars, but what they want here below is the disappearance of sexual taboos; in the case of our much-read contemporary Henry Miller, the taboos in question are those on incest and sodomy. Never mind how often they may have been violated, they have nevertheless survived ages and cultures as restrictions on unbridled fantasies closely related to the primary processes and heedless of the terrestrial consequences. They are basic human taboos. How deep is the mistrust of the consequences of their infringement is shown by the symbolism of the Oedipus story. Even unwitting transgression is felt to be no protection from the inevitable punishment, for the real enemy against whom the ban is directed is the unbridled instinctual urge that lays down its arms neither before one's mother nor the life of one's father.

The Utopia of the tabooless society breaks down on the fact that it is the vision of men who have instincts for the satisfaction of which – as we have seen – there are no firmly established boundaries. The necessity of restricting them in order to make social life possible is simply denied. Man as he was before the fall (or is conceived to be after the redemption) is not man, however. Happiness and trespass lie very close to each other; often they are so fused as to be inseparable. This is reflected in the experience of doubt, conflict, ambivalence. 'It can easily be shown that the psychical value of erotic need is reduced as soon as its satisfaction becomes easy,' Freud remarks, rather surprisingly perhaps to those who think of him only as a destroyer of Victorian sexual taboos. 'In times in which there were no difficulties standing in the way of sexual satisfaction, such as perhaps during the decline of the ancient civilizations, love became worthless and life empty, and strong reaction-formations were required to restore indispensable affective values. In this connection it may be claimed that the ascetic current in Christianity created psychical values for love which pagan antiquity was never able to confer on it.'⁴

We have seen waves of enlightenement in which it became evident that taboos, in spite of their claim to divine origin, derive from counter-forces in ourselves opposed to the instinctual forces, which resent such restriction. But increasing secularization, with the knowledge we have of the innumerable taboos that have existed all over the world in the course of history, does not diminish the compulsion to obey our own taboos. That only makes plainer the tragedy of the human situation – a tragedy inseparable from comedy as well as from mere sadness. Satisfaction in the absence of inhibition leads to unhappiness, inhibition without satisfaction does the same, and the dogmatically or ideologically assumed possibility of a satisfactory balance between them carries with it the dreadful imprint of boredom, and so cannot be regarded as a state of pure happiness.

A glance at history, at the spatial and temporal limitations of most taboos, makes something else clear. Any particular taboo is a component of a social order, is part of its conscience. Though conscience is said to represent irrefutable certitude, this is so only in relation to other certitudes, a system of knowledge into which one has to be initiated. This is provided by the family, clan, or the religious or ideological community. According to Mr J. W. Studebaker, United States Commissioner of Education, the chief concern of a country's educational system must be the implanting of beliefs. This is perhaps the only practice common to the post-Columbian inhabitants of the United States and the tribal cultures that preceded them. But when one considers, for instance, the sexual taboos that are legally anchored in the California penal code, where does the borderline between illusion and reality lie?

Even the briefest survey of the taboo phenomenon cannot omit reference to the fact that it exists, not just as a prohibition in the mind, but also as a human function that is exercised in practice. The basic purpose of a taboo being to prevent wishes from being carried out, power necessarily accrues to those who ensure that it is observed. It is noteworthy that the most ancient social institutions are associated with taboos. Priests presided over ritual cleansing, and the exclusive power to free men from the burden of sin eventually devolved upon them. The more inevitable infringements of bans are, the greater the power of the priesthood. As we live both in the shadow of tradition and in a mass society that has no historical precedent, we are surrounded by taboos in historical layers. The smallness of the change that has taken place in the way that power is exercised is illustrated by the resemblance between the trials of heretics in the Middle Ages and the terrorist methods of the present day. The more the individual is hopelessly caught up in a tangle of interdependences, the greater his dependence on taboos. The consumer society has its own taboos and, however profane they may be, it is dangerous to infringe them. As these taboos are subject to rapid change, 'adaptation' has itself become a supreme taboo, supervised by the Argus eyes of the communications system. One of the most shattering discoveries – often one is not sure whether to call it comforting or terrifying – is that men understand each other incomparably more quickly, immediately, and dependably by way of the similarity of their taboos than by that of critical judgement.

Amid the press of surrogate satisfactions, the perpetual stimulus of insatiable instinctual trends, and the cartelized or monopolized processes of establishing taboos, the matter-of-course way in which even short-lived ones are accepted is an indication of the effectiveness of the unconscious, the task of dealing with which has become no easier in consequence. Those who want light to spread must nourish the hope that a new taboo will be established, namely, tolerance. But that will be difficult, because taboo and tolerance seem mutually exclusive. So we can only hope that this unification of opposites will take place at least for a few happy moments.

# X

# Roles

*Worse than death*

Psychologically it is not hard to see why taboos and rules are obeyed and actively maintained, once they have been established, even though the logic behind them may not be at all clear to the outsider. Groups who are engaged in the same activity or share common aims or ideals are held together by identification. One might speak of an 'adhesiveness' of roles. The school child only reluctantly gives up the pre-school-age habits to which it is used. The ageing often die when their role habits suddenly become functionless on their retirement. They find it as hard to adapt themselves to freedom as the young do to adapt themselves to work; in both cases the new role is unfamiliar. New identifications involve a change in the unstable equilibrium between the id, the superego, and the ego; the challenge offered by a new role must also be reconcilable with the ego ideal, must open up a 'future'. The superindividual 'style factor' in behaviour is far more obscure to us than is the process by which the individual assumes and discards roles, and we also have no adequate knowledge yet of the extent to which the social style influences the individual's self-awareness.

A young married woman had three children. During her fourth pregnancy her husband was arrested for political reasons and sent to prison. She fled with the children, spent years in camps, suffered all sorts of indignities and injustices. Eventually her husband returned, and with great energy and industry the two built up a new life for themselves. The woman suffered, however, from her husband's sexual indifference. It was impossible for her to tell him this, or to make advances to him herself. 'It is improper for a woman to offer herself to a man,' she said. All the external sufferings that had failed to alienate the two from each other had not helped them to achieve sexual intimacy. The role stereotype of how a woman should behave as a woman was an insuperable obstacle; an impersonal social principle and this woman's self-awareness had fused into an indivisible entity.

A girl student slept with her boy-friend, who also slept with other girls. They discussed these incidents in great detail. The language they used, as was the fashion at the time among their contemporaries, was that of pimps and prostitutes. The code that governed their behaviour during these conversations was reminiscent of that of Red Indians being tortured at the stake; honour required that, however great the agony, not a muscle must twitch.

These two violent extremes of behaviour have one thing in common; they are not individual, but are dictated by roles. The feelings that a woman is allowed to display in her role as a woman may change, but not the overriding compulsion of the role itself. We have previously[1] drawn attention to the fact that this clinging to roles hampers empathy in relation to the other party. The first woman's husband was obviously also fulfilling a role with which he had his own individual conflicts. Thus there was a double clinging to roles in this instance that made empathy between the two parties impossible.

In comparison with the multiplicity of our feelings, ideas, wishes, role behaviour is very restricted; it permits us to display only what is collectively prescribed as appropriate to the situation. If an individual's behaviour is governed by his role to such an extent that he cannot show feelings that compete or contrast with it, that is a pointer to an immature personality unable to break through the infantile compulsion to identification and attain individual self-expression.

The more the tabooed area of 'honour' is involved in a personal conflict, the less room is generally left for individuality. To revert to the two women mentioned above, the feeling that their honour would be irretrievably stained (in the case of the first if she 'offered herself' and in the case of the second if she showed the slightest sign of revulsion or distress) struck at the very heart of their self-feeling and self-awareness; their self-knowledge, identity, self-esteem, were threatened with collapse. We are confronted with the apparent paradox that in one case infringing a taboo in order to take a step to obtain a freer understanding in sexual matters and in the other a retreat to intimacy from a remorseless banalization of the sex act were both impossible for the same reason – the ego ideal did not permit it. In both cases the ego ideal coincided with the type of role prescribed by the group. This was taken up into the super-ego where, alien as it was (because of its inaccessibility), it nevertheless exercised the function of dictating what the self should be. Many group moralities encourage this by declaring that the group (clan, race, nation) is everything and the individual nothing. Thus the individual must develop no critical ego; instead, he must identify himself completely with his role, for taking any other course would bring him only harm.

## Searching for new collective attitudes

We have quoted examples of what two groups have recognized as typical feminine behaviour. Their repertoire of roles of course included corresponding patterns of behaviour for 'husband' and 'lover', and in both cases the male and female patterns geared into and supported each other. A much more obscure question – to reiterate – is that of how role patterns originate. Why was a collective taboo that restricted sexuality followed within such a short space of time by another that called for promiscuity? When the life of an individual is looked at a little more closely, all theories based on 'a swing of the pendulum' turn out to apply to no more than a single component of the situation, for both patterns of behaviour reveal a deficient capacity so to incorporate biological needs into the ego as to establish an equilibrium enabling the individual to cope with her situation in life. It should be added that both women became neurotically ill as a verifiable consequence of the irreconcilability of the requirements of their role with the demands of their critical ego. The latter had manifested themselves during their development, but had never been able properly to break through. The resulting neurotic illness can thus be regarded as a protest – an unsuccessful one – against a mutilation inflicted by society, its imposition of a role. So far as the symptoms are concerned, it was regressive, but in so far as it was a protest that brought about the conflict, it was progressive. An apparently 'better adapted' individual would not have experienced it; he would have shared in the collective neurosis without showing any sign of personal discomfort.

However, the sum-total of the frustrations not consciously articulated in the ego of the members of the group expresses itself in an attitude of collective quest, a readiness to accept new binding collective patterns. That is one of the reasons for the dropping of accustomed patterns of behaviour and the adoption of new. If the social processes as a whole are relatively stable, if they cause little unrest, psychical frustrations can be tolerated for long periods without breaking through traditional forms; but if the basic economic structure, the conditions of production, are shaken, the resulting insecurity can easily set changes of behaviour in train. These considerations make the process to some extent intelligible (but not self-evident, which really means not understood). The rise and fall of large groups involved in radical changes in the productive process are bound to cause anxiety on the one hand and tremendous libidinal expectations on the other. We have identified the tendencies to make increasing demands and to press for immediate instinctual satisfaction, and manifestations of elementary fear, as collective id and primitive ego reactions in the constitution of our society.

*Group need of a boundary line*

Many new groups and sub-cultures succeed in developing traditions and surviving for generations; many quickly collapse, and many are variations on the same theme, such as adolescence. Adolescent groups dissolve as their members are absorbed by other groups; as soon as a new generation is faced with the same problems, the accent shifts and the implied comment on life changes. But all these group formations, whether big or small, invariably feel the need clearly to mark themselves off in some way from outsiders. In this respect the interesting psychological fact deserves to be noted that it is only in appearance that the demarcation line is laid down in relation to the outside world. Incorporation into the group also means recognition of a demarcation line within the individual, separating the part of himself that he keeps for himself from the part that is in contact with the group. The two women mentioned above could not reveal to their partners inner needs of theirs which were out of harmony with their group's role stereotype. An intense fear of being *touched* made them conceal that part of themselves that could not be fitted into the role, and this made that part of their personality an alien, disturbing factor.

Groups that have developed over a length of time and acquired a strong collective identity have little tolerance for ways of life that diverge from their own. They generally develop great intolerance for and a collective fear of contact with outside groups. Alien ways of behaviour are disapproved of and tacitly result in exclusion. Also there is a great deal of watchfulness for signs of that part of the personality of members of the group that does not fit in with recognized group behaviour. The arrangement of mirrors which used to enable one to look out of the window from behind the curtains and see what was going on in the street outside – it is still occasionally to be seen in Switzerland – was a symbol of this continual watchfulness. Orwell's 'Big Brother' is no fiction; he has always existed. Sometimes he is only a harmless nuisance, but at other times he and his obvious paranoia grow to enormous proportions within a group. To quote an innocuous example, in the United States milk consumption is one of the behaviour patterns by which virtue is publicly displayed and judged. But what is a family to do when all its members – father, mother, and child, even the dog – dislike milk and never drink it? The obligatory bottle nevertheless appears on the doorstep every morning. What happens if father finally pulls himself together and cancels the order? The expression of dis-approval on the milkman's face is identical with that of the head of a strict religious community faced with the apostasy of a hitherto re-spected member. A subversive character has revealed himself; one knows what to think of such an individual in future.

In old-established groups newcomers are accepted only after a long period of mistrust. Being accepted by the group implies readiness to discard previous orientations to newcomers and to identify with them; and even then a residue of contempt for the 'naturalized' remains. Few social organizations have succeeded in bringing about real tolerance between neighbouring self-centred groups within the framework of a larger unity. In these cases selfishness and group-centred orientation have to be overcome by overriding agreement on aims important to all. This process can be seen in the development from ethnocentric patrio-tism to federalism. But new frontiers of alienation form between the larger units.

As the reaction of social fear of contact is practically ubiquitous, its motivation is to be sought, not in the peculiarity or special characteris-tics of the things to which the individual has to adapt himself, but in the process of adaptation through which the novice has to pass. Xeno-phobia is based on the fact that divergent opinions and ways of life threaten to disturb the uneasily maintained equilibrium between the prohibitions and concessions in force in one's own social order. Marriage outside one's own social group, or earning a living in a way considered inconsistent with one's status, meets with especial disapproval, for instance.[2] The strong inner coherence of castes, classes, religious denominations, and also of occupational groups with long traditions – to say nothing of linguistic groups – creates a sense of security. Only the sensitivity displayed towards divergencies betrays some part of the effort it cost to establish self-identity by way of conformity. The alien is not only without, he is also permanently present within. The trouble taken by the tone-setting classes to influence the young by way of education and to indoctrinate them with the approved morality and code of behaviour shows us that conditioned reflexes are involved in this process of cultural adaptation; and this can mean only the organization of the individual on a psychical level that to a large extent excludes the critical ego. The potential ego of every individual is thus declared to be an enemy alien, and every step taken by it in the direction of 'enlightenment' begins by running up against the resistance of accepted opinion.

*Mass regression*

Every new street or traffic artery, every new industry or administrative centre, makes revolutionary inroads into the statics of group orientation. Behaviour once tabooed becomes ubiquitous, and new taboos compete with the old. The loss of validity of established patterns and rituals has, however, indisputably resulted in signs of disorientation. When we recall that man's instinctual structure remains unchanged in spite of all the cultural changes that it feeds, these signs of disintegration will direct our attention to the biological levels of regulation. The specific ties to behaviour patterns associated with definite roles that exist in every group are obviously the expression of a biological law in human life. All the ways by which non-human forms of life establish and seek to maintain co-operation and coexistence also apply to that social animal, man; the only difference is that in the human case the tie to those laws is looser. The collapse of the delicate and more sensitive structure manifested in the individual by regressive, primitive behaviour is also discernible in regressions at group level, all the way from the primitivization of ideas in disciplined bodies down to the formation of gangs and the increasing narrowing of horizons to selfish group interests. The strange thing is that this orientation by the 'hand-to-mouth' principle is perfectly compatible with far-reaching bureaucratization. Bureaucracies are formal organizations; however hard they try to conceal their techniques from public view (as Max Weber saw so clearly[3]) and develop an autonomy of their own, they remain administrative bodies and no more. They merely administer; the 'capital' comes from elsewhere. They are therefore able to serve a terrorist régime just as well as a freer society. As their growth has more than kept pace with the growth of societies and their functions, the secret influence that they exercise has grown enormously. Hence the desire of politicians and governments, not just to control them, but to secure their absolute loyalty.

*Managers and apparatchiks*

We have said that on the biological plane the historically constant factor that causes unsettlement is the fragmentation of the instinctual equipment, corresponding to which on the psychical plane there are ego capacities of very different kinds. We shall now take a closer look at one of these, namely the 'tool brain'. Culture, including language, is always tool culture. In contrast to earlier cultural phases, the phase of industrial development has led to a chain reaction, an extraordinary increase in the interdependence of man's tools. Industrial production assumes the existence of a tool-making industry, an ever-increasing number of tools that make other tools. Their total availability represents the degree of the industrialization a country has attained. The reification of man runs parallel with the specialization of technical production (and of course the scientific research that precedes it). Physical and human productivity are planned by the same tool brain.

The repercussions of the self-generating process of technological advance on existing social relations were neither intended nor foreseen. The displacement of old social arrangements by new ones does not, however, take place rapidly or at once, even when imposed by ruthless methods of dictatorship, as is shown by the modern history of Russia. The attack on private property as a means of signalling status turned out to be a double-edged enterprise. Whatever socially pathological paths property relations may have entered upon in the course of the feudal and bourgeois ages, however provocative the situation was and still may be, property is an offspring of the biological function that causes the more highly organized members of the animal kingdom to express their individuality by marking off their 'own' territory. This cannot be abolished by decree; on the contrary, the primary social reaction to the infringement of an established property system is the fight-flight reaction.[4] Even when an upheaval leads to the overthrow of existing property relations, this is immediately followed by new arrangements, a new distribution of territory. The increasing disappearance of visible property as a sign of power has by no means led to a diminution of the aspiration for possession and power. Power no longer goes with the passive possession of land, but with the functional possession of administrative position. In the Western world the characteristic man in possession is the manager, in the east he is the *apparatchik*, the party bureaucrat. The tool that he uses and applies his intelligence to perfecting is a bureaucracy.

When a social upheaval begins, the traditional social groups and their institutions resist it, or try to transfer the old relations between governors and governed to the new forms of production. In our world this first phase is by no means concluded. In countries such as Saudi Arabia or those of South America the process has been retarded at the cost of increasing social disintegration. The self-feeling of the men employed in industrial production stubbornly insists on their right to have their say. At the same time the newly established relationships always fall short of the ideal that led to their establishment. But new forms of bondage are easier to associate with men's self-feelings, because the new privileged caste that proceeds to establish itself has emerged from their own ranks and its exercise of power has no flavour of alien rule. The ruling classes in the days of feudal society and of the capitalist-imperialist bourgeoisie had that flavour because of the social fear of contact that they showed.

*Readiness to obey and the trend to terrorism*

The formulation of this new self-feeling and its claims is influenced by ideologies that have grown with the growth of science and industrialization and preside over the shifts in power positions that have taken place in the guise of attempts to give them meaning. As industrial technique irresistibly displaces not only the traditional techniques of producing and using tools but also the techniques of socialization of the obsolete social order, and as it gives rise to great new power conflicts, a new sense of power has developed among the masses and a sense of impotence among those still loyal to the ideas associated with the old order. New experiences of unpleasure are also associated with this self-feeling; and not the least of the functions of the ideologies (as of the traditional religions) is to help to deny these or hold out the promise that things will be better in the future.

We use the ominous word 'masses' here only to indicate the quantitative increase in population without any qualitative implications. Masses on this scale are a new historical phenomenon. They make new demands on the tool brain; new techniques are required to provide for their needs. Thus concern for the special forms taken by traditional styles takes second place to overall conformist planning.

Shop-window displays provide an environment very different from the 'local colour' of the past. The guiding principle is planning, in which the individual appears as a numerical unit, at best as a type, a typical representative of an income bracket. It has been shown that the masses can be split up into categories on the basis of which the individual can be 'objectively' planned for, whether as a consumer or a voter. This puts new power into the hands of the mass planners of all kinds, which is then reflected in the ideology of the moment. Nevertheless it is impossible to shut one's eyes to the fact that all this planning is based on little historical experience. The best technical planning cannot do everything; its imperfection is reflected in a sense of insecurity, often obscurely felt and in any case hard to express in words, that has led to a regressive willingness to obey on the one hand and a similarly regressive trend to terrorism on the other. The appearance of archaic forms of rule by violence, equipped with the most modern tools and accompanied by the apotheosis of a leader and the demonization of competing outside groups, is tangible evidence of this regressive social trend, one of the concomitant phenomena of which may well be the successful carrying out of a huge electrification programme.

We are deliberately conducting this survey in dry, abstract terms without quoting controversial examples. As we are trying to gain a clearer view of at any rate some of the determining factors involved in the interaction between the constitution of society and that of its members, we must try to maintain critical detachment from conflicts conducted at a higher level of emotional excitation. Our principal theme throughout is that the challenge that proceeds from the evolution towards consciousness is inherent in all the gropings towards a new order, and the development of the tool brain is one of the elements in this process. At the same time we cannot conceal from ourselves the dimensions of the opposite trends. The self-awareness that enables us to organize our conduct independently of orientation by social role, that is, reveals a degree of insight into the dynamics of the psychical processes, plays a feeble part in world events, as it always has done. Optimism on this score would be wishful thinking, a distortion of reality. Freud described the situation as follows: 'Each individual is a component part of numerous groups, he is bound by ties of identification in many directions, and he has built up his ego ideal upon the most various models. Each individual therefore has a share in numerous group minds – those of his race, of his class, of his creed, of his nationality, etc. – and he should also raise himself above them to the extent of having a scrap of independence and originality.'[5]

### A disappointment

The great disappointment of the twentieth century is the realization that technical progress, though it brings with it many conveniences and 'freedoms from' – leisure, for instance, freedom from work – nevertheless fails to provide that 'scrap of independence'. To revert once more to the two women we mentioned above, the student displayed an extraordinary freedom from inhibition in relation to the long-tabooed field of sexuality; the wife and mother, barely ten years her senior, might well envy her this. But the younger woman had unexpectedly succumbed to a new bondage to roles which helped her not one whit towards independence – towards 'freedom to'. 'Freedom from' brought no relief to the ego, which should have been free to make its choice.

Thus we see that the possibility of advance to critical awareness of one's situation is continually sacrificed to the assumption of roles and stereotyped prejudices. The compulsions at work here derive from older levels of evolution and long historical ages; they provide over-powering competition for the more conscious level of decision. The sense of the danger we experience when we lose contact with the group as soon as we behave reluctantly and more independently is based on pre-experiences that made their imprint at the time when our psychical personality was being built up. The predominant role played by our super-ego in making decisions in the social field bears witness to this. It issues its orders unconsciously and rapidly, overwhelming the ego, which in any case is more slow-moving, because it has to find its way between alternatives and contradictions, which in collective stereotypes and patterns of action are not felt, or not yet.

Also life is made harder for our contemporaries by their situation between a past and a future. On the one hand adaptation to the con-ditions of an industrialized mass culture is forced on them by the social equilibrium in which they live, while on the other they are still partially tied to traditional values and the organizations whose task it is to maintain them. This increases the inner incoherence of the individuals on whom the burden of decision in this phase of history lies. The naïve assumption that because the individual is a somatic unity he is also a psychical unity can lead us hopelessly astray. Great and small alike take refuge in appalling oversimplifications, idealization, and demonization. The idea that there are 'two souls' in the human breast is inadequate to describe the situation. Perhaps we shall come closer to the truth if we speak of the 'momentary personalities' with whom we are frequently confronted who borrow their impulses from the immediate situation and change these in a fashion as protean as the situation itself without the individual moments ever growing into a uniform history. History assumes memory; under the pressure of our mass civilization this seems to be restricted to specialist knowledge; there is no similarly sharpened memory for one's own affective structure, for the self and the inevitable crises and breaks in its development.

*The parish-pump outlook*

It would be an undue restriction of the concept of the role if we refused to concede that it can be functionally associated with the 'scrap of independence and originality' which, when it is attained, makes de-tached insight possible. Insight into the possibility of different choices does not necessarily disturb integration into a role. No role can without violation of the truth hope to offer the key to all the possible situations concealed in it. Anyone who tries to hide behind his role in this way ends by concealing his own self in the role. This concealment of the self is sometimes displayed in grossly distorted form in the role of the judge, who sees himself defined in his legal code and bends reality accordingly. But the uncertainty of role behaviour in a world of unforeseen conflict situations encourages anxious withdrawal into stereotyped action and opinion distressingly deficient in originality.

The extraordinary lack of friction in mass societies controlled by huge bureaucracies is a frequent subject of complaint. What this reveals, however, is a poverty of experience in handling new situations; satisfaction with roles in this context indicates an increased fear of responsibility, which is vaguely delegated 'upwards'. This encourages a poverty of imagination to which consideration of a better way of responding to problems does not occur.

At the higher level – where a similar tendency, this time to 'pass the buck' downwards is possible, prevails – answers tend to be sought along the lines of the tried and tested 'parish-pump' traditions of the past. Control of public expenditure, as was demonstrated recently by Hellmut Becker and Alexander Kluge[6] in their study of its effects on cultural policy, follows the principles of the absolutist petty state of the past, and this in turn follows the pattern of the domestic economy of an old-fashioned paternalist household. Every society must of course budget properly, but forms of decentralized control are conceivable that would result in a great diminution of friction. That would involve greater responsibility at the horizontal level, however, and in particular much greater openness about the control of expenditure and responsibility for it. Both are repugnant to a hierarchical bureaucracy, in which there survives so stubbornly the paternalist form of organization, the relationship of dependence on a father who can give or withhold at his pleasure and whose resources and income are kept more or less secret from the rest of the family. To the public, parliamentary budget debates rather suggest dependence on the good or bad moods of the paternalist 'state' (that is, the bureaucracy), which enhances its power by allowing the various groups to compete for its favour like hostile brothers. Should a budgetary expert dismiss as childish this outline of the emotional side of an administrative system that claims to be completely objective, we should not allow ourselves to be misled by his skill at preparing financial estimates but should, instead, find out something about him as an individual. We should very much like to know about his feelings when he negotiates with claimants, for instance; a sense of paternal responsibility is certainly involved, but there must also be a sense of pleasure in the exercise of his power. There is no need to go to the top or even the senior level; every official who possesses and exercises the right to inquire whether this or that telephone conversation was really necessary is exercising paternal supervision. That is the only way by which order is established and people are educated to responsibiity or held blameworthy. But the 'parish-pump' conditions of the relatively poverty-stricken states of the past are transferred to an affluent society whose 'impoverishment' lies elsewhere, for instance, in the excessive pressure on the people at the top; the secret satisfactions that derive from identification with a powerful father are the most effective defence against a more efficient distribution of responsibilities.

It is well known that the huge bureaucratic apparatus of the paternalist state and all the private apparatuses erected on its pattern conceal an enormous amount of waste, the result of a smoothly operated system of avoiding responsibility that evades control. Intelligent understanding is the weaker partner; there is no experience of the possible satisfactions that would be obtainable by a redistribution of roles in harmony with the demands of the situation. Merely imagining an adult society – a society organized on the principle of equal responsibility – makes one dizzy; and, as it makes one dizzy, the idea must be a fraud and a swindle. This is another manifestation of the fear of losing contact in an environment that requires fundamental emotional reorientation. The primitive pattern of education – that of obedience to paternal commands – has left too deep an imprint on the ego ideal of every individual. Having been accustomed throughout his lifetime to hierarchical conditions, he can conceive himself only in the role of 'ruler' in his turn, and he tries as hard as he can to live up to it. The paths that he follows are well trodden. The idea that society might move up the ladder of maturity from the paternal family pattern to the stage of adult agreed decision has only very rudimentary achievements to its credit. The violence of the opposition encountered by the trade union movement (even among the working class) is attributable not only to economic reasons but also to the shock to the sense of order of the bourgeois leaders of society (and the self-ideal of the lower classes based on that pattern) caused by the idea of 'brothers' uniting against the father. We may suspect that the acquisition of equal rights by women – their acquisition of a collective role imprint really equal to that of men – will deal paternalism its death blow. But only if early upbringing is no longer overshadowed by the father-figure – from whose shadow women have hitherto never escaped – will it be possible for the paternal role not to be imitated in every sphere of life, but for authority to arise from a horizontal balance of forces. In any case, the attitude of claim and protest directed to an authority above is now directed at a fiction, because the man who exercises authority is not 'the owner' but an official who, when he surrenders or loses office, is a human being of exactly the same proportions as those who 'threaten' him, to use the animal behaviourists' term.

*Enlightenment up-to-date*

Our previous observations can be summed up by saying that old role patterns have shown a durability that has survived far-reaching changes in social reality. Though they serve the needs of a dead order and fail to serve those of the living one, they are still adhered to, because the unpleasure of experiencing the new and the disturbing extinguishes curiosity. And not only that. Roles have a protective function which the individual cannot do without so long as the world outside his familiar surroundings remains alien and threatening. Role behaviour causes curiosity to fade, and is often suppressed by certitudes dictated from above. In firmly established social orders roles can be well adapted and appropriate; but when the foundations are shattered the strangest behaviour patterns emerge, in which diminution of anxiety is sought regressively. The consequence is that, just at the time when social experimentation, a firm step forward, is called for, the institutions in whose hands decision lies adhere to the old pattern while unrest is aimlessly wasted in ties to fugitive roles. At all events, much more originality is expended on atoms than on human emotions. The tool brain prevails at the expense of insight into the self. Here lies the great division that used to run between man's instinctual nature and his conscience. Now it runs right through the field of action of the ego itself. Once more we see how emotional maturation has failed to keep pace with man's technology and his mastery of nature. The decisions we make under the influence of the new social reality bring us remorselessly closer to the key issue. Do they increase our awareness of our self or do they conceal it from us? Do they promote or hinder the trend to consciousness?

Evolution to consciousness is enlightenment. The implications of the word have greatly changed. It used to foreshadow the reign of a sovereign 'reason'. Looked at in retrospect, the sovereignty of reason to which the men of the age of Enlightenment looked forward (like the sovereignty of mind of the German idealists) seems very much tied to its time, influenced by the idea of the sovereign, the absolute ruler. Similarly, our view of man must be influenced by the social situation, among other things by the growing consensus that society can be kept alive only by the functional interdependence of all its productive elements. We therefore do not take refuge in any abstract concept of reason, but speak of an ego capable of attaining critical self-awareness in relation both to what it has learnt and to what it perceives and feels in the self. The ego has its own history, in which it has continually opposed the instinctual forces, making use of social rules and injunctions in the process, and it has often suffered defeat and passed through long periods of subservience before being again able to take the initiative. To think of reason as a human characteristic with a process of maturation leading to a fixed goal is to us a romantic dream. It is a monumental error that survives in many theological propositions and above all, to our misfortune, in the field of jurisprudence, which is the reason why jurisprudence has contributed and still contributes little to the integration of a new society but a great deal to its state of disintegration and confusion. The administration of justice is in the hands of a bureaucracy that works, not for the maintenance of the state, but for the maintenance of itself, and it is the most dangerous of all bureaucracies, as has been demonstrated. It no longer possesses the creative power of making explicit the social sense of justice, putting it into words, and, instead of searching for the fundamental rights and wrongs of the case at issue, administers a fictitious justice dictated by prevalent ideologies and propositions regarded as self-evident.

Thus enlightenment, enlightenment about the nature of man, in contemporary terms means insight into the dependence of human decisions on the basic facts of man's instinctual constitution and the destinies of the basic instinctual drives as shaped by the conditions of the social environment. Consequently, instead of relying on the self-realizing power of reason, the task is patiently to investigate how much reason man's actual environment permits him to show. The great regulators are still the prevalent role patterns, the type of equilibrium prevailing between instinctual demands and the countervailing social necessities – or what are regarded as social necessities at any particular time. Role behaviour thus depends on a continual resort to prejudices. This makes it incumbent on us as far as possible to make accessible to understanding the dynamic processes involved in assuming a role and the prejudices associated with it.

## Cast-iron alibi

The term 'social role pattern' as used in the modern social sciences refers to a complicated pattern of obedience. When assuming a role we receive a system of guidance to the social world and of binding instructions on how to behave in it. 'The functioning of society depends upon the presence of patterns for reciprocal behaviour between individuals or groups of individuals. Patterns for reciprocal behaviour are institutionalized (formalized) as status roles.'[7] The concept of status role originates with Talcott Parsons.[8] Status is defined as a 'position in a definite social pattern . . . as distinct from the individual who may occupy it . . . a collection of rights and duties'.[9] R. K. Merton uses the term 'status set' for the various social positions that an individual holds at the same time, and the term 'status sequence' for the various positions he may successively occupy in the course of his lifetime. 'Status in action' thus amounts to playing a role or, alternatively, to put it in a less friendly-sounding way, 'normative behaviour' that accentuates the 'dressing up' element involved and the element of dignity the role confers. The more successfully this normative behaviour acts as a social regulator, the better it succeeds in settling all sorts of conflicts; the less the friction that arises in reciprocal role behaviour, the more stable will be the social situation as a whole. The problem presented by the evolution to consciousness and the impossibility of obtaining a comprehensive view of the determining influences in our mass societies can be stated in a nutshell as follows: How can an inter-locking system of roles and status positions be established that will not solely or predominantly follow the hierarchical pattern? As we have seen, the one-way system of orders from above and obedience from below is no longer adequate. The alternative principle would be far greater initiative at all levels in contributing to the formation of standards and the attainment of integration by consent. This assumes a change in the self and in the sense of responsibility of every member of the group. Stated in psychodynamic terms, it means a diminution of the absolutism of the super-ego, in relation to whose commands the ego plays the part of a disciplined and unquestioning subordinate; a strengthening of the ego capacities, both in dealing with the instinctual impulses and their derivatives, the affects; and the ability to respond adequately to the demands of the environment without blind obedience to its taboos. This, however, assumes education for independence; and included in what we mean by independence is a capacity for intuitively understanding others instead of primarily seeing in them the attributes of their roles and allowing them to act as triggers for the release of our own affective behaviour.

We cannot leave the sociological definition of role without some further comment. Psychologically the discussion of roles is incomplete without recalling the 'double roles' that we continually play. It is not only spies and agents, intriguers and hypocrites, who play double roles. What we have in mind will become clear if we consider the way in which a role can be used as an alibi. The police officer who carried out his duties in an exemplary manner and in the course of them murdered a thousand 'enemies of the state' with his own hands was, during the period of his life in question, swimming on the crest of the wave of his time and not, as moralists have subsequently tried to persuade us, in the scum in its wake. The use of roles for the satisfaction of eccentric appetites is a constant temptation; at many moments in history it has made a wholesale break-through at all levels. A field-marshal, a man of great taste and sensitivity, who took his staff on a tour of the cathedrals of France and acted as an expert guide for their benefit, was capable of signing (even if he did not draft) the following army order: 'In the eastern area the soldier is not only a warrior who fights according to the rules of war, but also the representative of an inexorable national idea and an avenger of all bestialities committed on the

German and related nationalities. Therefore he must have full understanding of the necessity of severe but just retribution on Jewish subhumanity.'

When a temptation offered by a role is succumbed to, a step is taken into the pathological. The fragility of a role's purpose is much greater than we admit. It is in institutionalized roles that preverbal brutality finds its organ of speech. However far removed our way of thinking may be from its primitive origins, we must never fail to take into account the unchanging nature of instinctual forces beneath the surface of civilization; privilege is primarily based on physical prestige, with intelligence trailing a long way behind. Those who have been only partially and imperfectly socialized have been 'groomed for barbarism', as Jürgen Habermas says, are ready when a 'changing of the guard' takes place to avenge themselves for the frustrations imposed on their instinctual impulses by reason. But the objectives and the methods chosen by the vengeance for which man's indomitable instinctual nature yearns are prescribed by the restrictions, the cruelty, inherent in society itself. The repetition-compulsion of history is based on the chain of reaction by which cruelty, whether in open or clandestine fashion, is handed on. This explains the twin roles which the 'momentary personality' is able to play in such conflict-free fashion. In one role, as a member of a disciplined body, he submits to the most severe restrictions, and in the other he gives way to unbridled destructivity, and he rationalizes both with idealistic pathos. The instinctual renunciations imposed in one field are compensated for by unrestricted instinctual satisfaction in the other. If his own face vanishes in the uniformed ranks, so does the reality of the victims of his killings and violence; it becomes merely a fetish object for his own autistic drive.

*Transcending roles*

Such a solid bond between id and super-ego is established in these masochistic and sadistic automatisms that all that is left over for the ego is the humble task of devising plausible excuses. But, as regressions of this kind are not conceivable without a predisposition of the personality brought about by education, it is a mistake to concentrate only on the psychopathology of the individuals concerned. The collective responsibility of the society in which such things take place cannot be evaded. Its system produced these personalities.[10] Their excesses are comparable to an inflation; the currency remains the same.

At the other end of the scale of possible patterns of behaviour is the possibility of acquiring ego control. The human being can identify only with objects with which the outside world presents him. He must be taught how this process, which originally takes place without the intervention of the ego, can be brought to the level of conscious reflection so that it may be accepted or rejected. He must be taught how to assume a status and exercise a role in such a way that his 'scrap of independence' can become a firm possession on which he can build. The rational-sounding argument that under a reign of terror our critical independence is weak and fearful is beside the point. When independence is a functional element in society and hierarchical compulsions are resisted in 'peace time', we can count on 'excuses' for the blind outbreak of instinctual nature having smaller chances of acceptance, though this assumes that such independence will be accompanied by a diminution of the fear of man's instinctual nature. Where there has been education to independence, intuitive understanding, empathy, is possible, because the overriding compulsion of taboos has been broken. When empathy is encouraged, tolerance follows as a consequence of insight. When insight is possible, it will include insight into man's instinctual nature and exclude man's self-idealization as a being who should be free of the instinctual urges he describes as 'base' and 'sinful'.

Realization of the fashion in which we are tied to roles can lead to our making a distinction between our public and private roles. But what is the meaning of the latter? 'Private' roles are also socially prescribed. With more development conscious reflection becomes 'engaged', and our 'scrap of independence' surrenders to the resistance of our role behaviour. Thus the role is further consolidated, and at best the fusion of role and understanding becomes a model.

Transcending the roles and sets of roles that we fulfil assumes a life-long effort on our part, for we are never fully aware of the influence on apparently totally unconnected 'private' decisions of trends that we develop in exercising our roles. A questionnaire about the death penalty was sent to all the professors of surgery at German universities, and the replies were unanimously in favour of it. The reaction that that was only to be expected shows that unconsciously we do not underrate the influence of an individual's main role, and grant that it allows little elbow room for his individuality – that is, provided that one is not the individual referred to. We are not concerned here with the rightness or wrongness of the death penalty, but with the unanimity of the replies. Why should the choice of the profession of surgery determine in advance its members' attitude to the question of the appropriate penalty for an act of grave asocial aggression? However 'natural' and 'obvious' the outcome of the questionnaire may seem to us to have been, no pressure in favour of unanimity seems to have been at work in this instance. What the unanimity illustrated was the over-riding imprinting power of roles. The objection that surgery is chosen as a profession only by a certain character type is not very convincing either. It is possible that those who later become surgeons are psycho-genetically characterized by a strong attitude of curiosity and have strong constitutional aggressive impulses, and that in the course of a long learning process they succeed in converting their aggression into the specific skill required by their role. Why should this learning capacity end with the 'delicacy of touch' required of surgeons and the taming of their aggressive trends in diagnostic precision? An alternative sugges-tion seems not too far-fetched. Their unanimity in favour of the death penalty seems to point to a strong counter-cathexis of the ego against the pressure of aggressive trends. In their professional role those trends have to be rigidly controlled. But the idea of the death penalty for murderers provides an opportunity for a scrap of satisfaction for pre-social instinctual trends by guiltless (because socially sanctioned) identification in fantasy with the executioner. If we assume the validity of this interpretation, we have yet further corroboration of the univer-sal presence of the basic infrastructure beneath the level of social status attained.

Roles, apart from leading to group formation, provide ready-made techniques for controlling instinctual impulses in social life. At the same time, however, they perform a kind of 'blind eye' function, for they provide outlets for crude, selfish, instinctual wishes to emerge under respectable moral auspices. That is not the least of the reasons for the satisfaction that men find in them. Greater awareness of the extent to which we are acting roles or being our true 'selves', and of the strength of the temptation to use the role as an excuse, is certainly bound in many situations to increase the number of renunciations imposed on us. This process can be successful only if the renunciations are of a type capable of yielding satisfaction. There is no doubt that the possibility is largely dependent on the way in which we are initiated into our roles.

# XI

# Prejudices and Their Manipulation

'Freedom is a very great reality. But it means, above
all things, freedom from lies.'

D. H. LAWRENCE[1]

## Human rights v. prejudices

So enormous is the power of prejudice that any attempt to gauge its
influence is bound to fall short of the reality. Every psychological
theory of prejudice fails to do justice to the extent of the phenomenon;
the reality is always far worse. Exaggeration is unfortunately practically
impossible in this connection. Our daily lives are filled with choices
imposed by prejudice. The gulf between a conceivable and desirable
reality in which men had succeeded in overcoming the prejudices that
divide them and reality as we know it is obvious if we glance at the
constitutions of modern states. The fundamental rights proclaimed in
them are in striking contrast to the tradition of prevailing prejudices.
Article III of the Basic Law of the German Federal Republic, for
instance, states: '(i) All men are equal before the law. (ii) Men and
women have equal rights. (iii) No one shall suffer disadvantage
or advantage by reason of his sex, extraction, race, language, birthplace
or origin, faith, or religious or political views.' A state that declares its
basic principle to be such freedom from prejudice thereby proclaims itself
to be the enemy of all traditional prejudices. The fundamental rights of
which it becomes the guardian have a double function, however, the
protection of prejudice and the prevention of its unjustifiable application. While having prejudices is no crime, their militant propagation
at the expense of others is an illegitimate incursion into the others'
freedom. The Brockhaus Encyclopaedia defines fundamental rights as

the 'unassailable and inalienable right to freedom from state inter-vention or compulsion that everyone possesses by reason of his human nature; these rights are not granted or lent by the state, but must be acknowledged and guaranteed by it'.

But to what extent do the representatives of the state act on these principles, and to what extent do its citizens act in conscious awareness of such freedom and obligation to tolerance? Or do the constitutions of states tell us, not so much about what happens in practice, as about the moments of insight in which the 'founding fathers' allowed them-selves to be guided by their critical ego and their intuitive understand-ing of the reality of others? Are these solemn declarations not similar to those of a conclave, made far from the tumult of the world and having no real impact on contemporary passions? The power of interests, which are much closer to the instinctual infrastructure of mankind, easily reduces such basic principles to scraps of paper. The discrepancy between the intellectual efforts of the drafters of constitutions and the slight proclivity of the common man to behave in a manner appropriate to the ego and defy prejudices and selfish behaviour even when the latter threaten their long-term interests can only be sorrowfully noted. No alternative to this remains open to us. In justice to the ego, we must accept things as they are without discouragement and stick to our aims through phases of frustration. We are ourselves part of the state, even though its actual as distinct from its paper constitution increasingly excludes us from involvement in its affairs. Nevertheless it is in our power to observe its basic principles, and thus help to influence the degree of self-awareness in which society lives, for that is the real social medium. The basic concept underlying the legal constitution of the state is on a higher level, its ideal being the overcoming of self-centredness. Whether this is to remain empty verbiage or to become a principle of self-orientation depends on the friendliness or hostility to consciousness of the groups that constitute the state. If the structure of the state is authoritarian, awareness of prejudices is difficult to come by, because to a large extent they coincide with the dictates of authority about which no doubts are permitted.

The proposition that all men are equal is itself a prize example of a prejudice. But the principle that they should enjoy equality before the law is an achievement which required the breaking down of a whole chain of dominant prejudices dating back to primitive antiquity. It demonstrates the strength of the evolutionary growth of conscious-ness. The principle of equality before the law throws light on the dis-tance that separates human from animal societies. It took thousands of years for it to be enshrined in legislation. Not until 1861 did Tsar Alexander II grant personal freedom to twenty-three million serfs who, with their children and children's children, had hitherto been the personal property of their landlord, who was also their judge. In Germany serfdom was abolished in Baden in 1783, before the French Revolution, but it was not finally abolished until the revolution of 1848. In countries in which an absolutist feudal aristocracy still prevails the slave trade still survives, in spite of all declarations of human rights. It is a long road that leads from the death of Spartacus (71 B.C.) by way of Magna Carta (1215), the Habeas Corpus Act (1679), the Bill of Rights (1689) – in which equality and liberty were first stated to be innate and inalienable human rights – and the French Revolution to our own Basic Law. That the struggle to ensure these rights is not yet over is reflected by the abstention of the Soviet Union and other states from the vote for the Declaration of the Rights of Man at the United Nations on December 10, 1948.

A prejudice can be plainly seen to be a prejudice only when its origin has been discovered. The principle of equality before the law can be established only when the reasons given to justify the previous in-equality have become manifestly untenable. To those privileged under the old system (by God's grace, by reason of their birth), this means an upheaval of the whole social order that guarantees them preferential treatment before the law. Thus establishing the principle of equality involves a major struggle for power and is associated with a whole history of revolutions and counter-revolutions. Every conflict of collectively shared prejudices is, however, a grim struggle, not only for external power, but also for inner certitudes. Those who adhere to group prejudices gain certitude from them, inner certitude about the 'higher' order on which their claims to power and social status depend, whether they rely on the mythical advantages of their family tree, fair hair, or any other characteristic that appears to demonstrate their manifest superiority, while the same prejudices compel the unprivileged to reconcile themselves to the marks of their inferiority.

From the psychological point of view, we must distinguish between two aspects of prejudice. The first is the economic function it fulfils in mental life. The relationship of senior and subordinate that is established between a prejudice and the ego reflects an actual power relationship in the outside world. The prejudice ensures frictionless adaptation to the hierarchy of subordination, sparing the ego the conflict involved in deviation or revolt. Secondly, there is the part played by prejudice in the guidance of psychodynamic processes. By that is meant the part it plays in the stabilization of psychical equilibrium. A prejudice spread throughout a community will have a similar effect on many of its members but a different effect on some. In one instance it may associate itself with other prejudices or with instinctual surpluses seeking discharge, while in another it may remain relatively uncathected and have little practical importance.

The relatively stable cathexis that accrues to a group's central prejudices and the reactions that this leads to in character formation often provide sure clues to the group's trends. The way authority is exercised in it, the extent of its tolerance, its severity, its restrictions, its repudiations of instinctual drive, are all more or less deeply implanted in the character structure of its members, enabling one to say: 'Tell me what your prejudices are, and I'll tell you in what kind of political system you feel at home.' Thus prejudices represent an important aspect of obedience, an aspect that extends deep into the sphere of unconscious psychic regulation.

## Obedience to prejudice

Picking up the thread of our earlier reflections, we can recognize engulfment in prejudice as the result of learnt obedience and obedience to conscience. Associated with every firmly established prejudice is the tendency to react in the manner dictated by it. Prejudice treats its object as one familiar to it from its own experience, though in reality the process is prescribed by external or introjected authorities. All doubt about whether they are right is stifled. Where certitude prevails doubt is excluded, and this *limitation of the possible* is the essence of the matter. We are guided by such certitudes in innumerable situations. We experience the world piecemeal in a series of *a priori* prejudices. 'Certitude' gets the better of critical judgement – often in spite of directly conflicting experience. A familiar example is the anti-Semite who will not allow anyone to say anything against his only Jewish friend, though this does not in any way affect his overriding anti-Semitism. The pseudo-logic with which such inconsistency is defended lies behind the saying that there is an exception to every rule. What can certainly be described as prejudice is surrounded by a wide and hazy marginal area; superstition and articles of faith, illusory ideas and lofty ideals, and not least scientific first principles, should all be examined with the same open-mindedness.

Thus the prejudices it obeys reveal something of a society's state of psychical equilibrium and the means by which it maintains this, particularly through the concomitant affects. Adherence to prejudice can be consistent both with peaceability and with destructive aggressivity; thus it makes a great difference whether prejudices are cathected by libidinal or aggressive instinctual components, and also whether a prejudiced attitude (for instance, a principle of absolute non-violence associated with metaphysical rewards and punishments) binds the two instinctual components or tends to dissociate them. Does the non-violence taboo, for instance, involve violent repression of the aggressive side instead of integrating it? In general it would seem that the process of dissociation prevails and fans the unrest in the world. The extent to which the prejudice-guided mode of thought is able to impose itself in mass societies largely suppresses the impulse to objective judgement, and this applies at all status levels. The concomitant emotions are left unquestioned too, because the valuation contained in the prejudice makes them seem self-evident. Great alertness is required to detect the situations in which we can be misled by prejudice – and that cannot be expected of everyone; nor can it be held against him that he does not feel under an obligation to be completely honest with himself and does not, what with manipulated information and the gaps in it, follow a path other than that which is suggested to him. Nor is it evidence of limited intelligence; rather, it is evidence of deficient education in making use of it.

One of the psychodynamic characteristics of prejudices is their power of permanently binding cathected energy to the ideas contained in them. The libidinal component is undoubtedly deeply involved – we are fond of our prejudices and are reluctant to give them up; but this libidinal cathexis frequently opens the way to aggression. The object associated with the prejudice can then easily become an object of hatred, of surplus aggressivity looking for something on which to discharge itself. From the aspect of narcissistic instinctual satisfaction, prejudices often turn out to be a positively ideal solution of the economic problem; both instinctual components obtain satisfaction, though at the expense of the object distorted and alienated by the prejudice.

This gives us an important criterion. If we adopt an opinion based on prejudice, we may merely have made a mistake. If we are able to discover and correct it, we did not so much succumb to a prejudice as jump prematurely to a conclusion. Our opinion was not cathected with instinctual energy, and it played no significant part in our internal economy. But ridding our mind of error begins to grow difficult when our prestige is involved in the erroneous view, that is, when our narcissistic cathexis is faced with the threat of a humiliation.

Distinguishing between the functions of objective judgement and those of prejudice is even more difficult in the daily business of the courts. Our law books are riddled with prejudices which have nothing to do with principles of justice – on the lines of our Basic Law, for instance – but everything to do with the psychical economy of the groups who succeeded in codifying their prejudices into law. The grotesque sexual bans imposed under Puritan influence, which were carried to such extremes that in some places kissing a girl in public was a punishable offence, show that collective neuroses, and even perversions, can be given legal sanction. There would be no difficulty in demonstrating the absurdity of many prejudices enshrined in our legislation and showing them to be what they are, but that would bring us into conflict, not only with unwritten taboos, but also with taboos written into the legal code, which is the greatest reinforcement that prejudice can have.

Once more we may recall Pascal's remark that the greatest crimes have been considered meritorious by those who committed them, and that it is 'custom alone that decides what is right', for it is custom that provides the 'mythical foundation of its authority'. A prejudice can be very accurately defined as an accepted opinion based on insufficient evidence, sometimes associated with a system of punishments and penalties. Prejudices that leave a mark are the result of the compulsion to use neurotically fixed defence mechanisms. Even the most absurd laws in their way contribute to maintaining equilibrium, and this makes it difficult to disentangle them from the rational elements with which they are intertwined.

Thus cathected prejudices are components of the mechanism by which the ego seeks to come to terms both with the way in which authority is exercised in the social world and with the domination of the instincts. It is a primitive method, on the level of that of neurotic symptom formation. The most important consequence is that the ego weakens itself in defence mechanisms instead of strengthening itself by integration. Warding off what is hidden behind prejudice, avoiding anxiety-rousing insight into reality, which is always strange on first acquaintance, weakens the forces of the ego and makes it doubly reluctant to bring the concealed to light. It is a vicious circle. The history of science, with its long struggle against mythical authority, demonstrates the power of the ego to destroy customary modes of thought (and thus undermine social orders); that is, the power of the ego when it begins 'analysing' instead of using up its strength in defence mechanisms. Those who loudly proclaim their hostility to any kind of analysis of human behaviour (which is of course yet another prejudice) generally omit to mention that the results of analysis generally point to the necessity of a new order. But it is easier and more comfortable to use the ego defensively than to apply its forces to the investigation of reality, particularly when the nature of man himself is concerned.

Granted the human sense of strangeness in the world, the comfort of the certitude that prejudice provides is indispensable in the long period of individual growth and development, and if the analogy does not seem too bold we may assume the same to be true of the youth of humanity as a whole. To put the most favourable construction on the phenomenon, we may say that prejudices are like certain drugs; in moderate doses they provide relief, but in toxic doses they ruin the lives of those who indulge in them. But it is far harder for the psychologist and the sociologist than it is for the pharmacologist to determine the toxic dose, for they have to estimate this, not from the relatively easily ascertainable variations of physiological reaction, but from the extremely fluid relations of interdependence that prevail in individual societies. The Areopagus of extinct gods who have been worshipped in the course of the ages shows that men have always been conscious of their weakness; but the ways in which they have sought to cope with the unknown and the terrible have varied between the extremes of fearless inquiry on the one hand and concealment by projection on the other, between gentleness and charitableness and draconian severity, both to themselves and to others. It seems reasonable to conclude from this that none of the solutions to the human problem that have been offered can or should be universally applied. The difficulty of the task cannot be evaded. But condescending contemplation of the prejudices of the past is insufficient preparation for the careful study of those in which we ourselves have taken or still take pleasure.[2]

George Bernard Shaw, speaking in a voice very different from that of the preambles to our modern constitutions, said: 'We must face the fact that society is founded on intolerance. There are glaring cases of the abuse of intolerance; but they are quite as characteristic of our own age as of the Middle Ages.'[3] Intolerance and ignorance go hand in hand; and sometimes, as we have pointed out, they establish a vicious circle, one continually reinforcing the other. Human societies are so intolerant because they are so ignorant about themselves, and keep themselves so ignorant. As we have pointed out, the importance of intolerance to the social economy can be traced back to a biological root; it helps to maintain group equilibrium, and without such equilibrium social life relapses into anarchy. The purpose of any particular prejudice is to safeguard its holders against disturbance from the alien outer and inner world. This is generally brought about, not just by one prejudice, but by a whole set, originating in the processes of identification by which we adapt ourselves to our environment. Freud describes identification as 'the assimilation of one ego to another one, as a result of which the first ego behaves like the second in certain respects, imitates it and in a sense takes it up into itself'.[4] Identifications are indispensable for finding one's own identity but, if the ego becomes so firmly tied to another ego that the tie cannot be undone, a false identity, a false personality, is formed whose further development is blocked. The word 'false' should be treated with caution, however. We all have unresolved ties resulting from identifications. Our objective is to establish the neurotic, diseased form of tie, the total subjection that expresses itself in prejudices we are unable to shake off.

*Pseudo-rationalism*

The arsenal of arguments with which prejudices are defended is virtually inexhaustible. Often they are used with an agility and resourcefulness that takes the ground from under the critic's feet. The skilful demagogue is often a past master of this art; he has the laughter on his side, and uses it to spare his audience the unpleasure of examining reality and give them the pleasure of being able to identify themselves with the 'winning' side. This sharp-wittedness, which is often nothing of the sort but really its opposite, is an extraordinary phenomenon, after all; it strikes us as so natural because we are so easily able to practise it ourselves, or at any rate to appreciate it in others. Everyone can recall his astonishment at the fertility of his own imagination in inventing excuses in an emergency in his school days; necessity is the mother of invention. How does that come about? As we have previously mentioned, fear paralyses the more differentiated psychological processes and provokes primitive reactions such as aggression or flight, or in extreme cases panic, a pattern reminiscent of the tropism of the simplest forms of life. Here, however, we see fear stimulating the ego to considerable feats of ingenuity in the invention of plausible excuses. The paradox can be explained. The lie invented by the ego – and the content of many collective prejudices is a lie – corresponds, not with the facts of reality, but with wishes and ideas about reality as it might be. If the premise that I was the victim of aggression were correct, the conclusion (that I had to defend myself, and that it was as a consequence of this that the other party got a black eye) would incontrovertibly establish my complete innocence in the matter. But that is generally not the situation when pseudo-rationalism sets out to buttress prejudice. Where prejudices are at work the ego is faced with the task of warding off guilt and fear of retribution. What takes place is comparable with motoric flight. The ego is subjected to ruthless instinctual wishes and has to bring what actually happened (or is going to happen) into harmony with the standards of reality. Thus there are two sources of fear that have to be avoided; fear of internal impulses and fear of external sanctions. In this situation the prejudice brings notable relief. It permits a certain amount of instinctual satisfaction at the expense of, say, an outcast or some subordinate, and explains why this is innocent, not punishable. Prejudices that perform this function spare the ego a lot of defence work and help it in its task of securing pleasure and avoiding unpleasure. The disastrous result is that they strengthen self-feeling without strengthening the ego. The ego does something of which it is capable, namely thinking, not in its own cause, however, but in that of an unconscious motive and, so to speak, in a 'predigested', collectively accepted, secret language. We have already come across the several instances of such servile ego work.

The situation is aggravated by the interpretation put upon reality by the convincing though unsound arguments used to buttress the prejudice. These serve the need to cover up and obscure the desire for unilateral, selfish instinctual satisfaction and ward off retribution, felt to be just retribution for real guilt. In doing this the ego may have recourse to whole sets of prejudices that mutually support each other in a chain of so-called evidence. The more self-evident these prejudices seem to us to be when they are presented to our minds, the more easily this can happen, and this will always be the case when they enjoy wide collective dissemination and are linked with approved affect directed at approved objects.

## Influencing the man in the street

If we were in a position to be able to consider everything objectively before making up our minds, there would be no prejudice. Our capacity for objective judgement is, however, limited in two respects. We live in a world in which an incalculable number of choices have continually to be made, and if we subjected everything to objective scrutiny we should get nowhere. Even in our own personal lives we find ourselves confronted with unprecedented situations in which we have to make up our minds, though very well aware that we have never been in such a situation before and lack the capacity for judging it objectively. Also it is not rare for us to lack the courage to use the capacity even if we possess it. Courage in this context means solidity of ego structure, the ego's ability to hold fast to its object in spite of the intervention of the super-ego and the id (and also of course intimidation from the social environment) and the ability to deal with it according to its own standards. In making most of our decisions, however, as we saw in Chapter I, we inevitably fall back on conventions, customs, the experience and opinions of specialists, and hand over responsibility to them. We put our trust in accustomed rules and signals and try to make surprising and unfamiliar situations less alarming thereby. That does not necessarily mean that we are led into error, though of course this can occur. Factual opinions that I take over from others put me in a position of dependence on them, of course, but that is inevitable in a world in which the division of labour prevails. But when I take over other people's affective judgements the danger of being led astray increases rapidly. The division of labour necessarily involves reliance on the experience and opinions of others. But the combination of this with the frequent necessity of the wholesale taking over of affective attitudes is the most dangerous conceivable social constellation. It is the situation in which we live.

The other limitation of our power of judgement, contrasting with the multiplicity of outside influences to which we are subjected, derives from the relative monotony of our instinctual trends and the paths by which we seek their satisfaction or repression as the case may be. Here the issue of courage arises again. We do not dare admit to ourselves the motivations of our actions, and consequently we project them on other men and institutions. We displace into the outside world the terrifying insights we catch brief glimpses of in ourselves, and then note with relief that it is not ourselves but others who are capable of such brutal, barbarous, and disgraceful impulses. Not content with cleansing our self-image by projection, we further buttress ourselves by identifying our purified self-ideal with individual or corporate models and believe them to be capable of sweet reason totally uninfluenced by emotion. This defence against critical observation both of the self and of others is a more frequent and more permanent element in our lives than considered reflection.

It is a truism to say that we do not like looking men and things courageously in the eye, but there is more to it than that when we discover the reason. Our capacity for critical assessment is entwined in affective judgements, emotionally charged prejudices, which we cannot give up without experiencing acute anxiety. Even the first step generally fails, namely, the realization that the anxiety stems from intimidations and threats of punishment dating from childhood, and that the reality of the situation that rouses it may not be dangerous at all. The taboos and fears that we carry about with us from childhood contain a lot of magical ideas. They are still cathected, and their irrationality continues unchanged to hamper our capacity for critical thought as soon as the latter approaches them. As we have seen, however, the form taken by our defence against the instinctual side of our nature is moulded by the existing system of social values. As infringement (often only in thought) of stereotyped judgements threatens a loss of status and prestige and hence of self-valuation, the ego withdraws from the test of such dangerous reality and seeks security in prejudices. If magical threats involving a great deal of anxiety are implicated, the prejudices condense into the great taboos. The ego carries out yet another task. It has to preserve its self-respect in the face of this feeble retreat. This it does by an ingenious step in adaptation – it adopts the taboos as its ideal. That is the trick performed by subservient reason in order to restore the pleasure principle. It would seem not impossible with the aid of critical insight to arrive at a satisfactory solution of the problem of sharing out property and responsibility, or of freeing the racial and minority problems that exist in many societies from the projections with which they are burdened; it would seem not impossible to devise ways and means of coping with the effects of irrational events, for instance, to consider the most sensible frontiers to establish after a lost war with a view to avoiding involvement in new projections and counter-projections which must eventually erupt in further violence. The reason why these things do not happen is that prejudice is quicker than thought. It is formed before thought can intervene. The affective attitude to these problems follows selfish principles, even though the tribute it thus pays to the pleasure principle is exceedingly short-sighted. Thus, when we accept the views we are offered in such situations, we can be certain that they will not be detached and objective, but one-sided and fallacious. It must of course be admitted that, when once powerful collective moods have developed, testing reality can be a task that makes heroic demands on the individual, and in practice it may be condemned to futility over long periods.

The pseudo-rationalism of toxic prejudices is an instrument of government. The primitive subsoil, inimical to consciousness, from which they grow should never be lost sight of and its influence never be underrated. Relations between rulers and ruled are power relations, and as such are by no means tied to enlightened understanding. The ancient sign language of power is still at work in the most complicated social organizations just as it once was in the horde or clan, and determines who is the stronger and who the weaker. Pseudo-rationalism works in favour of the group which in existing conditions enjoys a preferential position for fulfilling its instinctual wishes; the manipulation of prejudices serves to protect its members from the resentment of their unprivileged fellows. As this process of manipulation goes far deeper than the level of conscious calculation, it would be wrong to describe it as a tactical method; it is, rather, a dynamic process that runs though history like a thread.

We must be prepared for the criticism that our analysis fails to do justice to the mind and spirit of man, and that we are on the way to reducing him to a creature of mere instinct, making history only a business of drives and being driven. The word 'reducing' must be accepted, in the sense that any analysis of complex facts is likely to hit on a new and unsuspected system of cause and effect – in the present context the permanent involvement of instinctual forces far removed from consciousness. They are the biological foundations of our life, and only a part of them can be transposed into conscious freedom. The animal part is generally despised and looked down on (generally in pre-conscious dependence on the established régime, as exemplified in ideas about being 'the agents of civilization', for instance); even among those who proudly withdraw themselves from earthly instincts and talk of mind, spirit, purpose, and other such things, as if these were freely available, the situation is not much better. The inevitable relapse comes when these high-minded gentry feel it to be their self-evident duty to behave like 'strong' and 'valiant' beasts of prey, slaughtering their fellow-men in the service of the 'spirit' and for a 'just cause'. This behaviour turns out to be compatible with their honour. We do not accept the invitation to regard mind and spirit of this kind, either in one way or in the other, as being immune from having political and social consequences, even though this should earn us the rebuke of undervaluing it in our balance sheet. If we are following a single thread, it means that we are trying to throw light on a single factor, with no megalomaniac pretensions to explaining everything. It is not always night, after all, and it is impossible to say that there will never be a state of freer interdependence between older levels of organization and historically younger ones which will enable a balance to be struck that it will be possible to regard as 'right' after critical examination and not merely because it accords with ideological wishful thinking.

The obverse side of the proud emblem of 'the free spirit of man' is lamentation about the impotence of the human spirit. That is a venerable paradox, but it should not be taken as being necessarily true for all eternity. What is required instead is the development of a methodology, a system of purely pragmatical rules, enabling us to distinguish between pseudo-rationalism and the genuine article. Social order is a necessity, but there is no such thing as the best social system for mankind; a society that came close to this ideal would permit a great deal of critical ego, would know how to track down and expose defence mechanisms, and would give ego obedience precedence over the taboos. With these rudiments of a methodology for unmasking questionable claims to authority (and equally questionable surrender to illusory beliefs in other, consolatory worlds) we are searching for the principles of a socio-psychological method of analysis which purely empirical investigation is unable to supply. In social philosophy idealism and pessimism have come to terms. 'Pessimism became a rationalization of the disquieting state of reality. It helped to shift the blame for the absence of the benefits expected from technological process on to the nature of the world instead of attributing the source of the growing evil to a social organization in which technology has shot up over man's head.'[5] The development of technology has changed man's self-awareness only to the extent that it has increased his feeling of power. The sensitive pressure on the accelerator pedal that causes the horse-power to spring to life is an experience closely related to that of flying dreams. Insight into the motives by which the individual has always been guided and his behaviour determined is not increased by these mechanical aids. On the contrary, the danger of self-deception has if anything been increased, because the techniques of handling human beings have grown side by side with industrial techniques. The persuaders threaten the critical ego in old roles and new; equipped with the findings of behaviour research and dynamic psychology, they keep the individual tractable. Knowledge is of course not the sole privilege of pure intellect; it is not seldom a professional secret of skilful incumbents of roles.

The more realistic the anthropology on which the methods of the manipulators are based, the better they are able to manipulate prejudices. That has now become a matter of general knowledge among managers of all kinds; here psychology has made a really epoch-making breakthrough. To the unpractised ego plausible presentation brings darkness just where light ought to be shed; this makes the real world as inaccessible to it as did the demonology of the old days with its sacred, unenterable precincts. Nevertheless the possibility of evading these conscious or unconscious traps exists. It lies in the development of the critical ego capacities and their coherent organization, which provides the only means of seeing through the taboos in which pseudo-rationalism wraps up the facts. The points must be established at which the umbilical cord of interests joins the similarly shadowless world of conformities. The art of measuring the rationalizations of prejudice against reason can, however, be most successfully practised in the observation of one's own behaviour. This again assumes society's teaching the individual how and when to give up identifications, and which ones, and how they should be transcended in order, as Nietzsche put it, to become a 'universally right-seeing eye'.

Vulnerability to prejudice is no less a problem than that of giving it up. If it is encouraged in the early years while the child, still a stranger in the world, is naturally thrown back on identifications, social standards extinguish the sense that one could become a self, or even that one ought to. The greater the fear of the model that identifications have to diminish, the more powerful they are. Thus the greatest tendency to prejudice exists among communities based on fear. Toxic and ineradicable prejudices can consequently be described as the result of over-identification. Even the slightest degree of uncertainty causes unpleasure, in which the individual regresses to mimicry, to identification with the model. If he has not been taught how to tolerate unpleasure, or if all non-conformity is threatened with severe punishment, relapse into prejudice is the only way left of saving some rudiments of the pleasure principle.

Whenever one is faced with a decision the initial reaction is unsureness. But this unsureness, this ignorance, alienates us from the majority to whom the situation obviously presents no problem. Fear of inferiority is a strong (if not one of the strongest) motives that cause one to take refuge in the conflict-sparing certitude of prejudice. 'Men seem to carry about an agonizing fear of the "I don't know" inside themselves,' says Hofstätter in describing this situation, 'as if hardly anything were so painful as having to admit to ignorance. I believe that that brings us to the root of that strange phenomenon, public opinion. Inner tensions associated with the state of suspension involved in not knowing are at once greatly diminished when a patent remedy is hit on.'[6] Prejudice releases us from this 'state of undifferentiated tension';[7] it gives us direction, and a pattern for action in emergencies. Unsatisfied trends which have been looking for an object immediately bind themselves to the certitudes and hopes that the prejudice promises, and anxiety is diminished. Hence the method of the demagogue, as Hofstätter points out, is artificially to increase the sense of uncertainty before offering his solution. Intensified anxiety lowers the threshold of regression, and the tendency to identification increases to the point of psychical symbiosis.

### Sacrifice of the intellect

The paternalist society made ample use of prejudice. Its socially formative certitudes converged in the belief in a father God by whom these certitudes were consecrated. The distinction between profane knowledge, which was liable to correction, and sacred knowledge, which required the sacrifice of the intellect in this world, is not an ancient one. Until the advent of the great discoverers of scientific laws, profane knowledge took second place. The highest prestige was enjoyed by the incumbents of roles which by virtue of the divine blessing or birth put them closer to the father God than ordinary mortals. This is not the place to discuss the subterranean survival of this hierarchical pattern of authority since the Reformation, the American Declaration of Independence, the French Revolution, and through the permanent scientific revolution of our time. The fact remains that the decline in the prestige of sacred knowledge and its representatives continues irresistibly.

The scene has changed to the extent that rebellion against the father has lost its central importance. Religious tyranny gave birth to religious heresies – going all the way to fanatical atheism – which yielded nothing to it in intolerance. When we come across this antithesis to paternal absolutism nowadays it is no more than an anachronism. The social processes that led to the growth and development of industrial mass society continually and often unintentionally eroded the image of the venerable, omniscient, omnipotent father. There is every sign that paternalist ideas in church and state hardly affect the lives of the masses and have ceased to awaken any response in them. True, residues of magical modes of thought have been greatly reinforced in our time. Sectarianism as an expression of group neurosis and over-dimensional ideals that can also be regarded as group neurosis still hold many under their spell, some permanently, some only briefly.[8] But in populations counted in millions many are still only few. The 'grey' masses of our huge, amorphous cities are indifferent to all claims based on paternalist authority.

The nation is still referred to out of habit as *la patrie*, the fatherland, land of our fathers, etc., but the passive, demanding attitude to it betrays a deeper tie; it is nuzzled against as if it were a mother goddess with innumerable breasts. As national and private undertakings grow more closely interlinked and those in positions of responsibility grow more and more remote, the technical landscape takes the place of mother nature. Booms and crises are only superficially regarded as 'artificial', the result of decisions made within society; in the fantasy world of the salary and wage-earner they have a quality resembling that of the vagaries of the weather. They are accepted rather like the fat years and lean years distributed by the mother goddess, and are responded to either euphorically or dysphorically instead of being taken as a challenge to social criticism as in the age of class struggles. The concentration is on technical development, not on bringing about a change in men's minds; technology is relied on to bring about incubator conditions. Only a few regard this, as Henry Miller does, as an air-conditioned nightmare.

*From divine state to divine bureaucracy*

However hard politicians and employers may try to keep the paternalist principle alive – and the trade unions need it too in their role as contracting parties – the millions are no longer interested, their frame of mind is quite different. To their basic expectations the idea that the chief aims in life are independence and aggressive competition are totally alien; and conditions are such that for most of them these are very unrealistic aims in any case. That is why campaigns for higher wages, for instance, no longer resemble a fierce conflict with a severe father figure; regression has gone deeper than that and left the structure of the super-ego, the sense of duty, responsibility, and self-restraint behind. Production is lavish, they drink lavishly from the mother's breasts, and the objective is the somnolence of society. Demands and claims are made on a level that makes a differentiated experience of life superfluous. The state of mind we are describing has a vague quality, it is in the air, but we cannot localize it like a pin-prick. All the same, these intangible moods are basic; they make us see the world with different eyes, they make the world itself seem different. They are an all-pervading phenomenon, specific and at the same time non-specific (that is, not localized) reactions to environmental conditions as a whole. They originate in a 'processing of information' about inner needs and outside conditions, which are worked up into a total impression, a complex of feelings that awaken echoes of affects and hopes. Circular arguments of course establish themselves in the process, giving greater clarity and durability to the moods and helping to stabilize them. The paranoid, euphoric, depressive, aggressive, total climate of the culture is easy to detect but harder to describe convincingly. The fundamental mood of regressive, passive expectation of happiness is not dissipated just because activity and initiative appear in places. Only in extreme cases is the depressive individual completely paralysed by his state of mind; in ordinary circumstances, though shadowed by depression, he takes an active part in life, but his activity and capacity for experience are coloured by depression, despondency, and complaint.

The dissemination of an infantile demanding attitude, the withdrawal from the paternal world of articulated effort and its risks, can – if it develops into a salient collective characteristic – have no cause other than the devaluation of all the characteristics that the paternalist culture once had. When social processes as a whole allow few opportunities for initiative because the productive apparatus requires and produces unindependent masses, the spirit of rivalry (to take just one point) can no longer be satisfied by the development of the individual's initiative, but turns into envy and 'begging behaviour' resembling that of nestlings on the approach of their parents bringing food. This may have been the plight of members of hierarchical bureaucracies ever since hierarchical bureaucracies began, but now it is the plight of the bureaucratized, administered masses. It is not just one type of human destiny among others that influences the general mood; it has become the general destiny. This has brought about a fundamental change of scene.

The development of this new homogenized state of dependence has run parallel with the break-up of the paternalist world and all its apparatus. The latter has been replaced by a 'park' of independently producing machines; the sources of energy that guide the whole thing and keep it going remain hazy. The suckling gets its milk, but cannot ask where it comes from. All it insists on is that it should get it, and it does so imperiously. It would be easy to dismiss this as a cheap analogy, but that would be underrating the continuity of psychical processes. Regression is a harking back to patterns of experience that remain alive beneath later ones by which they have been overlaid. If the individual is driven back to them in an emergency, they are fully revived. Regression serves to evade reality, but it leads to a resuscitation of realities that were once experienced and are now emotionally relived. This leads to a vigorous double life. At the conscious level argument takes place with the more or less rational symbols of everyday speech, but expectations are simultaneously awakened that do not derive from rational calculation. Susceptibility to prejudice and emotional pliability are ruthlessly exploited, for instance, in campaigns for higher wages or higher sales: the practitioners of the art have learnt skilfully to adapt themselves to the now general expectation of compensation in this world for the unpleasure experienced in it.

As we mentioned in the chapter on the 'invisible father', we are far from overlooking the effects of our constitution on the sheer increase in population and the adaptation that has had to be made to industrial civilization. The survival of institutions such as the family, the churches, and national units as guardians of order cannot blind us to the fact that they are no longer central to people's lives. Their libidinal cathexis is steadily approaching zero. We are told, for instance, that barely one per cent of the German Protestant population goes to church on Sunday. The modern forms of propaganda used by the churches or the army do nothing to change the situation; they arouse no deeper interest than propaganda of other kinds, though the great majority of church members take incomparably more pleasure in a well-written report on the test of a new car model than they do in a Sunday sermon. We state this without irony and without pleasure, but we state it; it is, indeed, a fact familiar to everybody, though it has not, apart from some expressions of backward-looking wishful thinking, received the attention it deserves.

*Blows to pride and the response*

The new patterns of prejudice illustrate the 'oral' character of the regression that has taken place (in succession to the characteristic striving for 'anal' security of the paternalist society, with its approval of possessions acquired as the result of hard work). They circle round the 'standard of living' complex and everything associated with it. As against the ascetic, anti-self-indulgent trend of the bourgeoisie, with its concentration on percentage yields, the emphasis on consumption has brought a more cheerful, more relaxed note into daily life. After successive waves of destruction and devaluation, the moral considerations associated with the values of the traditional paternalist society, in which the head of the family ensured its security, are no longer listened to. Widespread dependence on allowances and pensions gives the state a primary maternal aura, and a complaisance towards its biddings is therefore expected which would be more in place in the nursery. In bourgeois society conflict centred round succession; the younger generation struggled with the older for accession to the latter's authority, its role privileges, of which the greatest was the control of its property. In industrial mass society the struggle is for a permanent security of quite a different type; permanent security means being looked after for life. This is producing a completely different view of what success consists of – namely, securing oneself a place at the breasts of the administrative goddess as early in life as possible. This necessarily brings about a new kind of 'good behaviour' which did not exist in a society in which feudal and aristocratic, bourgeois and proletarian claims to authority conflicted with each other.

This revolution is as plainly reflected in the cathected content of old prejudices as it is in the nature of the new. One no longer attaches oneself to anything that does not in some way give physical satisfaction or partake of the nature of a toy. When a new technical gadget is successfully launched with the aid of the prejudice mechanism, prestige is associated with the toy, whether it be a camera or a private bar or a private swimming-pool. But, in accordance with the satiety curve, satisfaction of the impulse predictably leads to loss of interest, which has to be stimulated afresh by the offer of something new.[9] This is in striking contrast to the paternalist society, with its ideal of stability accompanied by simultaneous frustration of physical sensual pleasure.

In the consumer society prejudices change continually in accordance with fashion, but they are continually renewed. They do not go deep, but the readiness to follow them remains constant. Hectic mobility in the search for satisfaction and boredom when it has been obtained are the two poles between which the consumer oscillates as soon as he is released from the unpleasure of production.

Here, then, we have a psychical condition characterized by the fact that the greater part of its content is introduced from outside and also by a far-reaching withdrawal of the libido to a narcissistic cathexis of the physical self. We set out on this survey of it in order once more to illustrate the extent of the regression that has taken place. This regression is a consequence of the loss within a few decades of an environment by which many generations were formed. We are not here concerned with investigating the type of character formation associated with the age before the population explosion and the development of modern science and its exploitation, that is, the character structure of the paternalist society; we are concerned with the relative consistency of the response to the new fundamental conditions of life, which have produced a new type recognizable over and above all individual variations. Numinous and profane forms of authority formed a unity that left no one unaffected. The age of the Enlightenment in all its manifold aspects shattered that unity which, so far as the masses are concerned, has left behind nothing but puzzling traces expressed in an almost unintelligible language. Attempts to revive the past are bound to fail, for the evolutionary step towards greater consciousness is irreversible. The symbolic language hitherto used by religion has ceased to be intelligible in a world in which the outlook from which the images stemmed has disappeared. It does not follow, however, that the area of experience that has hitherto been covered by the word 'religion' is being buried by this. That depends on other lines of development which are not regressive but provide a means of expression for the growth of consciousness.

Science has not only made man more confident and given him independence, it has also struck blows at his deepest feelings. Freud[10] mentioned three such blows to pride that broke through powerful barriers of prejudice. These were (i) the cosmological blow administered by Copernicus, who removed the earth from its central position in the universe; (ii) the biological blow struck by Darwin with his discovery that man is 'of animal descent, being more or less closely related to some species and more distantly to others'; and finally (iii) the psychological blow involved in the discovery of unconscious mental activity that disputes the rational ego's authority over the self. 'For this mind is not a simple thing; on the contrary, it is a hierarchy of super-ordinated and subordinated agencies, a labyrinth of impulses striving independently of one another towards action, corresponding with the multiplicity of instincts and of relations with the external world, many of which are antagonistic to one another and incompatible.' This succession of narcissistic blows had to be coped with, and we can observe regressive and progressive attempts to do so taking place side by side. The validity of science is simply denied, or the distinction between science on the one hand and religion on the other is persisted in, or the human state is philosophically exalted. The challenging discoveries of science are made to seem innocuous by the defence mechanism of encapsulating and isolating them, regarding them as having no bearing on our knowledge as a whole, or solace is found in phoney attempts to demonstrate that there is no inconsistency between science and traditional religion of the type of *The Bible as History*. Another, and the most common, form of defence is withdrawal of interest from the disputed area, indifference to all attempts to find a unifying principle of order in the universe. This appears in the attitude of passive, vegetative dependence we have described, combined with the anarchical protest that breaks out when the sources of satisfaction do not flow with sufficient abundance. It is also reflected in behaviour during the crises of adolescence. The uncontrolled oscillations of mood and affect familiar to us at the age of puberty sometimes take the form of blind group tantrums characteristic of infantile protest behaviour.

Coping progressively with the humiliating blows to human pride calls for a new approach recognizing both the limitations and the infinity of the knowable. There is certainly no need for any sacrifice of the intellect. As an example of responsible faith we may quote one of the last letters of the physicist Max Planck, written on June 18, 1947. 'I can assure you that I have always been of a deeply religious disposition,' he wrote, 'though I have never believed in a personal God, let alone a Christian God.'[11] After what has gone before, it cannot be regarded as a disparagement of religious experience if we describe the doctrine of men being the children of God as childish. The child experiences a pre-verbal sense of security with its mother, and then another, associated with the business of practical living, with its father. In both cases the sense of security is embodied in real persons, but there is nothing to show that the 'world' is governed in a fashion analogous to that of the human family. Our first experiences of order are associated with human social arrangements; we have, indeed, constantly reiterated, in the light of social trends that are causing them to disappear, how essential to the satisfactory development of the child the two parents are in their different roles.

No one who has not had direct experience of security in the person of a model can learn to tolerate the greater doubts and uncertainties that result from conscious thought. This conscious thought must renounce identification of the unknown and the unknowable with the authority of an omniscient father. It must renounce security by prejudice. 'In the struggle for the good,' Einstein wrote, 'teachers of religion must have inner greatness and drop the doctrine of a personal God, that is, renounce the well-spring of fear and hope from which the priests of old derived such tremendous power.' Since the liberation from serfdom a struggle has been in progress for man's religious liberation, and the indifference of the masses to religion shows the difficulty of the task. Max Planck's and Einstein's religious attitude derived, not from obedience to conscience, but from obedience to the ego. Undoubtedly this represents an advance towards the fatherless society; not to a society obliged to kill the father in order to establish itself, but sufficiently adult to be able to leave him in order to stand on its own feet.

Here too we must be careful not to suffuse the word 'progress' with any optimistic glow. It is meaningless to say that being adult is better than being a child. First one is one and then the other, each in its own due time. If we look at the pathological symptoms of our society as dispassionately as we look at ancient times, we shall be able to distinguish between two types of fatherlessness. In the first the father-figure is lost at the time when the child vitally needs him for the building up of its identity (in his absence it becomes dependent on the mother for the whole of its lifetime). In the second the father has not been lost, but the individual has achieved a self-identity that enables him to shake off the father-figure and think not exclusively in categories of paternal authority. Only a society in which this second type prevails will be able to enter fields of development in which it feels itself to be responsibly adult and independently inquiring.

### Prejudice and conscience

Let us once more revert to the prejudices that are tied to the conscience.

A study of four hundred students quoted by Gordon W. Allport in his book on the nature of prejudice[12] showed that among those in whose education religion played a big part there was a much greater tendency to prejudices in general – in relation to race or minorities, for instance – than among those in whose childhood religion played a smaller part or none at all. Allport gives a warning against generalizations, however, for a strong tendency to (genuinely Christian) tolerance was also present among those brought up on traditional religious lines. Further investigation was therefore required to establish whether the prejudices concerned were included 'undogmatically' in a peaceable character or were a pretext for sadistic aggressivity.

Broadly speaking, however, the predominant feature in religious education to absolute obedience was the threat of merciless punishment. This is bound to lead to a traumatic fixation on infantile defence measures with the consequent trend, which we have by now sufficiently emphasized, to crude and aggressive acting out.

The obverse side of this religious authoritarian style of socializing human beings is that it cannot teach them to accommodate themselves to the ambivalence of their feelings. Integration of the instincts into the ego is hampered by the more archaic form of defence against them, by the mechanisms of repression, denial, and projection. These mechanisms are consolidated before the maturation of the ego and remain out of its reach. This type of religion has paid heavily for this. Apart from its promises of salvation, in the past it provided an outlet for brutality in the practices of the institutions that supervised religious taboos.

The modern secular religions, the state ideologies, have given a new lease of life to this process. They are very successful in manipulating people, because they take into account the individual's state of dependence in a culture in which the division of labour is highly developed. By sanctioning the release of repressed and therefore blind aggression against a scapegoat they give the tamed, passive citizen the sense that his ideal of being strong, active, and independent is attainable after all. The enthusiasm, or rather the self-sacrificing devotion to the requirements of their leaders, that German soldiers showed in two world wars must have been rooted in a surfeit of peace-time experiences in which so much passive submission was required without the stimulus of adventure, that is, without the possibility of maturation by way of protest. The need for adventure and risk-taking was the more frustrated as new relationships of dependence were very effectively combined with still intact paternal authoritarianism. Martin Wangh[13] has drawn attention to the specific consequences of deprivation of the father who is idealized because he is on active service followed by the severe narcissistic blow that ensues when he returns home in the role of vanquished instead of victor. He quotes a study by Leslie T. Wilkins[14] 'which shows statistically that British children who were aged from three to five during the worst war years had a delinquency rate nearly 40 per cent higher than corresponding peace-time generations at the age of seven and between the ages of sixteen to twenty'. If this points to increased difficulty in social adaptation, to disturbances in the building up the super-ego, it follows that this generation will, in the event of economic crises, show a great proclivity to prejudices, though for reasons quite different from those of individuals subjected to a sadistic super-ego. The content of these prejudices will offer them the prospect of wiping out the narcissistic blow represented by the humiliation of their national pride incarnated in their father.

## On being confronted with prejudice about oneself

One cannot want to have prejudices; at most one can want not to have them. One has them before one is aware of it. The psychical processes of identification that lead to them are older than the capacity for critical reflection, and they continue after the critical conscious has developed. Prejudices complete passive adaptation to the forms of instinctual outlet prescribed by the social environment. When the ego impinges on the decrees of prejudice, unpleasure and fear are experienced, depending on the amount of cathected energy tied up in them. The point at which harm is done is reached when efforts to attain an independent orientation to reality are hampered by anxiety. The trends of the developing individual are met by prejudice (and still more by a set of interconnected prejudices) in two respects. All patterns of behaviour acquired through identification contain a variegated mixture of practical knowledge and group-specific and individual prejudices taken over from the model. Their adoption establishes affective understanding with the model figures in the individual's immediate environment and with the members of the group in general. Adhering to them protects the child, whose critical faculties are still weak, from hostile impulses from the environment. Prejudices set limits to spontaneous reactions and provide guidance for practical action. They do nothing to strengthen the critical capacities of the ego, but reinforce self-feeling because of the appreciation that is shown when the individual does what is generally approved and is considered right and proper. If there is no education in asking questions about the world, that is, if the models are themselves not capable of asking such questions, an obedience to prejudice sets in that cuts short the process of maturation, and adaptation follows the path of social automatism.

That is one possible line of development. Another use of prejudice is to provide an outlet for the discharge of the surplus instinctual energy accumulated by repression resulting from the group's standards of behaviour. With a certitude similar to that of magical modes of thought, prejudices create the feeling, not only of what is right and good that is incorporated into the ego ideal, but also of the evil that is characteristic of alien objects. The surplus affect that cannot be openly tied to objects within the group, let alone ruthlessly satisfied by them, can be uninhibitedly lived out upon these alien objects. Perfectly mild and civil individuals of whom, as the saying is, one would never believe such a thing, often turn out to be capable of performing unbelievable horrors upon aliens who have been declared to be evil. Our age has not been spared instances of this.

From the psychological point of view, the most important feature in this is the process by which objects are alienated by prejudice. They can be alienated in the hostile sense, but they can also be alienated by idealization. They may perhaps be strange or different from what one is used to, but without the obstacle of the prejudice it would be possible to get to know and understand them better. That, however, is not allowed to happen, because they have become a means to an end. But for their aura of dangerous and incalculable hostility, one's aggressivity would lose the prospect of satisfaction. The fantasy is free to indulge in acts of cruelty against the alien object. As the two antipodes of instinctual life, Libido and Destrudo, never completely lose connection with each other even when dissociated (which gives precedence to the aggression arising from frustration), and as they are directed at the same object, sexual desire distorted into hatred is found to be the other surplus driving force.[15]

There is a reciprocal relationship between the extent to which unworth is attributed to strangers, 'out-groups', and the accumulation of surplus instinct brought about by restrictions within the 'in-group'. The amount of uncompensatable frustration within the in-group determines the strength of the surplus aggression and the need to bind it to something ('if there were no Jews, it would be necessary to invent them'). A dialectical process takes place. One group of prejudices enforces repression and creates the surplus drive excluded from satisfactions; a second group creates surrogate objects for its satisfaction and channels the instinctual surplus in their direction. The same economic principles also apply to surplus libido. Unsatisfied needs for tenderness and genital sexuality easily become bound to surrogate objects which are 'alienated' from their true nature and given another similar to one's own. Anyone who has observed how a dog or cat can satisfy the emotional needs of its owner and has listened to the way in which the animal is talked to will know what is meant. Both the sentimental humanization of pets and the aggressive, destructive alienation of 'out-groups' are misconstructions based on the same dynamics of prejudice.

Finally we come to the highly cathected prejudices, that is, those associated with strong affect and tied to the conscience. They are closely connected with the feeling of identity, the inner perception of ourselves that tells us: This is I, and this I shall remain. The individual grows up with these prejudice structures, which enjoy social respect and mutually support each other, and he often does so without difficulty or objection and takes a great deal of satisfaction in the behaviour that they call for. Perhaps no one is unfamiliar with the vague sense of inner emptiness and helplessness that sets in when some encounter or experience puts us on the trail of some central prejudice by which we are bound. If our thinking ego is able to face the arguments that have shattered our previous certainty and allows itself to be convinced by them, the anxious void – in which one feels oneself to have been robbed – is succeeded by a new sense of liberation and identity.

The formation of identity depends on the individual's self-feeling; it does not without previous inspection adopt a social identity, meaning by that inconspicuous adaptation, undisturbed capacity for work and pleasure, and whatever other factors may be statistically taken into account in defining the socially healthy. Successful conformity certainly creates a feeling of self and identify, but this is the first stage in the individual's life history. The identity required of the mature individual is the result of *active* adaptation both to the outside world and to the world within. This means that the forces of the id and the acquired stereotypes of value and behaviour have to be subjected to active critical control and as a consequence either modified or given up. But, as life is a state of unstable equilibrium in time, or, in other words, readaptation has to take place in each of its phases, this can be successful only if the stabilities attained can be carried over into new ones that have to be established. The sense of security derived from infantile defence mechanisms and the identity feeling which derives from them – and at that phase is inevitable – has to be sacrificed to the unstable equilibriums of an ego development which sometimes finds itself running into culs-de-sac and sometimes proceeds continuously. Identification with the father has to be found, to be supplemented and superseded in its turn by identifications at the horizontal level; and finally the 'scrap of independence and originality' will demand its appropriate place in self-awareness and hope for recognition and friendly reception.

Not that the ego can or should shake off all the habits that originated in identification, but it should progressively gain an influence over them. Where parts or central areas of the character remain excluded from the development of this increasing sensitivity of perception both of the self and of others, and are unable to meet the challenge of adequate adaptation, a partial stoppage of development can be said to have taken place, a toxic immobilization arising out of prejudice.

Our character, that is, the characteristic behaviour we display to the world, is determined by the work of integration done by the ego as a whole, its unconscious as well as its (more meagre) conscious components. Self-perception and perception of the outside world are interconnected; the accuracy of our perception of the human environment depends on that of our self-perception. A distorted picture of the human environment is always the result of a refusal to believe in processes inside ourselves; instead, we delude ourselves that they are at work in others. No one escapes the anxiety experienced on realizing the uncanny fact of affective distortion of perception. This anxiety derives from resistance, dealing with which is the central content of psycho-analytic treatment. Confrontation with the self-deception resulting from prejudice is often signalled by so much anxiety that massive resistance blocks all attempts to break through to it – yet another illustration of the tremendous influence that prejudices have on the human internal economy. Those who are contemplating subjecting themselves to analysis invariably express fear of loss of the self, that is, their identity. 'What will become of me?' they say. 'What sort of unknown person will it turn me into?'

This is only one example among many, though it is an impressive one, because the psycho-analytic objective is obviously to help an individual who desires to be freed from restricting or morbid disturbances. Similar anxieties are, however, felt by most people, particularly the young, when considering what career to adopt. The choice is often very difficult, especially if practical considerations can be left temporarily out of account. The individual is then faced with the ordeal of choosing what in many respects is a permanent identity and of accepting limits on his self-ideal without surrendering himself in the process. What he is in search of is a new identity which, though distinct from the old, nevertheless leaves the latter with all its value, and it is far harder to find this than to dismiss what he does not want. Often it is restrictions as such that are shunned, because these are felt hitherto to have been repressive to the self. To many the idea of entering the Society of Jesus, say, or a military academy, or the state administration, is intolerable, for they resent the discipline that would be required of them; in psychological terms, they resent the interference with their identity involved in moulding it in accordance with a model, an ideal type. In the three examples we mentioned the values and the freedom of action that is permissible are indeed to a large extent prescribed, and the individual is expected to find his identity within firmly established guiding lines. The so-called liberal professions promise far more 'freedom'. 'The psychological poverty of groups'[16] begins where restriction of freedom in a tedious job allows little elbow room for self-discovery. The individual is then robbed of his 'nature' without the consolation of identification with a group that gives him social prestige.

Exclusion from groups – and hence also from the prejudices that they vigorously defend – sets other prejudices in motion. Those who reject groups as incompatible with their identity tend to succumb to the prejudice of condemning them out of hand. All Jesuits tend to be regarded as crafty and capable of anything, all officers as presumptuous and obedient dummies, all administrators as dry-as-dust bureaucrats tied up in red tape. When one examines these prejudice-based aversions a little more closely, it is surprising to find that objective considerations based on the undeniable restrictions involved in joining a strict religious order, for instance, play a very minor part in their motivation in comparison with phobic anxieties dating from traumatic experiences in childhood. It is like going down into the cellar, which was such a frightening experience in childhood that one avoids doing it even as a grown-up; moreover, everything associated with it is avoided as being dangerous. It should, incidentally, be added that we do not deny the unpleasing and pathological deformations of character that can be brought about by membership in orders, cliques, and so-called élites. These dangers arise, however, only in cases where infantile experiences fuse with existing collective prejudices.

## Brief apologia for gossip

Obviously we can escape prejudice only by resolutely mustering all our counter-forces, but nothing in the world is so deadly earnest that it cannot be the subject of satire. That is the function of gossip.

The less power we feel in ourselves to free ourselves from conventions, the more devious are the routes by which we avenge ourselves on them. One of these routes is gossip. When we gossip we are concerned, not so much with the facts as with the affects that they rouse in us; we are concerned with the gaining, not of knowledge, but of pleasure. We are concerned with establishing, not the true nature of the object of our gossip, but with enjoying what he is believed to be capable of. Prejudice helps in this process.

Pleasure in gossip is the obverse side of our insuperable disappointment at all the thrills, the exciting playing with danger, that have eluded us in life; when we have found a suitable hook, we can use it to hang all our unpleasure on; also it gives us the prestige of being 'better' than the victim, because we do not dare do what he did or is alleged to have done. The need to devise platforms of prestige which can be used to transform disappointment into a sense of power is positively inexhaustible. These platforms have to be continually invented and enjoyed; one instance is the official receiving a caller who is seeking something from him; he sits without raising his eyes from his desk for a moment, as if the caller were a beggar. If the latter falls for the bait and gets angry, the pleasure is increased. Gossiping is one of these ways of gaining enjoyment for one's pride for which there are no opportunities in actuality.

The 'fundamental democratization' of our times expresses itself in, among other things, unlimited curiosity. Gossip has long since been commercialized and sold as a 'service'; it has become part of the communications industry. This reflects the survival of a timeless need adapted to the process of urbanization. Passers-by and neighbours have become so anonymous that it is impossible to gossip about them, though the village and small town still provide opportunities. But, in spite of all the gossip in the press, spontaneous gossip still flourishes undiminished in offices and groups of all kinds. The alienation to which the major scapegoats are subjected takes place here on a minor and more subtle scale. All breaches of social rules – or what can be interpreted as such – are greedily seized on and, with the aid of the aggressivity that is always lying in wait, are used for delivering 'pin-pricks'. The vocabulary of popular characterology seems to have been ready made for the expression of prejudice; ambition, craftiness, cowardice, and so on become the total verdicts on those who become the targets of gossip.

Gossiping is generally thought of as an especially feminine characteristic, but those who have ears to hear will recognize this as a male projection; men and women are equally susceptible to its attractions. Both sexes alike desire, at any rate in fantasy, to share in the forbidden and the sinful and in the pleasure of punishing it. Though gossip may sometimes be troublesome, and sometimes poisonous and dangerous to the extent that it may ruin a reputation, it is nevertheless an indispensable safety valve for those held in the bondage of society, and it prevents worse, the complete unison of prejudice. It should also be recalled that there is an idealizing kind of gossip, arising from and promoting a collective popularity. This is by no means confined to girls' boarding-schools; enthusiastic multipliers of the phenomenon are ready and waiting everywhere.

The tendency to aggressive gossip thrives most luxuriantly in 'closed' groups the members of which have ample opportunity for keeping an eye on each other and observing how they keep to the rules, that is to say, in village communities, long-established urban residential areas, and in sects, orders, and offices. What the actual content of the gossip is basically does not matter; the essential thing is that there should be a common victim on whom it can be centred. The intensity of participation runs parallel to the affective frustration that the group as a whole does not admit but cannot escape. Assiduous gossip is a way of temporarily forgetting one's miseries. The power of the powerless is that of taking people's characters away. Where the ego has been strengthened by libidinal fulfilment and the primary instinctual wishes have been reasonably satisfied, the need for the aggressive conspiracy of gossip diminishes. Thus it constantly happens that it is the freer individual who falls victim to gossip.

The relative harmlessness of ordinary gossip lies in the fact that the victims are not fixed, do not have the permanence of the major scapegoats. Gossip gives everyone the pleasure of a fleeting reinforcement of the feeling of being a member of an in-group ('we are better than others') and the opportunity of emotional discharge in moderate doses; he can also temporarily be a victim himself. This easily rousable susceptibility to prejudice is to be encountered everywhere; it prevails naked and unashamed even in the most distinguished assemblies. In the form of snobbishness and the sarcastic witticism it produces a notable increase in narcissistic pleasure and – if one possesses the art of getting the laugh on one's own side – results in an increase of prestige. Here too the ego becomes the willing servant of the pleasure principle.

As we have already observed, successful adaptation by way of general education to an intellectually demanding environment by no means necessarily involves affective maturation or increased self-perception. The ineradicability of gossip provides confirmation of our view of the character as a very loose association of vectors of potential reactions. In the eyes of the observer (and most certainly also in those of sharpened self-perception) these often seem not at all to fit in with each other. They mark levels of development reached in periods of life that lay very far apart from each other. The pleasure we all take in gossip illustrates our regressive proclivity to give up the more rational forms of human coexistence in favour of more primitive pleasures; and, as we all enjoy it so much, it is doubtful whether we really wish to be so adult as to give it up altogether. That would involve the sacrifice of too much pleasure.

# XII

# Two Kinds of Fatherlessness

*From Oedipal rivalry to sibling envy*

The ominous word 'masses' has recurred several times in the course of this book. In common parlance it has long since come to have qualitative rather than quantitative implications, and when it is used it is important to establish the state of mind of the user. This can vary all the way from a triumphant identification, an inflationary 'we' feeling (we, the victorious masses of the revolution, the victorious army, the winning party), to anxiety, which in turn can range from resignation on the one hand to a sense of dangerous exclusion on the other. At one end of the scale the individual has the exultant feeling of merging with the ocean in all its moods, and at the other he feels a solitary dwarf threatened by an incalculable giant.

As fatherlessness – meaning the loss both of a primary relationship and of a model that has to be outgrown – is a condition which will have to be borne and coped with by the societies of our time, and as society nowadays is mass society, we shall conclude our socio-psychological reflections with an attempt to contribute to the clarification of the concept of 'mass' as an affect-influencing reality.

Depending on whether I accept or deny belonging to the masses, I feel them to be powerful or myself to be impotent. The politician with the majority on his side is convinced of the intelligence and insight of the masses, and their support of his declared aims confirms him in his view of their correctness and gives him the feeling of legitimization. His defeated opponent finds these conclusions difficult to accept. He feels himself to be misunderstood, and the masses to be inaccessible to what he conceives to be reason. Meanwhile, in the expectation of better days, he consults the trends of public opinion in order to adapt his promises to them. The result is less a battle of political programmes than a kind of political roundabout, with public opinion chasing political promises which those who made them extracted from those to whom they were made. Thus politics moves further and further from the reality principle, a consequence of which is the application to it of the vocabulary of the variety stage. One politician is stated to juggle with facts or figures, while another 'steals the show' and yet a third skilfully walks the tight-rope. A politician adapted to 'democracy without freedom'[1] might perhaps best be described as an illusionist; he has mastered the art of manipulation, never gives himself away, and covers up tangible reality with convincing illusions. This is certainly a malicious oversimplification, but it is more than just a pleasing analogy, for there is a real correspondence in the methods of deception practised. We are of course all involved, since we permit such performances. Only an audience willing to regress to childhood gives the conjurer the feeling that his tricks are as good as reality. The sorrowful conclusion is that in a society which regresses in fantasy to a 'state that runs by itself',[2] a mother-goddess lavish with her milk, the political conjurer (demagogue) is bound to be successful.

The masses give an echo effect to the basic trends roused by the conflicts of interest that stimulate them. If I share in the collective excitement symbolized by acclamation or boos, I am borne along by the echo, while if I do not share it, if I listen to it from the outside, it strikes me as an overwhelming flood of emotion whose total lack of articulation and loss of individual characteristics are terrifying. This experience is by no means associated only with the behaviour of actual, visible masses; the echo effect also appears when all the newspapers say the same thing or the same subject produces the same reaction in all my associates. By many routes the mass media continually rouse reactions in us that identify us with the masses. If what is offered is to be successful, however, it must fall on fertile ground. The latter, a state of permanent nervous stimulation, is the counterpart of the feeling that in every area of activity the masses are competing with us.

Mass society, with its demand for work without responsibility, creates a gigantic army of rival, envious siblings. Their chief conflict is characterized, not by Oedipal rivalry, struggling with the father for the privileges of liberty and power, but by sibling envy directed at neighbours and competitors who have more than they. In contrast to the peasant, feudal, bourgeois-capitalist form of society, this represents a sweeping change in the total social situation, the effects of which – once one has become aware of them – cannot again be overlooked, because they are visible everywhere. On top of this there is the fact that the masses no longer vegetate in a state of vital deprivation, are no longer afflicted by under-nourishment and epidemics. Their instinctual surplus is a consequence of good physical condition and seeks satisfaction in horizontal encroachments at the expense of their competing neighbours. That society is at the same time fascinated by the idea of advancement does not seem to us to be inconsistent with this. People wish to better themselves, but that means that they seek, not responsibility, but advantages for themselves. 'One must have claims, but one does not have and does not want to occupy a position.'[3] The hierarchy in office and factory does not reach up to the level of paternal decision-making, and those who approach such an altitude often find it too much for them. It is significant that a term has been found to describe this condition; it is called the 'manager sickness', which is less an individual diagnosis than a description of a typical collapse under a typical social burden.

*The interested agents*

A structural characteristic of our competitive society is a combination of envy with an appetite for dependence, which as a result of the advent of the administered masses has superseded the old ideal of rivalry with the father. A withering away of the old roles of responsibility is a direct consequence of this. The weakening of the sense of responsibility is also reflected in corruption on a scale unknown in the days of the paternalist bourgeois state, and an obfuscation of ideas about what constitutes corruption. True, the inner-directed incumbent of public office was tied to a hierarchical system of territorial organization. He had less regard for the under-privileged and was overridden by the general trend to exploitation, but this did not lead to his personal enrichment. Even though his salary was Spartan, he identified himself with the principle of social order that gave him prestige. In an industrial mass society there is no place for such identification. The demagogues – politicians are becoming harder to find – and the representatives of interests, the lobbyists, have solid ideas of the gains to be expected from their job; as the interested agents of group or mass demands they do not feel themselves to be personally responsible.

This struggle for special interests has of course played its part in all societies, but there were natural limitations, in the literal sense of the word, on the demands that were made. The increase in productivity and in the human rate of reproduction, though the increase in the latter still outpaces that of the social product, has nevertheless given a new orientation to human covetousness. Its quality has changed; in the presence of the automatic machine the fantasy learns to expect automatic satisfaction, and all the more so as industrial labour, including administrative labour, is boring and monotonous. The demagogue with his election promises and the lobbyist both represent the basic mood of irritation that results from disappointment, but they are not catalysts of demands. They are not the representatives of any system, but only of conditions. Perhaps with this we have hit on a central sociological and psychological factor in present-day mass societies. The masses have brought conditions with them; there is no room for them in the traditional order, even less in the physical sphere than in that of mood and expectation. The result is a breakdown of order, a loss of orientation leading to regression to very archaic experiences, to the fairy-tale level, the conjurer's magic wand, the satisfaction derived at the mother's breast. Evolution towards a consciousness that would be adequate to these demands limps painfully in the wake of the growth rate of the masses; the critical conscious has not yet succeeded in devising an order capable of meeting the challenge due to regression through conditions.

*Loveless childhood and lifeless old age*

The life of the individual in mass society is pervaded by demandingness and the fear of being surpassed and left behind. Fear of old age has reached panic proportions; and the old are increasingly neglected and lonely and lacking in reciprocal contact with the younger generations. It is a bitter irony that this coincides with a big increase in the average life expectancy. The effort to remain young at all costs is a regressive character trait. Perpetual youth is an illusory ideal; as interdependence can be experienced only in sibling rivalry, when the individual reaches a certain age he simply drops out without trace. The individual would like to live without ageing; in reality he ages without having lived.

Other, apparently totally unrelated, trends illustrate the disturbance of contact between the generations. One of them is the trend to rationalize the sucking period. Bottle feeding is quicker, more uniform, than breast feeding, and is also labour-saving. The large proportion of mothers who can easily be persuaded not to feed their babies themselves shows that conditions are stronger than the impulse to comply with a system, here a natural one. The loss of social contact at the beginning and at the end of life have the same origin, narcissistic regression resulting from conditions in the main period of life. Another social loss is that of a model for the transformation of the ego into an old-age ego. The monotony of working life continues after retirement – in a void. 'Retirement bankruptcy',[4] both physical and mental, is not a natural phenomenon but the product of social conditions which irresistibly impose adaptation by self-alienation. At all events these social conditions are obviously stronger than the powers of critical resistance of which the individual might be capable, assuming he had the support of society. The decline in affective contact with the child and with the aged is in itself a process of de-differentiation in the social structure. It is characteristic of modern mass society, which is developing an amnesia for everything which does not function like itself. The frustrations of childhood are forgotten, the existence of old age is denied.

It is hard for the individual in the 'prime of life' to realize how it might be possible to find satisfaction in living within defined limits and getting used to them, for the area in which he lives and in which a more static way of life might be possible is perpetually subject to rebuilding and extension. In the most recent phase of development anxiety is increased by awareness of belonging to a rapidly growing world population; the masses of China, Japan, India, South America are no longer items of information one reads about in geography books but, thanks to the mass means of communication, have become visible reality. The question whether in the long run it will be possible to feed these human multitudes, and whether any room will be left for the individual, and if so what sort of room, rouses in us a sense of alarm at having so many siblings. These alien masses more and more tangibly restrict our 'Western' prerogatives. In one's own experience competition from the masses in one's own country sees to that.

*The detachment effect*

Another association is with the way in which the masses can be swayed. If the idea of being turned into a 'mass man' has any meaning, it can refer only to the fear that our proclivity to regression will get the better of our critical judgement and that we shall agree to tendencies imposed from above instead of examining realities for ourselves. The mere possibility of rousing similar affective reactions and moods in an incalculable number of human beings, with simultaneous lowering of the intellectual level – that is, anaesthetizing the critical capacity and conscience – is felt to be alarming in the extreme, as long as one has not oneself succumbed to the anaesthesia. Thus, in addition to the echo effect of the masses that we find so disturbing, there is also a detachment effect that has the same result. The detachment effect sets in as soon as I note that a large number of individuals are subject to identical feelings and impulses, which creates the impression of automatism. A reflex-like unfreedom is characteristic of all actions dictated by prejudice; the sense of danger arises from the unanimity of the phenomenon. If I fail to remain uninfluenced, or if such mass expression of feeling does not leave me cold, I incline defensively to fall back on an oversimplification, from their temporary uniformity of behaviour I infer a total uniformity of the individuals who make up the mass. That is the trap into which group psychology has all too often fallen. The detachment effect is misused as a judgement of value. The mass reaction is described as a natural evil to which 'others' have succumbed, but no explanation is given of why I remain aloof from it, as if that were perfectly natural too. Anyone who has unwillingly got involved in a crowd – in the rush hour, for instance – can easily see that the homogeneity is not necessarily as homogeneous as it seems. Each member of the crowd experiences his own detachment effect; he sees all the others as 'crowd' though he is a part of it himself.

If we regard mass behaviour as an inevitable mode of reaction that sets in either when a certain threshold of excitation has been passed or as the result of lasting stimuli, we give up the concept of ego obedience and are left with a pseudo-biology, a pseudo-individualism, and a bag of tricks by which mass behaviour can be produced. Masses – large numbers of individuals closely packed together – are, however, a product of social conditions. Undoubtedly reactions of the immature psychical organization, such as an easy falling in with trends, are encouraged in these circumstances. Strange or unusual conditions set defence mechanisms in motion which have their precedents in sub-human life (for instance, the flight-fight reaction). But it must be recalled that all environments are originally alien, and that familiarity is based on habituation. Men are not yet habituated to critical examination of the second natural environment, the technical one, populated by the masses. To the extent that cultural criticism hampers this, and succumbs itself to regressive, anxious withdrawal, it is a hindrance instead of a help. The mimicry of mass behaviour has strong phylogenetic roots, but it is not the whole biology of social man, of which his critical capacity also forms part. Only by making use of the latter can order be found in chaos.

In their hostility to the masses the cultural critics overlook the fact that there is always an element of pain or unpleasure in the loss of critical detachment, in the process of alienation from the self. The horror felt at 'not knowing',[5] when we are vividly aware of the self's inability to assert itself, shows us that the self-amputation of critical thought involved in the process of surrendering to mass feeling is a by no means unalloyed pleasure. The individual whose power of criticism is crippled, who is a casualty of high social pressure, is indeed speechless so far as his own conflict is concerned – he is probably totally unapproachable about it. But if we have an acquaintance whom we continually meet in a state of intoxication, it would hardly occur to us to attribute this to exuberant enjoyment of life on his part. If masses of individuals succumb to inhibition of thought, become automatized, it is not very reasonable to diagnose this as a biological defect, a constitutional addiction to dependence, instead of regarding it, like all forms of addiction, as having been conditioned among other things by social circumstances. Thought offers a wide field of libidinal satisfaction, and men do not surrender it without reason.

*Encroachment on territory and dissociation of instinct*

The error of perspective that causes all the other members of a crowd to look like mass men to each individual member of it brings us back to the subject of sibling rivalry, the trend to horizontal aggression. As modern man is continually confronted with anonymous or almost anonymous other men who reveal no certain sign of their status but in one way or another continually get in his way, his mood is one of diffuse aggressivity, only imperfectly controlled by manipulated slogans. The continual succession of new sources of stimuli constitutes a permanent encroachment upon what the individual used to claim as his own territory, at home, at his places of work and recreation, and in moving from place to place. Retreat into an illusory space of one's own (and a simultaneous aggressive invasion of the privacy of others) is to be observed whenever young or old go out walking with a transistor set blaring. A minimal territory of one's own is certainly one of the biological prerequisites of emotional equilibrium; the deformation of life that takes place in slums and mass camps provides ample evidence of this, and there are many new slums in the towering blocks that spring up round production and administration centres.

On the other hand, being cheek-by-jowl with a mob can be extremely enjoyable, in a football stadium, for instance, when the echo effect of unanimity of feeling carries one away and becomes an extension of one's own. Also, to avoid presenting a distorted picture, it should be added that none of the processes by which mass man and conformity are produced are one-way only; they also produce opposite effects. The means of mass communication, for instance, by no means exercise only the stultifying influence for which cultural critics hostile to the masses wrongly condemn them utterly. They certainly do exercise such an influence, but they also provide a large amount of information and stimulate liberal and tolerant thinking. Apart from irresponsibly improvized housing developments on the fringes of our cities, there are also admirable examples of creative imagination in popular housing. These things we must concede, because otherwise our criticism would distort the picture. If there were no counter-trends to the overriding tendency to human impoverishment in a comfortable but loveless mass environment, there would cease to be any productive purpose in criticism. That is not the case, however, though conditions are questionable enough.

We must bear in mind that the quantitative factor present whenever we have the experience of being confronted with 'the masses' indicates the limitations of the resolving power of our perceptions. When the individual is faced with a large number of unknown, unfamiliar individuals all in the same state of mind, they strike him as being a mass, even more so if their uniformity is emphasized by a uniform, for instance. This *de facto* merging of very different individuals into an overriding impression of homogeneity is what we called the detachment effect. The more my own state of mind differs from that which unites a large number of men, the more they become mass men in my eyes. It can regularly be observed that this experience of encountering 'the masses' rouses instinctual trends, and that these very easily become dissociated in relation to them. This is especially the case when one of the feelings roused is anxiety. The ambivalence characteristic of all our relationships with others is then displaced to the two extremes of enthusiastic acceptance or aggressive repudiation. The reactions of many drivers in heavy traffic show how the libidinal instinctual component is taken back into the ego in a state of hostile excitation and strengthens the narcissistic cathexis. The driver's nearest and dearest is then himself, and that makes his driving more aggressive and ruthless. This process of dissociation can be observed at work whenever a large number of approximate equals, individuals of the same level of prestige, are competing for privileges; a typical sibling rivalry that promptly ceases when someone who enjoys higher prestige in the particular field of dispute appears on the scene; in the instance we have quoted this would be the traffic police.

It is, however, questionable whether the police in general are still regarded as representatives of paternal authority or are not now seen in a much more intangible regulative context. To many, of course, the policeman (like the teacher) is a screen for the projection of aggressive feelings derived from experiences with members of the family in infancy. The attitude to officials, who similarly impose restrictions, is different. They are felt to be obstacles, and awaken an obscure sense of discomfort that cannot be attached to any visible, powerful individual. The system causes every variety of resentment and demandingness, but what sort of system it is, where its authority ends, when it is performing a necessary function and when it is exceeding its powers, is all very hazy and uncertain. Contact with it is generally confined to form-filling and making payments.

This reminds us of a process which Dahrendorf calls the division of labour of authority. 'In highly developed industrial societies,' he writes, 'we can observe a development, quite independent of the social character of their citizens, which can perhaps be described as a far-reaching division of labour of authority. As in the case of the division of labour in industrial production, this development has led to the creation of numerous specialist positions, each of which bears only slight traces of the process to which it belongs.'[6] Carried to its present degree of division and sub-division with all its manifold ramifications, this is a relatively new social phenomenon. Division of labour in the productive processes runs right back through history; manufactures existed in the ancient cultures of Mesopotamia. But, whether in ancient China or in the first wave of the industrial revolution with its coal barons and railway kings, authority and power were always associated with individuals. Where the last relics of feudalism have been extinguished, however, and new castes find themselves in the saddle, power does not derive from them; instead, they administer a power system, a flow of authority, fed by many channels of interest. The system is generally unravellable to them, and is certainly unintelligible to the man in the street. All attempts to describe the situation point to the conclusion that the determining influences in society are (in accordance with the tangible, pre-industrial world enshrined in our language) regarded as events similar to natural processes in order to make them accessible to our experience. 'No identifiable individual exercises power, and yet power or authority are exercised, but we can name only persons who do not have any part in it.'[7]

## Fatherlessness of the first and second degree

The detachment effect causes us to regard the large numbers of human beings employed in industrial production as 'masses'. Indeed, de-individualized masses strike us as being just as faceless as authority. We grow up from the power relationships of childhood, which are tied to persons, into an incomprehensible system of power relationships under which we spend our working life, the phases of our life in which our character has been finally formed. Thus we go through two contrasting phases. If we compare this with the uniformity of the paternalist structure of society – in which the relationship with the father was succeeded by that with teacher, employer, landlord, all the way up to the king – we are entitled to describe contemporary society as a fatherless society. When 'no identifiable individual' holds power in his hands we have a sibling society.

This is a condition for which society was totally unprepared. It developed as an unintended by-product of extreme specialization. Meanwhile it has grown into an overriding problem, to which that of productive relations must be subjected if we are to advance from 'conditions' to an orderly system. For the situation is having dangerous repercussions on the primary social group, the family. The emotional relations and authority structure of the family are being affected by the style of non-binding fraternal relations and the levelling out of manifest differences of rank. The division of labour in the field of authority obviously presents a real historical challenge to our active, productive capacities for adaptation (in contrast to mere passive acceptance of events). This kind of fatherlessness presents us with a problem to which we shall have to find the answer. But there is no cure for the fatherlessness and motherlessness in childhood which these social processes are helping to bring about. The individual who has not had the primary opportunity of forming secure object relationships, of coping reasonably well with his ambivalence in relation to one and the same partner, is bound to succumb to the emotional excesses described in Le Bon's *The Crowd* as if they were constitutional characteristics and not the consequence of society's blindness to the practices by which it itself produces them.

As we have seen, the increase in specialization has led to fatherlessness of the first degree; to the loss of the physical presence of the working father, or, to state the situation less one-sidedly, to a general weakening of the primary object relationships. The intervention of technical routine in the very earliest relationship between mother and child is no less fraught with consequences than is the disappearance of the later hand-in-hand relationship between father and child. Fatherlessness of the second degree dissolves the personal element in power relationships; one is aware of authority as ever, but it cannot be visualized. The fatherless (and increasingly also motherless) child grows up into an adult with no visible master, exercises anonymous functions, and is guided by anonymous functions. What his senses are aware of is individuals similar to himself in huge numbers.

The phylogenetic roots of the intensification of narcissistic and aggressive trends that takes place in all experiences of being encroached upon are, as we have said, not difficult to discover. The chance neighbour who infringes on my minimal private territory becomes an invader, an enemy, who triggers off aggressivity or aggression. In spite of the fact that we thereby put an excessive burden on ourselves, coexistence at excessively close quarters requires us to suppress our primitive affective reactions (flight or fight tendencies), and this applies also to competition at close quarters such as takes place in specialist fields. Unconscious aggressive tension is undoubtedly increased by this repression, and is further increased by the libidinal frustration of coming across those similarly aggressive-minded in everyday life.

Mass sporting events, with their emphatic promise of libidinal satisfaction, thus have a remedial effect in the economy of mental life. The individual is able voluntarily to open up his own private territory to others and allow his neighbour to come close to him in the guise of a friend. The detachment effect vanishes, and mass participation sets in. Aggressivity is able to concentrate and discharge itself on the opposing team. This communal experience had predecessors in festivals of all kinds celebrated throughout the ages, but we should not overlook its surrogate nature. Festivals, providing the magnificent experience of temporary liberation from the duties of everyday life and the all too severe demands of the conscience, are of course a pointer to the oppressive nature of the restrictions from which they provide a temporary escape, and this is certainly also the economic function of the great sporting and other similar events of our time. Their frequency, which is tied to no natural rhythm, and the avidity that is felt for them demonstrate an increased need for close contact, even though it is anonymous and momentary. The lack of stably developed primary object relationships, the cold climate in the family group, in which people have little or nothing to say to one another and indeed have little in common to talk about, steers affective expectations in the direction of stimulating mass events.

A vicious circle has established itself. The individual condemned by the specialized nature of production to a mass place of work, though he needs a familiar place, a home, in which he can feel that his ego aspirations, conflicts, and hopes as well as his instinctual wishes will be recognized and accepted, and where he will meet and react to the similar personal needs of his partner, is obviously not held in this place of intimate relations, but is driven back again to the places of mass pleasure. Understanding the problem can begin, however, only if we refrain from moral condemnation of this behaviour and cease nursing the illusion that, if he only wanted to, if only he were more interested (or in whatever other terms the reproach may be framed), he would be able to lead a rich and satisfying private life. The spread of television has effectively demolished the idea that the mass of individuals have full freedom of choice and ought to be able simply to ignore the facts of the social situation. In the case of television good and bad effects are as closely interlocked as they are with any other tool used by the individual. The bad effects arise from the way in which it is used, not to increase one's knowledge of the world but merely to secure illusory satisfaction. The individual uses it at home to divert him from home. This cannot be laid at the door of the inventors of this ingenious device. The lack of resistance with which the viewer allows the flood to flow over him every evening is connected with the strain to which he has been subjected during the day. The uncreative, monotonous nature of his work leaves behind no problems worth thinking about, but a sense of irritation that sets up a demand for contrasting experiences, for a counter-stimulant to release the tension that has been built up. The dispersal of the primary group as a result of the division of labour, responsibility, and power has impoverished the capacity for differentiated intellectual and emotional contact and the development of an affectionate or stimulating atmosphere. Behaviour at home too is passive and anaclitic, dependent on the provision of material that provides the illusion of escape; the demand thus created is sufficient for the industry that caters for this need, in this case the information and fiction industry.

We cannot sufficiently reiterate that we are not here concerned with denunciation of evil, let alone the moral satisfaction of demonstrating the impasse in which we find ourselves. We are concerned with gathering basic facts which must be understood if changes in social conditions are to be brought about. If it is desirable that society be changed, there must first be methodical investigation of actual social living conditions and their affective repercussions, and of the influence of both on the formation of our consciousness.

In this context it must also be appreciated that the modern ideological mass movements, looked at from the same psychodynamic point of view, must be regarded as releasers of tension. In his play *The Rhinoceros* Ionesco describes the transformation of alarm resulting from the detachment effect into the pleasurable merging in a new mass identity.

When such an ideological mass identity ends in defeat and disaster, as it did in the case of Nazism, the detachment effect is retrospectively re-established more strongly than before. A feeling of helpless impotence makes it almost impossible for former members of the mass to remember their rhinoceros period and the beliefs and hopes associated with it, and to feel their way back to their feelings and motivations at the time. This cannot be dismissed as merely simulated stupidity. With the loss of the mass identity, part of the memory is lost also. The analogy with the amnesia that covers the years of early childhood, from which only fragments of memory stand out, is plain. There is also a trace here of the reluctance we previously mentioned to regard oneself as a creature affected by time and to learn the behaviour appropriate to the different stages of life. Identification with the Führer and the mass ideals he imposed was always in the background a process of compulsive adaptation accompanied by great anxiety (even when the individual joined the movement very 'obediently' and shouted loudly with the rest). Mass dictatorship was a continuation of group dictatorship. Severe discipline in infancy created adaptation to drill and regimentation and an identity that was able to make only feeble attempts to pass beyond the first stage of enforced identification. Intensification of the demands for obedience in society as a whole then led to mass regression to the level of automatic obedience to orders. Orientation remained rigidly bound to prejudice, and the forces of the ego were used up in pseudo-rational justifications. When the pressure to obey was suddenly removed the individual no longer understood himself. He was as alien to himself as was the power that imposed the adaptation on him.

*Chimerical ego ideal*

The eruptive spread of mass automatic obedience illustrates yet again how the limits of later potential development are almost inevitably set by infantile experiences. Even what at first sight seems to be relatively gentle pressure on the child but nevertheless conceals a remorseless threat of withdrawal of love can result in identification having the same intimidating effects as severe corporal punishment. Both stifle curiosity, the proclivity to inquire and search, and tend to make it impossible for affective models of behaviour and prejudices ever to be driven out. Self-understanding consequently remains vague. The sparse signs of independent ego development correspond to an ego ideal that is remote from reality, and the individual compensates for his impotence by megalomaniac fantasies. The idealized Führer fitted perfectly into this distorted, chimerical reality. It now becomes clear to us, however, why the Führer idol that was so frenziedly worshipped vanished so completely from the scene after its collapse, though this certainly provides no guarantee that the appearance on the scene of a new one might not be greeted with similar enthusiasm. The model was idealized to unattainable heights, calling for passive, feminine, adoring dependence, not a challenge to rival it.

Childish competition with the father leads to incorporation of his values in the conscience. Real experiences with him set the pattern for later reactions in the social field. In particular, they determine the emotional attitude to the world of work and involvement in society in general. The imprinting influences of the mother precede these; they originate in the most intimate relationship of all. No matter how much developments in our specialized mass society may cause the occupational roles of men and women to be assimilated, a natural, biological difference remains. To the extent that utilitarian considerations tend to wipe out the difference, they must inevitably lead to pathological individual developments. No social arrangements can ever adequately take the place of the intimacy of the mother-child relationship; the child can acquire basic trust with its mother and with no one else.

The painful experience of ambivalent feelings, the first rivalry conflict which remains the model for all later ones, arises later in contact with both parents. Unless distorting social influences make them unsuitable for the task, all parental substitutes are able to do less for the child than the parents can do. There is no substitute for the father relationship either. If the father understands his role and can show the child its role, the seeds can be sown for the child's future independence of judgement and independence of character, and it can also be shown how to tolerate setbacks and disappointments. The father has to frustrate, but he can do so in a way for which there is no substitute, remaining conciliatory in his impositions. The emotional ties between parents and child, the conditions for the successful establishment of which are created by the parents, enable them to make educative demands on the child and to reconcile it to those demands.

We have sufficiently discussed the ways in which this pattern can be disturbed. All that remains to reiterate is that it is essential that society should become conscious of the unique situation of the human child. The central undertaking is the acquisition of knowledge about the human task of education. In the exercise of our social responsibilities as parents, teachers, magistrates, and so on, we must be capable of dealing with the child with intuitive understanding. Not till we have understood its dependence and its profound susceptibility to influence are we able to appreciate its unalienated needs and the nature of our own task of guiding it in the direction of critical understanding. The basic theme underlying all our socio-psychological ideas is that society must educate itself to subordinating all competing interests to the education to the child. That is no light matter, but it is essential for the survival of the specifically human way of life in the fatherless mass society. Our distance from that goal is one of the reasons for the mass levelling and the emotional bewilderment which can hardly be overlooked – they can in fact hardly be exaggerated. Seeking a way out by attempting to revert to obsolete patterns – the style of the peasant or bourgeois family, for instance – is condemned to futility. If it is true that fatherlessness (invading even the field of traditional religion) has to be tolerated in a world in which the division of labour has been extended to the exercise of authority and has to be compensated for by critical insight, it is also true that childhood without a paternal model can no more be tolerated without consequences than can life without a close relationship with the mother. In the framework of a society that is broadly organizing itself on a sibling basis the structure of the family will have to be reorganized and rebuttressed; a better, more real equilibrium, for instance, a real equality, will have to be established between husband and wife. Thus we are confronted with two kinds of fatherlessness. Gaining as thorough an understanding of them as possible is the remedy for a social pathological condition in which both father and mother are disappearing as the main bearings of social life.

## Disappearance without trace of the Führer

If the child has had a really living relationship with its father as with its mother and siblings, the father will remain with it as an inner object long after it has outgrown his immediate influence. The mass leader with his promises and threats is no substitute for him; in fact, surprising as it may seem, he is much more like the imago of a primitive mother-goddess. He acts as if he were superior to conscience, and demands a regressive obedience and the begging behaviour that belongs to the behaviour pattern of a child in the pre-Oedipal stage. If he fails, he is abandoned like a worked-out gold mine; he can no longer inspire loyalty when he has ceased to inspire fear and cannot keep his promises. *'Ubi bene* ... the rest of the proverb is superfluous.'[8] The tie to the Führer, in spite of all the protestations of eternal loyalty, never reached the level, so rich in conflict, where the conscience is formed and ties with it are established.

True, excessively close identification with the father and teacher has to be given up if we aspire to a selfhood of our own, but the difference between this and the disappearance of a mass ideal is obvious. We supersede our identification with our father in the right way if we look back on him lovingly and understandingly as a man with his own peculiar traits and weaknesses, in the wrong way if we remain tied to him by hatred, not wishing to be like him, but wishing to be different. In either case he remains inside us as a tangible part of our history, whether it is a part we accept or a part we try to reject. We have passed through identification with him in Nietzsche's sense, but he remains a permanent part of our being. How different is the end of the identi-fication with the failed mass leader, hailed by everyone as a glorious father so long as he was in power and ruled with the carrot and the whip. Suddenly no one wishes to be reminded of him; no one, it seems, has ever had anything to do with him. With the uniform one took off one wiped out that part of oneself, that chapter of one's history, as though it had never been. It is wrong, however, to maintain that no real identification took place, and that the masses merely adapted themselves hypocritically to a police and terror régime. For it cannot be denied that innumerable individuals agreed completely with the aims, values, privileges, and also with the disciplinary methods of the régime, and approved of them in private, when they were with friends whom they could trust, or were alone. All the same, after the collapse the identifica-tion ceased, though identification with great popular leaders in history has often survived their failure. Instead, however, after the end of the Nazi régime and other similar types of mass tyranny the great majority of those previously loyal to it extinguished their memory of it as a compromising thing. But, to revert to the words of Nietzsche that we quoted, did their memory yield to their 'pride', their self-valuation, or merely to the necessity of adaptation to a new political régime? This suggests that the new régime would meet with the same indifference if it failed to satisfy the need for milk and honey. Riesman's 'other-directed' type could be interpreted in psychological terms as the product of pathological social processes resulting in inability to defend basic trust against basic mistrust (in Erik Erikson's sense). Having never experienced firm object ties, the other-directed individual is an opportunist, not out of weakness of character, but because his character development has never attained stability. He is governed by pre-Oedipal wishes, external stimuli, without being able to organize these into a memory, in the sense of a consciousness, a self. He has no introjects to which he can look in situations that call for temporary renunciation and which would give him support in conflicts. He lives by the feeling of the moment, in accordance with the all-or-nothing law of stimulus and reaction, just as a suckling lives between hunger and satiety. The principle of accepting immediate renunciation for the sake of an ultimate aim, which was still characteristic of the struggles of the proletariat to obtain its social rights, is no longer viable.

Primary fatherlessness might be capable of turning enlightened democracy, with its rational division of powers, its basis in individual self-awareness, into an illusion. The sensitive spots of the masses of 'nobody's children'[9] who live in the moment with no sense of history are liable to exposure when their vegetative prosperity is disturbed. Dahrendorf[10] states the situation in sociological terms as follows: 'The inner-directed man needs democracy as a framework for the expression of his interests, values, and ideas. The other-directed man can live in a democracy, but does not need it. He needs society and, so long as society gives him the guidance and security he cannot find in himself, the political institutions under which he lives are a matter of relative indifference to him.' This political indifference recalls Harlow's experiments with rhesus monkeys, the incapacity for love shown by individuals brought up with surrogate mothers, whose capacity for experience did not extend beyond themselves. In the human sphere incapacity for love also means inability to transform primary impulses into interests, participation in the life of society; it means clinging fast to sources of nourishment and protesting when they flow too sparingly, with no consideration for social give-and-take.

Thus background motivations for the discarding of models and the process of reorientation can differ vastly. In one case the individual takes his prehistory with him into a new phase of maturation, while in another he fails to mature at all; instead, change comes from conditions, to which he passively adapts himself. If he makes a mistake, there is no conscience to prick him; at the worst, a new outside authority – for instance, a de-ideologization official, a purge tribunal – delivers a sentence to which the accused submits as passively and reluctantly as a child accepts a punishment it believes to be unjust. He still sees the world in terms of the power-impotence relationship, the only one he has truly experienced, and has never reached the stage of discovering the possibility of independent thought. Therefore, instead of exercising the latter, he projects outside himself responsibility for behaviour which suddenly turns out to have been guilty. It is the Führer who should be held responsible, he says, not the obedient children of the state who merely carried out his orders.

*Military digression*

Whichever way we turn, we come across traces of regressive behaviour, and note that in the mass adaptations in our society the regressions go very deep, that is, to primitive patterns of experience and behaviour. Submissiveness ensures satisfaction of instinctual needs, and total protection is promised. The protection is vigorously insisted on. The apparent paradox – in reality it is merely an unrelated juxtaposition in the poorly integrated psychical apparatus – is that this pliability can also be consistent with great bravery, the toleration of a total war, for instance, and fantastic feats of endurance in the desert or on frozen fronts. We cannot pursue this theme further here, except to point out one thing.

If we observe the war-time performance of the German soldier, we note that he was organized and led by an officers' corps the leadership of which was completely impregnated with the tradition of inner direction. The situation, however, was not that a caste of generals who were completely in line with the European military tradition were simply duplicated by paramilitary demagogues who secured control; or that side by side with 'decent' military conduct of the war there was a parallel movement, a double one, represented by the fanatical discipline of that *corps d'élite*, the S.S., on the one hand and the fanatical, uninhibited criminality of the same S.S. on the other. The situation was not so simple as that. The mentality of an organization that regarded itself as a heroic, monolithic *corps d'élite* and combined this with a de-individualized, destructive, and annihilating fury directed against the enemy was a phenomenon obviously closer to contemporary social processes, as is shown by the training and methods of the G.P.U. and the Commandos in East and West respectively. The tradition of chivalry, of remembering the dictates of conscience even in battle, is on its last legs, and the type of officer who was brought up in it is dying out, with other types belonging to the 'inner-directed' age.

But even this is not happening in the way in which a race dies out, for instance. Symptoms of degeneration appeared among the representatives of the correct general staff itself. They were in contact with the new way of thinking (pseudo-rationalism in the service of the primary trends) and were infected by it. This is exemplified by Field-Marshal von Reichenau's army order dated October 10, 1941, which said: 'The soldier must have full understanding of the necessity for severe but just retribution on Jewish sub-humanity. . . . Hence duties devolve upon the troops that go beyond the traditional, purely military duties. . . .'[11] Field-Marshal von Manstein followed this up on November 20, 1941, by stating that 'the Jewish-Bolshevik system must be exterminated once and for all.'[11] Here we can observe ancient caste prejudices against Jews and socialists, which had hitherto to some extent been kept in check by the organized conscience, linking up with the promises of the mass ideology. The rigid and restrictive rituals of the military apparatus involved a good deal of education in automatic obedience, the obedience of the circus ring, but this was more than counter-balanced by the simultaneous formation of conscience. The pressure of the super-ego, however, was unable to resist the suction of greatly stimulated instinctual trends. In a society predominantly guided by the super-ego no one would have dared think out to the end the consequences of the idea of doing away with the commandment 'Thou shalt not kill,' the idea of extermination. A mass leader who had never risen to the level of co-ordinated conscience formation, the spokesman of innumerable individuals who had become unacquainted with conscience, could do this and let them act accordingly. Even the generals did not resist this solemn and triumphant liberation from the super-ego. It was not so much the dying out of a race as a class of incumbents of roles ruining themselves. Thus there is reason to expect that a social structure the dominant tone of which is set by a mass of individuals released from responsibility and moral injunctions will, in the exceptional circumstances of war, result in the appearance of specialists equipped for total annihilation. Their training methods will be very strict, that is, they will amount to a process of education in automatic obedience verging on the limits of masochistic tolerance, to prepare the way for a maximum release of sadistic aggressivity in compensation for the unpleasure previously imposed.[12]

In comparison with these techniques, the old 'spit and polish' discipline seems mere playing at soldiers. But such phenomena, with their combination of submissiveness and the intensification of hatred that goes with it, are very directly connected with the process of mass formation. If the prototypes of the inner-directed character-structure desert, how much easier must desertion be for those used to dependence associated with clamorous demands.

To the mass leader everyone is a member of the masses. That is his detachment effect; he cannot tolerate the proximity of anyone who is not dependent on him or develops an interior system of responsibility that might lead to conflict, scruples, or doubt. The mass leader and his system require men completely trained in automatic obedience and as free from conflict as possible who will respond undialectically to certain stimuli. Responsibility remains the omniscient leader's exclusive prerogative, while the ego of the great majority remains tucked away, as it were, in an infantile hiding place. All responsibility is specifically delegated; Göring's words 'I have no conscience. My conscience is Adolf Hitler'[13] will be recalled in this context. When the most junior 'youth cub' in the movement carries out an order, he is thus able to bask almost priest-like in the reflected glory of his almighty leader.

However, the surrender of the conscience to the leader, who takes its place, is a phenomenon not confined to the conditions that prevail under mass dictatorships. The 'other-directed' man of our time, with its division of labour of authority, is attuned to psychical infantilism. This state, made up of a mixture of inhibition of primary development and regression, is at present the strongest and most uniform response

TWO KINDS OF FATHERLESSNESS

to a profoundly altered social environment. The individual does not grow into a system of values, ideas, and commandments guided by his personal models. The picture is rather of a manipulated conformity adopted for its own sake. A field of interests that is in intention totally non-homogeneous forms a fleetingly predominant pattern to which the personality living in the moment adjusts itself. In this process it is surprising to see persons who are in many respects recognizable as individuals turning into echo-persons in certain affect-cathected fields that might bring them into conflict with society. Perhaps it is this discrepancy between development into tangible individual personality on the one hand and role behaviour that picks up slogans just as easily as it drops them again on the other that is so characteristic of the mass of individuals of our time. But perhaps the training of the critical intelligence, which is inextinguishable because it is required for the functioning of society, may be a basis for the further evolution of consciousness. For this purpose, however, there must be a change in the direction of scientific inquiry, from external nature to the internal nature of man. It need not unduly disturb us that the process of acquiring self-knowledge also yields its private gain. That has been the case in all scientific advances. The 'human manipulators' in politics and advertising are alarming only to those who do not understand their methods.

## The economic significance of idols

No group formation can take place without the process of identification. The identification may relate predominantly to any of the three centres of impulse of psychical life, that is, to id wishes, to the demands of the conscience or super-ego, or finally to the achievements of the ego. Thus group formations look very different, depending on the principal level of the identification in force. In the course of history communities with strong super-ego identification have shown the greatest durability and the greatest capacity for the formation of tradition. A predominant identification with intense instinctual wishes is characteristic of highly rebellious groups capable either of carrying out a revolution or of succumbing to mob reaction, but the duration of such groups has been short. As we have seen, however, a great change has been brought about by the transformation of the social structure, the vast increase in numbers of those dependent on the anonymous

SOCIETY WITHOUT THE FATHER

system of division of labour and authority. In a society in which collective living conditions involve frustrations to which the majority of its members respond with regressive patterns of behaviour, a chronic challenge to identification with id wishes comes into play. This trend unites the masses, but is not characterized by rebelliousness against existing collective super-ego structures; it works rather as a permanent stimulus to an attitude of spirally mounting claims, a 'levelling up',[14] the demand for an ever-rising standard of living. The increasing productive capacity of the industrial revolution does not apply to these id wishes the brake to which they were subject in the pre-industrial age. Step by step it is able to satisfy many desires of the multitude, though to a large extent it does so with surrogate satisfactions. When revolutions now take place against still surviving types of archaic paternalist authority and privileges, they are guided by the aspiration for the standard of living of the industrial mass societies. This seems a liberation, and indeed is one. Where the old poverty still prevails, the new impoverishment of life in our technical civilization is not feared or suspected.

The fundamental process of identification at work in the big societies needs still further analysis, however. Identification means that we erect inside ourselves the object with which we wish to identify ourselves. The choice of a leader depends at least as much on the needs of the group as it does on the possession of outstanding qualities by the individual chosen. What is the group's objective? Immediate satisfaction of a collective instinctual wish? Fulfilling that wish in harmony with the recognized moral code? Or critical examination of the practicability or otherwise of fulfilling it? If we arrange our questions in that order, we see that with each stage the leader becomes an increasingly real object belonging to the outside world, a member of the group with whom communication about and discussion of conflicts and problems are at any rate theoretically possible, whose essence does not consist in his taking the 'lonely decisions' attributed to him by self-idealization and Caesarean apotheosis.

The primacy of id impulses survives in primitive moral codes which control instinctual drives by merely reversing them, as by substituting aggressive persecution of sexual desires for their satisfaction. At this stage the objects of the outside world are still predominantly a means for the satisfaction of instinctual needs or for resistance to them, as the

<del>290</del>

case may be. This can be observed in the course of the individual's development towards a morality closer to the ego. A rigid tie to pre-social instinctual trends and a moral attitude alien to the ego is often obstinately preserved in the course of advancement to prestige-giving roles and stands in the way of their more humane performance. The dominant factor in development of this kind is identification, 'the original form of emotional tie with an object'.[15] If the way of life of our society, the sum-total of its influences, restricts us to this form of social contact, advance to more mature object ties is prevented. Human partnership, for instance, will not be experienced as involving both detachment and community, but identification will 'in a regressive way [become] a substitute for a libidinal object-tie'.[16] This throws yet more light on why mass leaders leave so little trace and so little mourning behind when they disappear. The idealization to which they were previously subjected involved no libidinal relationship with the object, but only with 'the state of infatuation'. This process is not guided by the ego, but takes place as an object-blind break-through of intense instinctual wishes. The characteristics of the object merge in the projections contributed by one's own strong tensions. In the state of infatuation we see, not persons, but characteristics. The very similar cult of film-stars provides an excellent illustration of this. The strongly oral-regressive sexual expectations of the dependence addicts of our time are directed towards female idols with large breasts. They act like super-optimal dummies, releasers of instinctual feeling.

The economic function that this increased tendency to identification performs for the psyche is that of creating an imaginary fusion between the unclearly perceived self and the wishful image; as Freud says, 'the object is being treated in the same way as our own ego, so that when we are in love a considerable amount of narcissistic libido overflows on to the object'.[17] By idealization of the leader, for instance, self-idealization is made socially credible and is intensified. 'The object has been put in the place of the ego ideal.'[18] The detachment effect causes the individual features of the members of an ideologically united mass to recede into the wings, while the centre of the stage is occupied by the unanimity with which the multitude use the same object for the satisfaction of their narcissistic aspirations, putting it 'in the place of their ego ideal' and consequently identifying themselves 'with one another in their ego'.[19] The high degree of chance that is characteristic of the choice of such models or leaders becomes more intelligible when the parallel with the process of individual falling in love is appreciated. Attempts to establish the characteristic features of such mass leaders break down because the only thing common to them all is that they are the object of narcissistic instinctual trends. 'On the basis of present knowledge, it must be stated that in spite of intensive efforts it has been impossible to discover either a "gift for leadership" or a clearly defined multi-dimensional constellation of characteristics as specific factors. The study of small groups in approximately comparable circumstances has thrown up a series of qualities with significant frequency, for instance, energy, self-confidence, intelligence, articulacy, perseverance, and understanding of human nature, but that tells us very little. There are too many exceptions and opposite examples lacking in several and sometimes all of these qualities. The more the groups vary in membership, structure, purpose, and situation, the smaller is the correlation. No uniformity could be detected even in regard to the "charismatic" leader, quite apart from the fact that Max Weber's concept of this type exists at most as an exceptional phenomenon.'[20] Thus the role of popular idols, pin-up girls, leaders, is dictated less by their possession of outstanding qualities than by the instinctual tensions produced by the prevalence of a definite social type. All forms of effective propaganda therefore first attune themselves to the expectations of the public to which they are addressed and then base their principal themes on these, no matter in what field the hero is awaited.

Thus Freud's 'primary masses', whom we have previously mentioned, need to have incorporated in their guiding image a dream-like, omnipotent ego ideal, built up out of their frustrations and inhibited development. The peculiarity of our situation is that this form of idealizing object cathexis in relation to the social environment (and condemnatory object cathexis also) is making more and more obvious advances, while communication with others based on real, ambivalent contact is characterized by an increasing weakening of emotional cathexis. This could hardly have failed to occur, for libidinal object cathexis requires a constant object to which emotion is directed; only thus can identification develop into partnership, which presupposes the experience of a clear distinction between ego and object.

The weakening and above all the de-differentiation of emotional relations in the family group and the trend to mechanized work that leaves no trace of itself promote the accumulation of surplus libidinal-aggressive trends on the one hand while they hamper advance from identification to partnership (the development of object libido) on the other. As these processes lead to a general levelling, because the incumbents of influential roles are not exempt from them, the result is a noticeable impoverishment of affect in direct social contact at all social levels, a general emotional withdrawal from ties with work, and a tendency to illusory retreat to narcissistic ideal formation. These processes are followed, like an army by its baggage train, by a lavish supply of objects in which the dreamy ego ideal can take pleasure. The point about these reciprocal reactions lies in the de-differentiation of the psychical structure of the many, accompanied by extreme differentiation in production and administration. Thus we are faced with the necessity of dealing with two opposite trends of a kind for which there is no historical parallel.

*A successful compromise*

A backward glance at systems that have become historical is no sub-stitute for the task of investigating the ramifications of present-day social processes, but it can draw our attention to ideas for the ordering of society that have not been historically exhausted. We have said that the levelling process inherent in the attitude of demand combined with obedience is based on regressive trends. Now, obedience has always played a prominent part in the formation of the German national character. That character has not seldom simultaneously sought relaxa-tion of tension in unreal attitudes of demand, and sometimes the two have combined with disastrous consequences. Only exceptionally, and never in its guiding image, has this obedience taken the form of obedience to the ego; generally it has tended to be a synthesis of obedi-ence to the instinctual drives and moral obedience relatively alien to the ego. This expresses itself in the formation of group structures more or less following the pattern of the disciplined body. Asking for ex-planations is generally regarded as an offence against taboo. Obedience is regarded as being inherently one of the highest virtues, independently of whether the particular situation actually requires it or not. That involves restriction of the conscience to the actual function of obedience and implies recognition of the absolute superiority, privileged position, and exemplary qualities of the giver of an order. At the same time it exonerates the carrier-out of the order from all responsibility for its content.

That is certainly one of the reasons why no real need has been felt for coming to grips with our recent past, which surely merits the asking of questions. The insistence with which our former enemies keep reverting to the subject merely irritates. As, so far as the individual is concerned, the example for the carrying out of nearly all social tasks is set by disciplined bodies, he can conceive of social order only in the form of a hierarchical organization. Education, above all self-education to meaningful communication on the horizontal level that makes possible the asking of questions and the giving of reasoned replies, is becoming a highly important problem.

Margaret Mead devotes some interesting ideas to this subject in connection with the question of collective guilt.[21] The sense of guilt as we understand it, she says, is an inner experience that was given its imprint chiefly by the Protestant and Jewish middle class in Europe. In other cultures the individual reacts differently in situations that bring him into conflict with social laws. In Japan, for instance, it is shame, 'loss of face', that is most deeply felt. Collective guilt is described by Margaret Mead as the individual's sense of responsibility for the behaviour of his group, particularly his country. A sense of guilt of this kind can of course exist only where the content of the obedient behaviour that led to the guilt is consciously experienced and can so become a problem. Where obedience is itself an overriding virtue unconnected with the content of the orders which have to be obeyed, it follows that guilt or shame can arise only from disobedience. Society must therefore allow the individual the opportunity of constructive disobedience. It must strengthen his critical capacities, to make it believable that nonsense can be done, tolerated and disseminated at all levels of social life. When the parents act foolishly, sibling impotence is not enough. The individual must feel as adult as his seniors, must practise asking why, and test the soundness of the answers he is given. From this he must conclude that sometimes it is a duty to contradict and even to disobey. In view of the difficulty of getting objective information, this is one of the most important duties of responsible living in society.

In this respect the British seem to have achieved a successful compromise between the necessity of obedience and the equal necessity of its opposite. The citizen is socially bound in two respects. He feels a sense of personal responsibility because he has freedom to express criticism at any time and back it up, for instance, by voting for opposition candidates for Parliament. At the same time he maintains his identification with the nation, symbolized by the monarchy. 'The institution of the monarchy combined with the party system makes it possible for the individual citizen to be both individually responsible – because of the freedom to elect his representative in Parliament – and group identified because he is part of the nation supervised by the monarchy. This makes it possible for him both to exercise the most meticulous moral choice in approving or disapproving international acts, and still, the decision once taken, to accept full responsibility, which will be combined with active and effective guilt for national policies of which he disapproves.' In other words, if a spokesman of his government declared, as Hans Franck, the governor-general of occupied Poland, did, that 'in principle we shall have sympathy only for the German people and for no one else in the world', he could never detach himself from responsibility for the acts that followed such a declaration.

The behaviour pattern in our country, the authoritarian nature of its institutions that brooks no contradiction, made that possible, however. Guilt in Germany is associated, not with failure to exercise criticism, but with the crime of disobedience. If someone, whether soldier or civilian, receives an order in the course of his duties and conscientiously carries it out, that makes it *ipso facto* a moral and praiseworthy act. 'Obedience and conformity are rewarded; any initiative or deviation from duty or assuming individual responsibility is not rewarded.' Consequently 'the individual is absolved from personal guilt by implication in collective acts'.[21] The correctness of this analysis made in 1948 has been confirmed by the defence put up by all those tried for their actions under the Third Reich. Hardly anyone admitted any guilt; the only guilty ones were those from whom they took their orders.

British institutions seem to make possible a more successful compromise between the right to opposition and the supra-individual duty of obedience and responsibility. The emphasis is on the institutionalization of the individual's special rights. Only when these are recognized independently of status or class or caste and are firmly anchored in the social consciousness can there be sharpened perception for the question of when disobedience is socially destructive and obedience is the same. The antipathy felt in some quarters to parliamentary democracy, expressed, for instance, in references to parliament as a 'talking shop' (and of course nourished by the inability of deputies brought up in the habit of obedience to take proper advantage of the opportunities open to them in parliament), testifies to inadequate understanding of the necessary compromise. At the same time the specific symptom of democratic decay, the predominance of selfish individual interests, can be observed. So it is perhaps not very surprising that in countries in which individual ego development has been allowed to have *social* consequences only in recent or very recent times the lack of pliability in horizontal democratic thought and action is used by all supporters of authoritarianism as evidence of the deficiency of the system itself, and is politically exploited accordingly. Any kind of authoritarian régime seems to hold out the prospect of a return to the 'good old days', though in reality it merely reflects the inability to shake off the unsatisfactory habits of mind that went with them.

The British use of double identification is an example of a social system the possibilities of which have not yet been exhausted. It offers a contrast to double fatherlessness. A sibling society of adult citizens shares a sense of common responsibility symbolized by the monarchy. If we accept Robert Heiss's definition of a symbol as a 'condensed representation of an experience',[22] we shall not make the mistake of attributing a merely superficial representational role to constitutional monarchy in relation to parliament. It is, rather, the visible symbol of origin from the same father, the guarantee of a collective identity, a legitimization of all the children. The object that the individual citizen perceives in the symbolism of this type of monarchy is detached from the ambivalence of instinctual impulses, outlets for which are provided at other institutional levels and in everyday life; the 'condensed representation' symbolizes common origin and responsibility. The visible symbolism must have a deep phylogenetic root; it may have arisen from one of the basic 'releasers' specific to the human species. At all events the trend to symbolism can be seen in idols of all sorts. The striking feature of the British constitution is the withdrawal of the Crown from the exercise of the power that in the history of the paternalist type of government is symbolized by the authoritarian father.

The function expressed by the symbolism has changed. The role of the British monarch has become that of an 'enlightened' father, whose function is not to exercise unlimited authority but to guarantee the legitimacy of all the varied aspirations of the siblings up to the point at which the unity of the national group would be threatened. It would, however, be wrong to ascribe a preventive function to the symbolism of the Crown. This contains no element of deterrence, marking the limits of permissible behaviour; the symbolism works as an inner object influencing the character-structure of the whole group, rather in the sense of the instance quoted by Margaret Mead, as a kind of demonstration and guarantee that those who hold divergent opinions do not, despite their critical independence, wish to withdraw themselves from collective responsibility.

The safeguarding of individual rights by a collective super-ego which incorporates alertness for the preservation both of tolerance and of unity has resulted in a high degree of political realism in the political past of Britain right up to the voluntary dissolution of her Empire. The proclivity to take pragmatic decisions based on actual circumstances instead of being guided by ideal standards – undisturbed, that is to say, by the voice of a super-ego remote from reality – may be part of the same context. It seemed to us important to mention the system of ideas expressed in this separation of powers and their symbolic condensation as an alternative to the symbol formation of the regressive mass society. The symbols of the latter stand for identifying unison of instinctual trend; the processes of division of labour and of authority are causing the symbolic forms of expression of collectively valid super-ego demands to fade away. Even freedom, one of the surviving symbols that still arouse affect, is visibly becoming void of content, for there is an aspect of forlornness and abandonment about 'freedom from', which is its only conscious meaning; everywhere the individual is regressively retreating into ties and states of dependence. 'Freedom to' cannot be established solely on the instinctual level, it requires participation, involvement, and a visible symbol for the framework within which it is to be achieved. The symbol as the representative of directed experience then works as a catalyst, setting in motion development from the narcissistic level of experience of identification to the setting free of object libido. The latter involves participation, interest, perhaps passionate interest, in a relation of partnership, no matter whether this extends to the inanimate environment (which is then 'animated' by my interest) or to human ties.

It should be clear that we have not quoted the British example in order to recommend monarchy as a solution to the problem of the double fatherlessness of the people of our mass civilization. In the turbulence of the continuing industrial revolution with its profound impact on social structure, Britain must expect great difficulties in maintaining the vitality of the system of ideas that have hitherto prevailed. We have been concerned with the structure of mass society and the question of where firm ground can be found on which a counter-movement to the trend to regression can be based. It will be sufficient if we have made it clear that waiting for the appearance of 'great men' to do the trick is equivalent, in Samuel Beckett's phrase, to waiting for Godot. The work of the conscious, able to criticize a situation and change it, must be taken up and stimulated by individuals and the groups among which they live before they can reach the level of collective symbolism. Here again the British experience is relevant, for in Britain the change in symbolism from that of authoritarian ruler to enlightened, unifying father was fought for more consistently than elsewhere. When we consider that this was a process that took centuries, we can take some comfort in the thought that we too must exercise patience in regard to the problems that oppress us, and must think in terms of generations. But we cannot afford to be too quiescent in the matter, for in the past historical processes took place in a relatively constant cultural system that was closer to nature, and it is precisely the inconceivably rapid and continuous change of background that robs us of firm ground beneath our feet from which to consider the future. So that is only a feeble consolation.

### Sibling fear of ties

The presence of visible symbols indicates that social processes maintain their equilibrium round a nucleus to which the symbols refer. The more certainly the role associated with the symbol can be dissociated from its momentary incumbent, the more stable is the system. This is illustrated by the papacy as well as by the institution of monarchy. The zeal with which photographs of leaders, presidents, marshals, and generals are spread throughout offices, schools, and even living-rooms results from

the desire to establish a signal, the first step towards symbolization. But the process of condensation into a symbol cannot be brought about at will. In the major symbols instinctual, super-ego, and ego wishes seem to be united or, if not united, at any rate brought into a pattern reassuring to those who acknowledge them. Symbols are thus the mark of a reconciliation, their presence sets standards in everyday life. In minor, transitory symbols there is less condensation; they are super-optimal dummies representing actual libidinal or aggressive trends and they are fleeting, like will-o'-the-wisps. Super-ego symbols also continually recur, however; in times of crisis this role can be assumed by leading statesmen. It is interesting to note that the critical ego never appears in the form of a tangible symbol; it expresses itself, deals with symbols, but remains itself. At one end of the scale is the state of affairs in which no order has yet been introduced (its symbol is chaos), and at the other is that in which the constants in the social order have ceased to be inseparably linked with symbolic representation. The broad area in between depends on symbolism for the maintenance of order.

Let us now cite another experiment in social order, one that lacked any symbol of paternal authority, and collapsed. It makes it immediately obvious that fatherless mass society has not attained the state of development in which condensation of a social system into symbolism becomes possible. In central and eastern Europe after the end of the First World War the paternalist order of Kaiser, Tsar, and Emperor collapsed. To those brought up in Germany, Austria, and Russia their former rulers had 'been midway between supernatural and human father-figures',[23] and in the chaos and starvation or semi-starvation that followed military defeat in all three countries the short-lived experiment of workers' and soldiers' councils (soviets) took place. The Spartakus rising in Berlin in January, 1919, lasted for a week and ended with the brutal murder of Rosa Luxemburg and Karl Liebknecht, which set the example for both Fascist and other political murders in the decades that followed. In Bavaria the Workers' Republic lasted for barely a month, and in Hungary it lasted for four months. Then the 'evil spirit' was exorcized; in one modern history of the world the episode has not been considered worthy even of an entry in the index.[24] Only in Russia did a new state and social system arise out of the soviets. For years it remained bogged down in internal struggles for power until a new father-figure arose and created 'order' with one of the most fearful dictatorships known to history. The régime of Stalin's successors is still remote enough from the hopes that animated the peoples in 1918 and provided the impulse for attempts to build sibling government on the ruins of government by God's grace. Freud remarked that the blood of generations of murderers still flows in our veins. There has been a substantial addition to this genealogy since the end of the First World War.

While on the subject of things that are taken for granted, we cannot help noting that a usurper like Kemal Atatürk sent two million Armenians to die in the desert, an incident barely noted by public opinion; that under the Stalin régime millions died under a reign of terror in which no citizen had any security against the sentence of death or banishment; and that Hitler found no lack of Quislings ready and willing to aid him in his extermination practices. However repugnant these things may be in retrospect, they could happen and did; there was no collective symbol of resistance to which the subjected masses could hold fast. Even the perverse and sadistic element in these leaders is covered by the father image; public opinion, oscillating between horror and admiration, is willing to grant them a macabre greatness.

Very different was the unbridled, single-minded hatred directed at the heads of the idealists, such as the two leaders of the Spartakus rising, Rosa Luxemburg and Karl Liebknecht, who wanted to introduce a system of government by workers' councils. We are not here concerned with the clumsiness of all these attempts to achieve something totally new; compared to the tremendous mistakes that recur in history, they seem childish and harmless enough. Yet they roused this mighty howl of execration. As Paul Federn said in his study as early as 1919, the system of workers' councils 'jeopardized the security gain of the ancient wish fulfilment' to be dependent on a powerful father, for since time immemorial children have been accustomed 'to behaving themselves under the threat of the father's discipline and in awe of him'. If the social order had hitherto been similar to that of the family, the notable fact remained that 'the whole family did not participate to an equal extent in the social part of moral development. On the contrary, it is the situation of the child in relation to the father that provides the foundation for all respect for authority in him.'[25] The collapse of paternal authority automatically sets in train a search for a new father on whom to rely. Trying to substitute for him any other element in the family constellation, for instance, a sibling order, awakens deep anxiety, the reaction to which is irrational hatred of those who dare suggest such a thing. The weakness or fallibility of the father has to be made good and wiped out by putting in his place a new one of still undiminished strength.

This repetition-compulsion must have very deep roots. We are still to a large extent groping in the dark in this respect, but perhaps we can hazard a suggestion that may lead to a better understanding of the psychodynamic process that makes possible the permanent revolutions of our time and the fratricide associated with them. We have several times referred to one of the vital functions of the child's relationship with its father; it is ambivalent, and it also reconciles ambivalence. The father is experienced as permitting and forbidding, granting and withholding, and ambivalence of feeling is worked out and (with whatever degree of success) organized in relation to him. Conversely, the father's feelings towards the child are noticeably ambivalent; to put it in oversimplified terms, he relives himself in his child, and at the same time has a tendency to repress a potential competitor who theatens his position. In the political events of the present day the struggles of rival revolutionary and party leaders, and thus the whole problem of the father-son relationship as well as that of the rivalry of the sons between themselves, have assumed great, perhaps primary, importance. Let us therefore leave aside the other sex for a moment and consider this field of conflict by itself. It is a unisexual conflict. Homosexual relations between father and son are sublimated by cultural taboos which are of the deepest of their kind; sexual wishes openly directed towards the father are very remote indeed from the son's conscious, and they are rare even among overt homosexuals (at all events incomparably rarer than the negative Oedipal attitude in which the son imagines himself to be a daughter loved by the father). We do not understand the reasons for the intensity of the repression of such wishes, but in view of our constitutional bisexuality it would be exceedingly surprising if there were no trace of them whatever in relations between father and son.

Our constitutional bisexuality is channelled by culture. Direct sexual relations are fixated on the opposite sex and homosexual trends are desexualized. This process is not fully successful with all members of

SOCIETY WITHOUT THE FATHER

society, as we know. One of the fundamental tasks of human socialization is the individual's secure initiation into his sexual role. He is not
socially acceptable as a bisexual creature; instead, a male or female role
is imprinted on him. We know from psycho-analytic experience that
adaptation to this role is much more difficult than would seem from the
role habits that are so definitely signalled. We also know the fear of
alienation, of diffusion of the role status, that arises when the warded off
and not truly and securely sublimated bisexual impulses approach the
point of being admitted to consciousness. Even where they are acted
upon, in men's clubs, associations, and so on, intense anxiety and
revulsion prevent clearer recognition of the roots of the pleasure that
men take in each other's company. In contrast to the ancient world and
the cultures of the Middle East, for instance, in our culture 'moral
development' of this aspect of social relations is regulated by repressive
taboos and not by a process that allows sublimated feelings in this field
to be fully experienced as such. This may account for the vulgar and
smutty tone observed in many all-male gatherings, which partly arises
from the fear of homo-erotic impulses.

The paternalist pattern of authority as we know it exercises a
decisive influence on the fashion in which the sexual identity is built up
and bisexual inclinations are repressed. If the father image collapses,
as it did, for instance, with the breakdown of feudal aristocracy and
monarchy in Europe at the end of the First World War, this must
necessarily create an instinctual unrest extending deep below the level
of consciousness. Security in the role felt to be the most natural of all is
shattered by the loss of orientation towards the father. The relationship
of the sons between themselves is intensified and reinforced by the
libidinal and aggressive ties previously attached to the father.

Obviously the approach to a more highly erotically tinged relationship that conflicts with the most deeply unconscious ties with the sexual
role is very hard to tolerate indeed. Instead, envy appears in all its
violence; it is no longer bridled by paternal authority. Our conjecture
is that the attitude of aggressive envy of the now uninhibitedly contend-
ing brothers is reinforced by the anxious warding off of libidinal ties
with each other. We are familiar with another kind of defence against
homosexual wishes: the Don Juanism which is forced to conceal the
primary direction of the libido by unremittingly choosing new hetero-
sexual objects. We suspect that a similar evasion may be at work in the

campaigns of loyalists against deviationists, associated with sadistic methods of torture, that take place within military juntas and similar power groups that usurp the position of the traditional paternal authority without having found a new and secure framework for their authority. The endless ingenuity shown in the maltreatment of competitors, the humiliations imposed on them, and the pleasure taken in inflicting these things, seem to us to point to a pathologically transformed return of the repressed libidinal wish.

This recoil from even the attempt to achieve a satisfactory horizontal socialization, taken in conjunction with the regression to the oral level of satisfaction which we saw in the passively feminine, demanding attitude prevalent among the masses deprived of the father symbol, creates the impression of profoundly disturbed feelings of identity. Above all, the road to the fatherless society is signposted by regressive anxieties far more than it is by critical insight. This last part of our attempted analysis, our interpretation of the world-wide outbreak of manic barbarity, leads us straight back to the primary processes of socialization. All this is a forcible reminder of our terrifying ignorance about the conditions in which cultural adaptation takes place and the perpetually underrated strength of our instinctual nature. This remains true even if the theory we have just suggested is not accepted as valid. Society counts too easily on the domestication of man. The great upheavals of history show us that no part of his cultural adaptation is so secure that it can be relied on as a permanent human possession. The answer to the problem we have tried to suggest brings us back to the question of how the primary social institution, the family, can so develop as not to be exclusively dominated by paternal or maternal authority. The child's physiological need of protection is natural, and parental authority is natural too, but the family is also a union of father, mother, and child, and only when a moral symbol for that union has been found will it be possible to hope that the age of fatherlessness will cease to be an age of horror. Then it will also be possible to establish criterions for the essential social task of measuring regressive behaviour with greater precision. Humanity must be respected early if it is to be the direction-finder in conditions which it is impossible to foresee.

The same idea of union from the smallest human group to those on the largest, world-wide scale must lead to an integration between instinct, conscience, and ego such as was achieved by the great symbols of paternal authority. But the integration required will be closer to the ego than all previous principles of organization. It is therefore to be expected that the symbolism of the sibling organization will be less concrete.

As the masses must be roused from their dumbness, their enforced, vegetative passivity, and made articulate, it seems possible that the symbol-formation of the fatherless world will take place in language itself rather in any non-linguistic form. That itself would be an advance in the evolution to consciousness.

# XIII

# Epilogue

'All emancipation is the reduction of the human world,
of conditions, to man himself.'

KARL MARX[1]

## *Emancipation*

The author's motive in committing these ideas to paper was the desire for emancipation. Bearing in mind the impermanence of human moralities, emancipation implies a determination to explore one's subjective world and its relations to existing society. Both one's own character and the institutionalized features of the social environment can be shackles on insight and the action that should follow it, and both create the impression of being permanent, or at any rate of being beyond the individual's capacity to change. In reality the stability of both is being continually undermined; as an individual I change in time and have to cope with the process, while society is continually unsettled by the influence of new knowledge and new means of production, which lead to structural changes in it. So both as 'selves' and as incumbents of roles we are continually involved in processes of adaptation. This necessity becomes a source of conflict if we are not armed with knowledge and are willing to meet the continuous pressure of history with regression to infantile forms of adaptation and accept the relationship of dependency associated with them.

In the material field conditions have never changed so rapidly as in our own time. Our 'tool brain' has succeeded in mastering many natural potentialities and in adapting synthetic materials to our purposes, and many successful discoveries have encouraged the search for more. At the same time fundamental changes from which no one is exempt have taken place in the conditions of human coexistence. The necessary adaptations have obviously made excessive demands on the critical capacity both of individuals and of institutions. Regressive adaptation, that is, passive acceptance, predominates at the expense of constructive ideas for the organization of the new social world; and one of the consequences of regression is that ideas calling for active, constructive participation meet with no response among the masses. The principle by which they live, divested of its moral associations, is to let things slide. This points to a process of disintegration. The cracks in the structure are numerous. There is the discrepancy between the lavish production of consumer goods and the sterility of ideas about appropriate ways of living; between the organized demanding attitude and the almost neurasthenic breakdown of ties to responsibility; between the diffuse absorption in generalized activity and 'emotional involvement in living' (Victor von Weizsäcker); between an identity feeling that takes human frailty into account and the omnipotent ideal of perpetual pleasure; and above all between knowledge and a limitation of outlook that is deliberately chosen and felt to be acceptable.

Such discrepancies are of course as old as the history of human cultures; we believe that in our culture they have become accentuated by several degrees. The key fact is the contradictory nature of the trends. On the one hand we have the population explosion and the accelerated development of techniques to provide for its needs; on the other, stagnation or intensified regression in psychical adaptation to the transformation of society. The result is confusion of orientation. In conflict-laden situations the individual's choice is determined by ego fragments; such contradictory attitudes coexist in him and make him uncritical and defenceless against the influence of interests. As a consequence of the division of labour in the exercise of authority this weakening of the critical and integrating ego reaches to the level of those who exercise authority. The process of regressive adaptation is observable at all levels of society; this makes mass society a closed society. To the extent that regressive trends in adaptation predominate, a state of equilibrium is established that can develop in only one direction. There is resistance to critical examination of conditions and the unpleasure involved in that. Engagement is momentary, related to the immediate situation only; and choice swings to rapidly attainable pleasure gain. A balance of conformist adaptations that mean something only to fragments of the personality comes into being, and overriding critical integration of contradictory elements remains very weak. This, however, is a symptom of pathological personality development. If it is widespread, we have good reason to speak of a social pathological condition. Thus the task of emancipation lies in the analysis of the vicious circle of social conditions and the psychological reaction-formations to them. To liberate ourselves, we must first identify the pressures that society has itself created but for the time being is not prepared to admit to consciousness. Only careful study of this field of social pressure and the response it calls forth in human behaviour will create a basis on which organization can be built up out of 'conditions'.

## Remarks on method

The raw material for this book was provided by the psycho-analytic treatment of the mentally and physically sick. Thus the author relies on a limited field of observation. Instead of regarding this as a disadvantage, however, he takes the view that the patients concerned were highly qualified to testify to the conditions in which social adaptation, the development of individual character and behaviour, takes place in contemporary society. Much more morbid behaviour than was originally to be suspected turns out to be the outcome of an intensification of the situation in which we all grow up and live; it merely emphasizes the general.

The psycho-analytic technique offers two other advantages. The conditions of observation are constant, which is the fundamental requirement of all experimental situations. Also the relations between analyst and analysand are incomparably more continuous than in any comparable form of investigation. A total of about thirty thousand hours of this two-person relationship provided the raw material for this book. Also there is a very special quality about this relationship, and that brings us to the second of these two advantages. The analytic situation is often said to be artificial, dissociated from life, and what it produces is therefore held to be an experimental artifact. It cannot be denied that it is artificially produced and that we do not meet it in actuality, like systems of government or conditions of production. But are families, for instance, not founded? Are they not the product of a great variety of needs? Are we to say that human suffering arouses no desire to diminish it, and that therefore the relationship between patient and physician is an artificial one? Is it not rather one of the most natural relationships conceivable? Provided, of course, it does not become a self-alienating one, overwhelming the patient with technical apparatus and making him dumb and speechless. In its envy of the natural sciences, which deal with objects that have no power of speech, contemporary medicine has been led astray. It has concentrated on the X-raying of organs, while the X-raying of human behaviour struck it as unscientific and not worth while. It forgot that the power of speech is an essential human characteristic. In other sciences we get answers only to the questions that we ask, but man can speak for himself – if he is only given the chance. That sounds like a commonplace, and so indeed it is. But it does not mean that the obvious opportunity for diagnosis and therapy was therefore exploited. Here psycho-analysis made a discovery that was lying about in the street, only waiting to be picked up. The fact remains, however, that most physicians still do not take the trouble.

If we are willing to use what the patient has to tell us as a source of knowledge, a simple consequence follows, namely, the necessity of establishing a relationship with him of a special kind. For, if the difficulties and anxieties that he either met with or created for himself in contacts with other human beings could have been expressed as well as experienced, the painful detour of a symptom-formation would have been unnecessary. The detached but sympathetic relationship of the analytic situation creates conditions that make possible a return to the experience and its communication in speech. That is the second advantage of this method of observation; both the original experience and the responses that it provoked become accessible. We gain an insight into the aetiology of the condition as it is, and discover how and at what price an equilibrium was established between the context of the demands of the social environment and that of the psychical and sometimes the psychosomatic organization.

The ideas developed in this book are the condensation of experiences gained in contact with patients suffering from the most various neurotic symptoms. The author's experiences are of course not confined to them alone. He is himself a member of mass society. But he is grateful to his patients who forced him to turn his attention to a great many 'self-evident' propositions, as well as others that were not evident at all; he is in their debt for the light they were able to throw on many of these in the course of the therapeutic work. Our understanding of ways of behaviour we continually come across in ordinary life is notably extended if it is supplemented by observation of neurotic symptoms which present us with the familiar in intensified, or distorted, or cruder form. Neurotic behaviour reflects not only the individual's power of adaptation and resistance, but also the social standard of behaviour. The advance brought about by psycho-analysis lies in the fact that we do not take into account merely the obvious defects of society, the features of civilization that make us aware of its 'discontents', but that we pursue the reasons for discontents that are not yet or are no longer conscious. The neurotic suffers more than the well-adapted; but in many cases the cause of his suffering is present also in the well-adapted who, however, have gagged it. The vegetative inarticulacy to which social life is regressing is a central fact that is indeed worthy of study, for it is the great obstacle to emancipation.

There is, however, one criticism of this method that the author cannot overlook. This refers to the inaccessibility of the primary material – the patient's communications. This is inherent in the method itself. The dynamic relationship established between the two individuals involved is inaccessible to the observation of a third party. The reply is as follows. The two-person relationship between patient and physician is the *sine qua non* for the production of the material that has so extraordinarily expanded our understanding of the development of character into a behaviour pattern. The reasons why this is so, why a third party cannot be introduced as an independent observer, for instance, cannot be gone into here. Long therapeutic experience has confirmed that the introduction of a third party fundamentally alters the affective field. We have only to consider the step from the earliest relationship of all, the two-person relationship between mother and child, to the multi-person relationship with the whole family, or the intervention of a third party in a love relationship, to understand to some extent that the relationship between patient and physician requires undisturbed privacy for the performance of its specific task.

That being the case, it is evident that what is required is a control system tailored to fit the analytic situation, not a manipulation of the situation itself to meet the requirements of observation and control. The obvious form of control is comparison of findings with those obtained in similar situations, that is, empirical long-term correction or confirmation. But insights obtained in the psycho-analytic consulting-room have applications in other scientific fields in which different methods are used. From this point of view the author hopes he has suggested some socio-psychological ideas that could be taken up in the fields of sociology, education, legislation, and the political sciences. How in fact they can be 'translated' into those fields is a question of communication between the sciences, which is one of the main methodological problems of this age of specialized knowledge.

It should incidentally be mentioned that each of the principal themes dealt with in this book arose out of situations of conflict that regularly appeared in the course of treating patients. The (undoubtedly provisional) series of ideas that developed out of them shows how much insight into the processes concerned the individual can acquire when he is given the opportunity. Such insight leads to emancipation in two respects. We begin to see our human nature in a different light, as less fixed and more fluid than our character (and symptomatology) led us to believe; and we also see society in a different light, with greater understanding of its 'relations to man himself'.

### Detachment v. alienation

Efforts are also being made in other fields to attain new methods of self-knowledge as a means of emancipation from the conditions that drag us down with them. They are always connected with the conflicts which the critical consciousness has to work on when it has learnt to differentiate itself from impersonal processes. We shall conclude our reflections by mentioning one such method, which makes plain the convergent trends of the critical process in fields very remote from each other. We refer to Bertolt Brecht's 'new technique of acting which produces an alienation effect'.[2]

The way in which authority is exercised in society restricts our ability to form an identity by establishing a pattern of defence behaviour against trends and impulses to which the system responds by offering, not satisfaction, but punishment in some form. The psychical organization mediates between external and internal pressure by favouring the pleasure principle; it spares unpleasure by organizing defence at a level of perception or experience below that of consciousness. Contrary impulses from the instinctual sphere and contrary information from the outside world are denied in one way or another. The result is a cleaned-up field of perception that is freer of conflict than is reality itself, if by the latter is meant the sum-total of what we perceive both consciously and unconsciously. The gaps arising from the rejection of a certain perception are covered by pseudo-rationalism, the misleading conclusions of which are protected by high affective cathexis; touching them causes discomfort, and often fear so strong that the critical ego cannot cope with it. Brecht's idea was to bring this alienation to consciousness by a new technique of acting; he made the alienation discernible through the behaviour of the actor, which produced an 'alienation effect'. This behaviour of the actor and that of the physician in the psycho-analytic situation are very closely related. 'It is not his own part, so he is not completely transformed; he understands the technical aspect and retains the attitude of someone just making suggestions.'[3] In the case of the physician, this means that he feels his way into the patient's situation but does not make it his own, does not act for him or with him. Of this attitude of sympathetic understanding in which critical detachment is maintained Brecht writes: 'What is obvious is in a certain sense made incomprehensible, but this is only in order that it may be made all the easier to comprehend. Before familiarity can turn into awareness the familiar must be stripped of its inconspicuousness; we must give up assuming that the object in question needs no explanation.'[4] Thus the process involves a methodical search for what the alternative might have been, for every item of behaviour presupposes a previous choice, the motivation of which at first remains unclear. Brecht wanted the actor employing this technique to imply 'at all essential points . . . what he is not doing; that is to say, he will act in such a way that the alternative emerges as clearly as possible, that his acting allows the other possibilities to be inferred and only represents one out of the possible variants'. The author's purpose, like Brecht's, was to make the reader/spectator 'adopt an attitude of inquiry and criticism in his approach',[5] and to the extent that it has this effect the book will have achieved its purpose.

# Notes

## Chapter I

1. Quoted by Peter R. Hofstätter, *Psychologie* (Frankfurt, 1957), p. 20.
2. Margaret Mead, *Sex and Temperament in Three Primitive Societies*, New York and London, 1935.
3. See the detailed study by Manfred Pflanz, *Sozialer Wandel und Krankheit*, Stuttgart, 1962.
4. Theodore Lidz, *Zur Familienumwelt des Schizophrenen*, Stuttgart, 1959.
5. G. Pilleri, 'Biber', *Umschau*, 60 (1960), 420.
6. On the wider question of the extent to which the development of human and animal behaviour overlaps and similar genetic factors are common to both, see Konrad Lorenz, 'Die angeborenen Formen möglicher Erfahrung', *Zeitschrift für Tierpsychologie*, 5 (1943), 235; Otto Köhler, 'Vorformen menschlicher Ausdrucksmittel im Tierreich', *Universitas*, 9 (1954), 59.
7. Garrett Hardin, *Nature and Man's Fate* (New York, 1959; London, 1960), pp. 66 f.
8. Thus the word 'primitive' is yet another of the expressions of social unworth which we shall discuss later. See p. 12.
9. In speaking here or later of 'animals' as such, we are aware of the danger of such simplifications. There is no such thing as 'the animal', which is a very unbiological construction of the human mind, meaning merely the opposite of 'human'. (Rudolf Schenkel, 'Lebensformen im sozialen Feld und menschliche Sprache', *Homo*, 10 [1959,] 130.)
10. Rudolf Schenkel, ibid., p. 129.

## Chapter II

1. Theodor W. Adorno, 'Meinung, Wahn, Gesellschaft', *Der Monat*, 159 (1961).
2. Friedrich Nietzsche, *Jenseits von Gut und Böse* (Stuttgart, 1959), p. 78.
3. Sigmund Freud, *Thoughts on War and Death*, Standard Ed., XIV, 284–5: 'Thus there are very many more cultural hypocrites than truly

civilized men – indeed, it is a debatable point whether a certain degree of cultural hypocrisy is not indispensable for the maintenance of civilization, because the susceptibility to culture which has hitherto been organized in the minds of present-day men would perhaps not prove sufficient for the task.'

4. Romain Rolland, *Au-dessus de la Mêlée*, Paris, 1915.
5. *Thoughts of Blaise Pascal* (Kegan Paul, London, 1888), p. 279.
6. Karl Mannheim, *Man and Society in an Age of Reconstruction*, London, 1940.
7. Erik H. Erikson, *Young Man Luther* (New York, 1958), p. 36.
8. See III, note 7.
9. Sigmund Freud, ibid., p. 287.
10. See Alexander Mitscherlich, 'Neurosen und Psychosen als soziale Phänomene', in *Arzt im Irrsal der Zeit*, Göttingen, 1956.
11. Alexander Mitscherlich, 'Hindernisse in der sozialen Anwendung der Psychotherapie', *Psyche*, Vol. VIII (1954); C. de Boor, 'Widerstände gegen die psychosomatische Behandlung', *Psyche*, Vol. XII (1958).
12. B. Pasamanick, S. Dinitz, and M. Lefton, 'Psychiatric Orientation and Its Relationship to Diagnosis and Treatment in a Mental Hospital', *American Journal of Psychiatry*, Vol. 116, 1959 (quoted from M. Pflanz, ibid., p. 320).
13. Sigmund Freud, ibid., p. 287.
14. Sigmund Freud, ibid., p. 296.
15. Adolf Portmann, *Der biologische Beitrag zu einem Bild vom Menschen*, Festvortrag Regensburg, 1958.
16. Sigmund Freud, Standard Ed., XVIII, 19.
17. The ego is of course not a 'mental' agency totally divorced from the 'physical'. The unity of vital processes into aspects of which we gain insight seems to consist rather of biological processes (development of constitutional characteristics and the physical development of the organism) and conscious and unconscious mental processes (the correlation of which to physiological processes remains to a large extent obscure). It is this interaction between hereditary constitutional factors and the integratory work of the psyche to which Freud refers when he says: 'One is tempted to make the first factor – the strength of the instincts – responsible for the second – the modification of the ego, but it seems that the latter has its own aetiology and indeed it must be admitted that our knowledge of these relations is as yet imperfect' (*Collected Papers*, V, 321–2). The ego bears traces of its origins in the id – 'id and ego . . . [were] originally one, and it does not imply a mystical overvaluation of heredity if we think it credible that, even before the ego exists, its subsequent lines of development, tendencies and reactions are already determined' (ibid., pp. 343–4).

18. L. Bolk, *Das Problem der Menschwerdung*, Jena, 1926.
19. Adolf Portmann, op. cit.

## Chapter III

1. C. H. Waddington, 'The Human Animal', *The Humanist Frame* (edited by Julian Huxley) (London, 1961; New York, 1962), p. 70. See also his detailed discussion in *The Ethical Animal*, London, 1960; New York, 1961.
2. Julian Huxley, ibid., p. 7.
3. C. H. Waddington, ibid., p. 72.
4. C. H. Waddington, ibid., p. 73.
5. Sigmund Freud, Standard Ed., XVIII.
6. Peter R. Hofstätter, *Einführung in die Soḍialpsychologie* (Stuttgart/ Vienna, 1954), p. 356.
7. Gardner Murphy, *Personality*, New York, 1947.
8. Marcel Mauss has a similar train of thought in *Sociologie et Anthropologie* (Paris, 1950), pp. 289 ff.
9. Ferdinand Lion, *Jean-Jacques Rousseau – Selbstbildnis*, Zurich, 1960.
10. Erik H. Erikson, *Childhood and Society*, New York, 1950.
11. Anna Freud, *The Ego and the Mechanisms of Defence*, London, 1937; New York, 1957.
12. Harry F. Harlow, 'Basic Social Capacity of Primates', in *The Evolution of Man's Capacity for Culture* (ed. J. N. Spuhler), Detroit, 1959.
13. René A. Spitz, 'Anaclitic Depression', *Psychoanalytic Study of the Child*, Vol. II, 1946; and *Die Entstehung der ersten Objektbeḍiehungen*, 2nd ed., Stuttgart, 1960.
14. Michael Balint, 'The Three Areas of the Mind', *International Journal of Psycho-Analysis*, 39, 328–40.
15. Erik H. Erikson, 'Growth and Crises of the Healthy Personality', in Milton Senn, *Symposium on the Healthy Personality*, Macy Foundation, 1941.
16. Ibid.
17. *Archives of Experimental Medicine*, Vol. 1, 1961.
18. Cf. W. Rudolf's communication in *Mediḍinische Klinik*, Vol. 11, 1961.
19. See Helmut Moll, 'Kinderarbeit im 19. Jahrhundert', *Ärḍtliche Mitteilungen*, 46 (1961), 2257–9.
20. G. Rattray Taylor, *Sex in History* (London, 1953), p. 209.
21. Ibid.
22. Ibid.
23. Sigmund Freud, Standard Ed., XXI, 43.
24. David Riesman, *The Lonely Crowd*, New Haven, 1950.

Chapter IV

1. Ch. II, p. 11.
2. Erik H. Erikson, 'The Problem of Ego Identity', *Psychological Issues*, New York, 1959.
3. Georg Büchmann, *Geflügelte Worte*, 1879.
4. Max Weber, 'Über einige Kategorien der verstehenden Soziologie', in *Soziologie, weltgeschichtliche Analysen, Politik* (ed. J. Winckelmann) (Stuttgart, 1956), pp. 149 f.
5. Sigmund Freud, Standard Ed., VII, 169.
6. See Ernst Bloch, *Das Prinzip Hoffnung*, Frankfurt, 1961, and from a more clinical and pragmatic viewpoint Alexander Mitscherlich, 'Die Chronifizierung psychosomatischen Leidens', *Psyche*, XV (1961), 1–25.
7. Arnold Gehlen, *Anthropologische Forschung* (Hamburg, 1961), p. 77.

Chapter V

1. Sigmund Freud, Standard Ed., XIV, 119.
2. S. L. Rubinstein, *Grundlagen der allgemeinen Psychologie* (Berlin [East], 1959), p. 626.
3. Sigmund Freud, Standard Ed., XXII, 78.
4. Sigmund Freud, Standard Ed., XIV, 120.
5. The 'central and vital factor' in tenderness seems to lie in the 'comforting, protective presence that reassures the child; because this is manifested primarily and most directly by physical contact and also in speech, it is the former that takes the first place among the factors by which the need for tenderness is met. This also determines the choice of the organs of contact: the mouth and the hands . . . and feeding as the most vital function for the maintenance of life indisputably plays a part in the oral function.' Hans Kunz, *Die Aggressivität und die Zärtlichkeit* (Bern, 1946), pp. 77 f.
6. Sigmund Freud, Standard Ed., XXIII, 225.
7. Sigmund Freud, Standard Ed., XI, 136.
8. Ibid., p. 77.
9. Ibid., p. 133.
10. Sigmund Freud, Standard Ed., XVI, 416.
11. In *Handbook of Social Psychology*, II, 147.
12. Sigmund Freud, Standard Ed., VII, 267.
13. Cf. Horst-Eberhard Richter, *Eltern, Kind und Neurose*, Stuttgart, 1963. Richter traces the process of parental projection on the child, of which he gives striking examples.
14. Edith Weigert, 'Die Rolle der Sympathie in der Kunst der Psychotherapie', *Psyche*, XVI (1962).

15. Cf. René König, 'Soziologie der Familie', in Gehlen and Schelsky, *Soziologie* (Düsseldorf, 1955), pp. 149 ff.
16. See Hans Kunz, op. cit., or Peter Brückner, *Inhaltsdeutung und Verlaufsanalyse im Rorschachversuch* (Cologne, 1958), pp. 49 ff.
17. See Alexander Mitscherlich, 'Aggression und Anpassung I', *Psyche*, Vol. X (1956), and 'Aggression und Anpassung II', *Psyche*, Vol. XII (1958), where the problem is dealt with more fully.
18. Bronislaw Malinowski, *A Scientific Theory of Culture*, Chapel Hill, 1944.
19. Sigmund Freud, Standard Ed., XXI, 154.

Chapter VI

1. Friedrich Nietzsche, *Unschuld des Werdens*, II, Stuttgart, 1957, 25.
2. I Corinthians 13, 1.
3. P. 44.
4. Sigmund Freud, Standard Ed., XXIII, 225.
5. See, for instance, Peter R. Hofstätter, *Einführung in die Sozialpsychologie*, op. cit., p. 229: 'When Freud saw his patients, there was no food-shortage among higher society in Vienna. There was food and drink, tobacco and fuel; only in the sexual respect was there an occasional emergency. That was the situation from which the theory of the libido originated; it made the only shortage from which one definite section of the population was suffering the driving force of life as a whole. Today we can only regard this as an absurd generalisation, which nobody would dare offer the starving masses in Asia.' After what has already been said above, the reader may be left to decide for himself what is absurd or not.
6. Of the defence work of the ego – for instance, repression – Freud says that the essential fact is 'that the ego is an organization, and the id is not. The ego is, indeed, the organized portion of the id' (Standard Ed., XX, 97). He goes on to indicate the different functions of the psychical processes. Unconscious processes close to the instinctual source are reflex-like, tend to immediate discharge, while testing reality is the result of processes (perception, thought, learning, memory) which are of quite a different nature and do not try to help an instinctual tension predominant at a particular moment to achieve satisfaction regardless of the whole. The task of the ego capacities is rather to integrate the instinctual trends into the total process of living. They nevertheless remain in close functional association with the processes of the id. 'The apparent contradiction is due to our having taken abstractions too rigidly and attended exclusively now to the one side and now to the other of what is in fact a complicated state of affairs'.

7. Sigmund Freud, Standard Ed., XXII, 75 f.
8. Heinz Hartmann, 'The Mutual Influences in the Development of Ego and Id', *Psychoanalytic Study of the Child*, Vol. VII (1952).
9. See pp. 71-2.
10. Calvin S. Hall, op cit.
11. Friedrich Nietzsche, *Wir Philosophen* (Stuttgart, 1956), p. 535.
12. See Alexander Mitscherlich, *Leitwert Pflicht – Gehorsam*, in Hartenstein and Schubert, *Mitlaufen oder Mitbestimmen*, Frankfurt, 1962.
13. See Alexander Mitscherlich, 'Meditationen zu einer Lebenslehre der modernen Massen', *Merkur*, Munich, March and April, 1957.
14. Sigmund Freud, Standard Ed., XVIII, 69.
15. Sigmund Freud, Standard Ed., XXII, 91.
16. Sholom Aleichem, *Tewje der Milchmann* (Wiesbaden, 1960), p. 43.
17. *Sprüche in Prosa*, Part II.
18. Sigmund Freud, Standard Ed., XI, 150.

## Chapter VII

1. Erik H. Erikson, 'Growth and Crises of the Healthy Personality', op. cit.
2. Karl Bednarik, *Der junge Arbeiter von heute* (Stuttgart, 1952), p. 50.
3. Geoffrey Gorer, *The American People*, New York (*The Americans*, London) 1948.
4. See also Franz L. Neumann, *Angst und Politik*, Tübingen, 1954.
5. Ludwig Binswanger, 'Erfahren, Verstehen, Deuten in der Psychoanalyse', *Almanach der Psychoanalyse* (1927), p. 127.
6. Gorer, loc. cit.
7. Ibid., p. 30.
8. John Gunther, *Inside U.S.A.*, New York, 1947.
9. Ernst Michel, 'Das Vaterproblem heute in soziologischer Sicht', *Psyche*, VIII (1954).
10. David Riesman, *The Lonely Crowd* (New Haven, 1950), p. 22.
11. David Riesman, *Faces in the Crowd* (New Haven, 1952), p. 5.
12. Ibid., p. 485.
13. Carl J. Burckhardt, *Über den Begriff der Heimat*, address delivered in St Paul's Church, Frankfurt, 26.9.1954.
14. Gerhard Wurzbacher, *Leitbilder gegenwärtigen deutschen Familienlebens*, 2nd ed. (Stuttgart, 1954), p. 215.
15. Alexander Mitscherlich, 'Odipus und Kaspar Hauser', *Der Monat*, 3 (1950).
    Kaspar Hauser (1812?–1833) was a German foundling raised in solitary confinement until picked up by police in 1828.
16. Karl Bednarik, op. cit., p. 50.
17. Fischer-Bucherei, No. 413, pp. 32 f.

## Chapter VIII

1. Martin Luther, *Tischreden*, Blatt 66.
2. Ibid., Blatt 442b.
3. Ibid., Blatt 457b. Quoted from Dr Martin Luther, *Pädagogische Schriften* (ed. J. C. G. Schumann) (Vienna/Leipzig, 1884), pp. 273 ff.
4. Sigmund Freud, Standard Ed., XXII, 246-7.
5. Sigmund Freud, Standard Ed., XIV, 93.
6. Hans Thomae, *Der Mensch in der Entscheidung*, Munich, 1960.
7. Sigmund Freud, Standard Ed., XIV, 95.
8. Sigmund Freud, Standard Ed., XXII, 67.
9. Robert Waelder, *Basic Theory of Psychoanalysis* (New York, 1960), p. 169.
10. Sigmund Freud, Standard Ed., XX, 95.
11. See Sigmund Freud, Standard Ed., XX, 140. 'Anxiety is an affective state and as such can, of course, only be felt by the ego. The id cannot have anxiety as the ego can; for it is not an organization and cannot make a judgement about situations of danger. On the other hand it very often happens that processes take place or begin to take place in the id which cause the ego to produce anxiety. Indeed, it is probable that the earliest repressions as well as most of the later ones are motivated by an ego-anxiety of this sort in regard to particular processes in the id.' Freud also states that 'there is no reason to assign any manifestation of anxiety to the super-ego'.
12. Erich von Holst, 'Probleme der modernen Instinktforschung', *Merkur* (1961), pp. 913 ff.
13. Wolfgang Hochheimer, 'Probleme einer politischen Psychologie', *Psyche*, XVI (1962), 6.
14. Cf. Sigmund Freud, Standard Ed., XXI, 48: 'When a man has once brought himself to accept uncritically all the absurdities that religious doctrines put before him and even to overlook the contradictions between them, we need not be greatly surprised at the weakness of his intellect. But we need have no other means of controlling our instinctual nature but our intelligence. How can we expect people who are under the dominance of prohibitions of thought to attain the psychological ideal, the primacy of the intelligence?' The same applies to the inhibition of children's curiosity about sex, which is so important psychopathologically. The difference between the sexes is one of the first burning problems the child comes across when it begins its exploration of the world. If its curiosity is not satisfied with intuitive understanding of its needs, and if instead it is frightened off by prohibitions and their attendant anxieties, this will have far-reaching consequences on its capacity to use and develop its intelligence in orienting itself to its environment.

15. Goethe to Knebel, 8.4.1812, quoted from J. W. Goethe, *Briefe* (Munich, 1958), p. 662.
16. Friedrich Nietzsche, *Menschliches, Allzumenschliches*, II (Stuttgart, 1954), 204.
17. Bertolt Brecht, *Der Jasager. Der Neinsager* (Frankfurt, 1955), p. 245.

### Chapter IX

1. Sigmund Freud, Standard Ed., XIII, 33–4.
2. Ibid., p. 34.
3. Henry Miller, *The World of Sex* (Olympia Press, Paris), p. 122.
4. Sigmund Freud, Standard Ed., XI, 187, 188.

### Chapter X

1. Cf. Ch. III, p. 48.
2. Perhaps, however, in the midst of the reconstruction of the social scene we should keep open a dialectical way out for ourselves. The interest in past or obsolescent systems, even when these have no immediate relevance or validity for ourselves, helps to sharpen our view of order in human life.
3. Max Weber, *Wirtschaft und Gesellschaft* (Tübingen, 1922), p. 671.
4. See Wilfred R. Bion, *Experiences in Groups*, London and New York, 1961.
5. Sigmund Freud, Standard Ed., XVIII, 129.
6. Hellmut Becker and Alexander Kluge, *Kulturpolitik und Ausgabenkontrolle*, Frankfurt, 1961.
7. William F. Knoff, *American Journal of Psychiatry*, 117 (1961), 1010.
8. Talcott Parsons, *The Social System*, Glencoe, 1951.
9. Ralph Linton, *The Study of Man* (New York, 1936), p. 113.
10. Cf. introduction by Alexander Mitscherlich to Mitscherlich and Mielke, *Medizin ohne Menschlichkeit*, Fischer Bücherei, No. 332.

### Chapter XI

1. *A propos of Lady Chatterley's Lover and Other Essays* (London, 1962), p. 81.
2. In an age of intense competition between political systems and the prejudices associated with them the individual can easily find himself involved in conflicts with disastrous results to himself. Margret Boveri has amply documented this in her *Der Verrat im XX. Jahrhundert*, Vols. I–IV, Hamburg, 1958–1960.
3. George Bernard Shaw, introduction to *St. Joan*.

4. Sigmund Freud, Standard Ed., XXII, 63.
5. Max Horkheimer, 'Schopenhauer und die Gesellschaft', in Max Horkheimer and Theodor W. Adorno, *Sociologica*, II (Frankfurt, 1962), p. 116.
6. Peter R. Hofstätter, *Die Psychologie der öffentlichen Meinung* (Vienna, 1949), p. 3.
7. Ibid., p. 9.
8. 'Nor is it hard to discern that all the ties that bind people to mystico-religious or philosophico-religious sects and communities are expressions of crooked cures of all kinds of neurosis. All of this is correlated with the contrast between directly sexual impulsions and those which are inhibited in their aims.' Sigmund Freud, Standard Ed., XVIII, 142.
9. See Alexander Mitscherlich, 'Die Metapsychologie des Comforts', *Baukunst und Werkform*, April, 1954.
10. Sigmund Freud, Standard Ed., XVII, 139 f.
11. Quoted by Alfred Krämer, *Ärztliche Mitteilungen*, 46 (1961), 1962.
12. Gordon W. Allport, *The Nature of Prejudice* (Cambridge, Mass., 1954), p. 451.
13. Martin Wangh, 'Psychoanalytische Betrachtungen zur Dynamik und Genese des Vorurteils, des Antisemitismus und des Nazismus', *Psyche*, XVI (1962), 273–84.
14. Leslie T. Wilkins, *Delinquent Generations*. Home Office Studies in the Causes of Delinquency and the Treatment of Offenders, H.M.S.O., London, 1960.
15. See, for instance, Aldous Huxley, *The Devils of Loudun* (London and New York, 1952), or the ample material in G. Rattray Taylor, *Sex in History* (London, 1953).
16. Sigmund Freud, Standard Ed., XXI, 115.

### Chapter XII

1. Ralf Dahrendorf, *Gesellschaft und Freiheit* (Munich, 1961), pp. 321 ff.
2. Ibid.
3. Carl Linfert, 'Unbekümmerte Besitzer, oder: Wie lebt man von Ansprüchen?' *Der Monat*, 146 (1962), 7.
4. K. H. Stauder, 'Über den Pensionierungsbankrott', *Psyche*, IX (1955), 481–97.
5. Peter R. Hofstätter, op. cit.; cf. Chapter XI, p. 251.
6. Ralf Dahrendorf, op. cit., p. 349.
7. Ibid.
8. Carl Linfert, op. cit., p. 11.
9. Alexander Mitscherlich, 'Niemandskinder', *Die Neue Zeitung*, 3.5.1956.
10. Ralf Dahrendorf, op. cit., p. 344.

11. Léon Poliakov and Josef Wulf, *Das Dritte Reich und die Juden* (Berlin, 1961), p. 113.
12. See, for instance, Jürgen Habermas, 'Gedrillt zur Barbarei' (*Die Zeit*, 7.9.1961): 'Our society is structurally adapted to certain humanitarian rules – it cannot in the long run afford the breeding of terrorist subcultures. There is no such thing as barbarism in instalments. If permitted in one sphere, it will spread to them all.'
13. Hermann Rauschning, *Gespräche mit Hitler* (Zurich, 1940), p. 77.
14. Peter Härlin, 'Massenzivilisation gegen Vermassung', *Frankfurter Allgemeine Zeitung*, 18.1.1955.
15. Sigmund Freud, Standard Ed., XVIII, 107.
16. Ibid., pp. 107-8
17. Ibid., p. 112.
18. Ibid., p. 113.
19. Ibid., p. 116.
20. Kurt Lukasczyk, 'Zur Theorie der Führer-Rolle', *Psychologische Rundschau*, XI (1960), 185.
21. Margaret Mead, 'Collective Guilt', International Conference on Medical Psychotherapy, August, 1948.
22. Robert Heiss, *Allgemeine Tiefenpsychologie* (Bern, 1956), p. 199.
23. Paul Federn, 'Zur Psychologie der Revolution: Die vaterlose Gesellschaft', *Der österreichische Volkswirt*, 11 (1919), 571 ff., 595 ff.
24. *Historia Mundi*, Vol. XI (*Das 19. und 20. Jahrhundert*).
25. Paul Federn, op. cit.

## Chapter XIII

1. Marx and Engels, *Gesamtausgabe*, I (Frankfurt, 1927), 599.
2. Bertolt Brecht, 'Short Description of a New Technique of Acting which Produces an Alienation Effect', in *Brecht on Theatre* (translated by John Willett, New York, 1964, London, 1965), p. 136.
3. Ibid., p. 138.
4. Ibid., pp. 143–4.
5. Ibid., p. 137.

# Index of Names

# Index of Subjects